104974

92
JOH

Johnson, Mahlon,
1954-

Working on a
miracle.

$23.95

DATE			

WORKING
ON A
MIRACLE

WORKING
ON A
MIRACLE

Mahlon Johnson, M.D.

WITH THE ASSISTANCE OF
Joseph Olshan

BANTAM BOOKS
NEW YORK   TORONTO   LONDON   SYDNEY   AUCKLAND

WORKING ON A MIRACLE
A Bantam Book / February 1997

All rights reserved.

Copyright © 1997 by Mahlon Johnson, M.D.
Foreword copyright © 1997 by Abraham Verghese, M.D.

Book design by Donna Sinisgalli

No part of this book may be reproduced or transmitted in any form or by any means, electronic or mechanical, including photocopying, recording, or by any information storage and retrieval system, without permission in writing from the publisher.
For information address: Bantam Books.

Library of Congress Cataloging-in-Publication Data
Johnson, Mahlon, 1954–
Working on a miracle / Mahlon Johnson, with the assistance of Joseph Olshan.
p.   cm.
ISBN 0-553-10519-1
1. Johnson, Mahlon, 1954—Health.   2. AIDS (Disease)—Patients—Tennessee—Nashville—Biography.   3. Pathologists—Tennessee—Biography.   I. Olshan, Joseph.   II. Title.
RC607.A26J625   1997
362.1'969792'0092—dc21
[B]   96-49712
CIP

Published simultaneously in the United States and Canada

Bantam Books are published by Bantam Books, a division of Bantam Doubleday Dell Publishing Group, Inc. Its trademark, consisting of the words "Bantam Books" and the portrayal of a rooster, is Registered in U.S. Patent and Trademark Office and in other countries. Marca Registrada. Bantam Books, 1540 Broadway, New York, New York 10036.

PRINTED IN THE UNITED STATES OF AMERICA

BVG   10 9 8 7 6 5 4 3 2 1

For the woman who gave me life,
for the women who have given it meaning,
and for the scientists who have given us hope.

ACKNOWLEDGMENTS

In 1992 I was thrown into a new unknown world of souls who fought AIDS with valor and kindness that exceeds comprehension. This book is about their battles and their nobility, as much as it is a chronicle of my own struggles.

This literary effort could not have been sustained without the immutable faith of a mother, sister, and father who quietly endured the uncertainties of my physical well-being, my calls, and my three-year recording of this epic.

In dark hours, many, including Brenda Barnes, Robert Collins, John Chapman, Lisa Ellis, Fred Gorstein, George Gray, Linda Horton, Paul Kim, Don Pierce, and William Whetsell Jr., provided quiet support. Special thanks to David Page and Don Rubin for their concern and wise counsel.

Early on I was blessed with the assistance and encouragement of Lynda Shaver, who typed much of the first draft; Madison Smartt Bell and Susan Wiltshire provided kind and helpful advice then. The blessed and enduring inspiration of Raymond Bongiovanni (R.I.P.) continues to guide this book and our lives.

Additional thanks to Brenda Barnes, Linda Horton, Margaret Edwards, Doyle Graham, Barney Graham, George Gray, Kathy Neuzil, David Page, and Virgil Robinshan for review and helpful suggestions on parts of the manuscript.

I am indebted to Joe Olshan for overseeing the metamorphosis of this caterpillar of chapters into a more graceful and, I hope, readable work.

With boundless gratitude, I thank my agent, Mary Evans, for her faith in and support of this book.

Special thanks to Elisa Petrini, my editor at Bantam Books, for lending her considerable wisdom and talent to this project.

FOREWORD

———— ∞ ————

by Abraham Verghese, M.D.,
author of My Own Country

IN MY YEARS of caring for people with AIDS, there is a recurring but, thankfully, infrequent dream that I experience. I call it the "infection dream," and it begins with the fact that I have contracted HIV infection. It has none of the usual agitation or chaos of a nightmare; rather, in this dream I root around logically but with increasing desperation for a way to rewind the dream tape and take myself back in time to the before-infection moment, but I can't. There are no appeals; the finality of infection is pronounced by everyone I turn to. I'm stuck in the "after." I wake from this dream with my heart pounding. The relief I experience on awakening feels as if it were a true reprieve on my life given to me that night.

Unlike most dreams, there is a quality to this one that makes it linger long after the first cup of coffee and the drive to work. It replays itself as I go about my business of caring for persons with HIV infection, makes me realize that in my waking hours I really have no clue what it is like to carry the virus. For all the compassion I am supposed to have, for all the fearlessness of contagion I display in my clinics, for all the empathy I summon when I break the news to someone that the virus is in their body, there is still the reality that I am on the *other* side looking in. When I am conscious, awake, I never fully fathom what it is like to be infected; in my dream I understand perfectly.

Mahlon Johnson knows what it is like to be infected. I got to know Mahlon Johnson in 1994 when he called me after he had read *My Own Country,* my book about the emergence of HIV in rural Tennessee. I remember Mahlon's voice on the phone, quiet, tentative, fearful that he was bothering me. He introduced himself: a doctor, a neuropathologist, an associate professor at Vanderbilt University School of Medicine. And then, almost brusquely, matter-of-factly, he told me about being infected in an accident with a scalpel during a brain autopsy on a man who had died of AIDS.

The only reason he was telling me this was to establish his credentials for what he was about to ask me next: he wanted to write to the woman I called "Vickie" in the book, a tough-as-nails mother of two whose bisexual husband had infected her. The theme of my book was that the ridiculously large number of people with HIV infection I was seeing in a small rural community in Tennessee was a paradigm of migration revealed: native sons, mostly gay men, had left small-town Tennessee in a silent exodus years before; they had found themselves in the big cities, found the courage to live their lives; but tragically the virus had found them and they were now coming back to their rural homes, to their parents. They were not only infected but often very ill. But Vickie was an exception to this paradigm, as was her husband; he had never lived outside the area, although he had traveled to Atlanta and elsewhere. And Vickie, who had never traveled outside of a twenty-mile radius from where she was born, was infected by him; he also infected her sister. It is a tragic story.

There is a quality of spirit that Vickie possesses, an indomitability, a stubbornness, coupled with great heart—at least in my description of her in *My Own Country*—that Mahlon seemed to identify with. Her illness, her ability to forgive and then nurse her husband through his long illness and death, transformed her; she went from living a poor, turbulent, and unstable life in a trailer in a hollow to becoming a self-sufficient, outspoken activist, a fighter, and ultimately a nursing student determined to finish school. She went from being my patient to being my best friend and confidante, long after I had left the area for Iowa and then El Paso. It was as if the disease had given her purpose that was lacking before. I didn't know at the time of my phone conversation with Mahlon if these were qualities he aspired to or ones that he already possessed. I promised to forward a letter he wanted to send to Vickie. She, the recipient of many such letters after *My Own Country* was published, saw something special in him and called him. The two struck up a friendship that, I must confess, has made me envious. Once again I was on the outside of the particular nightmare they found themselves in. I could never quite be in their shoes.

A few months after Mahlon's call to me, he and I met in Nashville. He was only the second physician with HIV infection I had come to know. The other physician, Sandy Pomeranz, a gay nephrologist and in the last years of his life one of the best AIDS clinicians I had ever known, died a while ago in Phoenix. I found myself drawn to Mahlon the same way I had been drawn to Sandy: that sense of a comrade in arms now wounded on the battlefield. What had only been a nightmare for me as a physician had become true for them.

There were reasons I could relate particularly well to Mahlon. We were both in academia, doing research on AIDS. He was, I think, even more ambitious than the typical, driven Type As one finds in the best academic centers: when he was a resident at Vanderbilt he parked on old bread truck in front of the VU campus and lived out of it for years, showering in the hospital and using the truck only to sleep in and keep his few belongings in. His frugality and his single-mindedness were legendary. He had virtually no life outside of medicine. He did his residency and two fellowships at Vanderbilt and joined the faculty there. Although he gave up the bread truck and rented a studio apartment, his life continued to be his work. He published prolifically and brought in National Institutes of Health and Veterans' Administration grants and rose quickly to associate professorship. Typically, one of the publications listed on his curriculum vitae is a careful, unemotional paper documenting his own seroconversion, documenting the transmission of a virus from a dead patient to the prosector.

HIV infection changed Mahlon's life in two spheres: first of all, his single-minded pursuit of science became the single-minded pursuit of the science of his *own* HIV infection. And in the medical clinics staffed by people like myself, he quickly picked up on the nihilism that had infected AIDS care, almost a subconscious nihilism that said, no matter what you do, the trajectory of this illness is an inexorably downhill one. It was a nihilism that Mahlon would not accept. From the outset he has been determined to beat his HIV infection.

Most interested researchers at the end of the day go home to their families; most researchers do not take the virus home in their lymphocytes at the end of the day; most researchers do not set up intravenous infusions at night in their bedrooms. Mahlon, who scours the literature and abstracts till late at night, is aware of every reported advance in basic and clinical aspects of AIDS and he hunts down and speaks to the researchers involved. It is very difficult for another physician to resist speaking to a fellow physician with AIDS.

Mahlon had the advantage of knowledge of immunology prior to his infection. He began to read voraciously, to find leads on the many new and old drugs in clinical trials. He was willing to try theoretical combinations of drugs that were still years away from full-scale clinical trials. He was also young, in excellent physical shape from years of track and field and from pursuing a physical fitness regimen that has only become more intense as the years pass. He pushed to begin AZT and other drugs well before the "thresholds" of CD4 counts that most of us waited for. He began treating himself with IL-2 (interleukin) in concert with other new antivirals—all this well before the new protease inhibitors that are now changing the course of HIV infection. In the process Mahlon's CD4 lymphocyte count went from a low of 320 back up to 1,200, which is the upper normal level. IL-2 is difficult to use and causes swelling of the tongue and the whole body, but Mahlon persisted, coming up with his own treatment protocol. Several times I spoke to him over the phone when he was having the infusion and his tongue was so swollen that he was barely understandable, and yet he wouldn't dwell for a moment on the side effects, talking instead about the immunological battle raging within.

About a year ago he called to tell me that there was no longer detectable virus in his bloodstream when tested by the most sensitive PCR tests! Several bands on his Western Blot had turned negative. This was the moment when my own ingrained and subconscious therapeutic nihilism began to crack. I had been supportive, encouraging, but in my heart the experience of so many years didn't allow me to think Mahlon's experience would be that different from the majority of my patients. Mahlon became the first human being I had met in the thirteen years I had dealt with AIDS who *I* believed would beat the disease. Mahlon was being studied by Dr. Ho, a famous researcher in New York, and was also being studied by the NIH. At both places researchers were unable to find detectable levels of virus in his body. This was not only exciting news for him but electrifying news for all of us who know him and who work in this field.

Since then a new class of drugs, the protease inhibitors, has emerged; I want to emphasize that the developments with Mahlon antedated his use of protease inhibitors. Now, even in my clinic, I have a few patients in whom—through potent combinations of these new drugs with the older ones—the virus has declined to levels below the threshold of the test I use to detect its presence in the blood. A year after Mahlon cleared the virus—without protease inhibitors—the siren call has sounded in the HIV community: the virus *can* be checked with multiple drug combinations. It was the message being sung out at the latest AIDS meeting in Vancouver. But the saga of Mahlon's infection, his stubbornness in refusing to accept conventional wisdom, his faith in science, his self-treatment, and his perspective on what is going on inside his body make for a fascinating story—it is entirely different from anyone else's experience. Yet his results speak to us all.

But there is another story here. Unlike the great majority of

HIV-infected persons I see in my clinic, Mahlon had largely postponed his love life in the pursuit of his passion for medicine. Whereas others in my clinic often express regret for their sexual past, Mahlon's regret was perhaps not having much of a past to speak of. One of his regrets was that he had never been married, never had children. To his own surprise, I think, an urgent parallel part of his new life after becoming infected was the need to see if the possibility of marriage and children had ended. Dating someone *without* HIV infection was too daunting a thought. And so he found himself in a bizarre and interesting situation dating ''Dawn'' in Nashville—a destructive relationship that was destined to end. But after that came his friendship, kinship, bonding with Vickie and her children. It is not possible to imagine two more different people, two people so mismatched educationally and culturally.

Mahlon—even as he was searching for his cure—could not accept that Vickie should not also share the benefits he was experiencing, and so, at his own cost, he began flying her to Nashville to begin experimental therapy and IL-2 infusions. It was a raw spot in our relationship; I was concerned that he might endanger her in his zeal for treatment. Vickie smoked and I worried that the IL-2 treatment might exacerbate her chronic bronchitis, push her over the edge. I was wrong and he was right. Now when I talk to them, when I see them, I have the sense of looking at the last man and woman on earth. The survival of the species, the beating back of the deadly scourge seems for me now to depend entirely on what happens to them.

There are many unanswered questions. Does the virus have a safe haven in the body where it can hide? Can the virus, after years of dormancy in the body, relapse in the manner of herpes infections? How can this therapy, which is very costly, begin to impact the vast majority of the world's HIV patients who couldn't possibly afford the $15,000 or more a year that treatment now requires?

These questions and the science and humanity behind them are part of the story of *Working on a Miracle*. Mahlon is a meticulous scientist and writer and all along had been keeping a detailed journal of his experiences. In concert with another gifted writer, Joe Olshan, we have a narrative that tells us his story.

Mahlon *is* the much-talked-about cutting edge.

Mahlon's poignant personal saga, which has far from ended, is the herald call to the new era of AIDS.

Mahlon's story is the story of hope, of promise in AIDS care that is upon us.

We have finally turned the corner.

Abraham Verghese, M.D.
El Paso, Texas

WORKING
ON A
MIRACLE

CHAPTER 1

————— ∞ —————

A night of torrential rain. I was at the microscope, looking at sections of a brain tumor, when the phone rang. It was Beth Ann Jamison, a friend and infectious disease specialist with whom I was working on a study of brain lesions in AIDS patients. She was the clinician who cared for them in life, and I was the neuropathologist who cared for them in death, removing their brains to track down their killers.

"Mahlon," she said. "One of our patients just died. Obviously we'd like to have a post."

Beth Ann's manner was tentative because it was late and she knew that AIDS autopsies were demanding.

"So what's the deal with him?" I asked. Beth Ann told me that the patient was a Vietnam veteran who had been married to a wheelchair-bound woman. During a vacation in Hawaii, he'd visited a prostitute and several years later came down with Pneumocystis pneumonia, one of the defining illnesses of AIDS.

"I suppose I should do it tonight," I said, though it was getting close to eight o'clock.

"Well, Mahlon," she replied, "I leave it up to you."

I knew that the man's family would wait until morning to learn what had caused his death. But I wanted to close this chapter in their lives so that they could begin grieving, healing. Besides, in the busy morning, it was likely that I'd be called away from the autopsy by a neurosurgeon needing me to look at a brain biopsy. The work of the neuropathologist is divided between stories of the living and the dead. By examining brain biopsies, making diagnoses, you can predict the story of a person's life. By doing autopsies you can write his last chapter. Evenings were the best times to write those final words in uninterrupted solitude.

I turned off my microscope, put away the slides, and reached for my dinner, half a turkey sandwich left over from lunch. If I wanted to eat, I had to do it now, for the grisly case would ruin my appetite. Yet, as I headed for the morgue through the cold downpour soaking the campus at Vanderbilt University, I didn't mind doing the case. After all, I was in no hurry to go home.

WHENEVER I ENTERED the morgue, I felt reassured by the sweet smell of disinfectant. But that night, it was overlaid with the reek of formaldehyde, the smell of rotted human bowel and bile from an earlier autopsy. In the center of the room stood the gurney, covered with a faded blue sheet. Before heading to the scrub room, I stopped for a moment and lifted the sheet to meet my patient.

He was a large-boned man, perhaps about forty. His eyes, staring up at the ceiling, were sunken in and yellow. Yellowed skin, the telltale sign of liver failure, clung to protruding cheekbones. Parched lips, pulled back in a frozen snarl, revealed bloody, rotted gums. I was grateful to be facing him after his suffering had ended, at a time when I could view him dispassionately. For after death the body became a marvelous mystery, a collection of clues to solve the crime of disease, removed from the pathos of human suffering.

How different I would feel if I had witnessed his last two months of life, under siege by fungi, viruses, and bacteria laying waste to his organs, withering his body, and invading his brain. His last days, I was sure, had been spent in delirium, with spiking fevers and sweat-soaked sheets. The infiltrator of his brain would have garbled his speech along with his basic sensory functions, and killed in him any sense of pleasure. Now he was awaiting the final invasion, the invasion of my scalpel.

An autopsy on an end-stage AIDS cadaver can be a dangerous undertaking. The HIV virus replicates at an alarming rate. As the body's defenses collapse, HIV reproduces unchecked, saturating the blood with potentially virulent, drug-resistant strains of virus.*
After death, the corpse of an AIDS sufferer is extremely infectious, and unless it is incinerated or embalmed, remains so for several days.

---

* It wasn't until recently that the Centers for Disease Control determined that deep wounds and exposure to blood from end-stage AIDS patients could be associated with greater risk of occupational infection *(Morbidity and Mortality Weekly Report,* December 22, 1995). And, ironically, this same article suggests for the first time that AZT may have some beneficial effect in preventing infection.

So, before beginning an AIDS autopsy, I had to suit up very carefully, first putting on my blue cotton scrubs, then stepping into a protective hooded jumpsuit. I then donned arm protectors, a face mask, a clear plastic face shield, and two pairs of latex gloves. I couldn't help but feel claustrophobic in all this gear—but not afraid, not after years of such cases. Thus armed against the virus, I pushed the gurney into the autopsy room. There I saw Susan, a pathology resident I'd worked with for years, standing by to assist me.

The autopsy room is a world of stainless steel: stainless steel shelves and organ pans with an arsenal of knives, scissors, and forceps laid out carefully on a tray. Even the autopsy table, punctured with drainage holes for blood, is stainless steel. White plastic buckets filled with formalin await bodily organs to be pickled for a few days until they firm up, permitting them to be sectioned. Bottles of Clorox and disinfectant stand sentinel. In one corner of the room stood a massive metal saw, the "Butcher Boy," used to split bones and vertebrae. There was also a smaller, hand-held oscillating power saw used to cut open skulls.

Surrounded by so many sharpened weapons, I couldn't help but worry about the woefully inadequate protection of two pairs of latex gloves. For months we'd been waiting for the arrival of Kevlar gloves, supposedly puncture proof, like bullet proof vests, but they hadn't arrived. I remember growling to Susan, "How many damned government bids will it take before we finally get our Kevlar gloves?"

Susan shrugged.

I undraped the corpse. His emaciated face stared blankly at the ceiling. Trying to be gentle, I hoisted him onto the cool steel table; his whole body, stiffened by rigor mortis, shimmying with the movement. Then I raised his rigid head while slipping clear biohazard bags around it to catch the infected blood and bone that would spray once I started sawing. With another hoist, I placed a rubber headrest under his neck, propping up the skull. According to our practiced ritual, Susan handed me a scalpel and the surgical saw, but then slipped away into the corner of the room, seemingly wary of being splattered.

My first incision, ear to ear, splayed open the scalp, now thin like cheap leather after years of wasting. Blood trickled down over the white bone. Working steadily, I grabbed the scalp with the forceps to pull it off the skull. But it clung stubbornly, slipping from their grasp.

''Damn, these forceps are sprung,'' I told Susan.

Finally, after minutes of struggle, I abandoned the forceps and grabbed the slippery scalp itself. With folds of skin between my fingers, I peeled the scalp back from the skull. Blood continued to roll off the bone, pooling in a flap of scalp hanging precariously behind the head. My hands were completely bathed in blood, separated from the deadly virus by only a thin membrane of rubber.

Up until this time, everything, though delicately dangerous, had been routine. But then, in a split second, my fingers lost their grip and jerked into the path of my bloody scalpel.

Suddenly, splintering pain went right up my arm. The pain told me that the cut was deep, and for a second I stood there gaping at what I'd done. Then I saw my own blood seeping out and slowly filling each layer of glove that, by now, was filled with AIDS blood. My hands felt clammy and wet, and with a pang of panic I realized that, through the puncture in the gloves, blood was meeting blood in my wounded hand.

I leaped into motion, ripping off the gloves and rushing to the sink.

"Mahlon . . . what happened?" yelled Susan.

I didn't answer her, preoccupied with the sight of my naked hands covered in blood. I could feel my face flushing inside my mask as I opened the Clorox bottle and plunged my hands under a stream of bleach. I found the incision; it was deep in my thumb, now the source of a fierce stinging that almost masked the throbbing pain. Despite the terrible burning of the Clorox, I pulled open the wound so more disinfectant could penetrate the exposed tissue.

Then I realized that all this time Susan had been hovering around, calling out, "Mahlon, how bad is it? God, I can't believe this happened. You've got to stop and get it checked."

I turned to face her, peering at me from behind her surgical mask, her eyes popped in horror. "Right now?" I said. "Why? It's just a cut," though I knew the wound was more than superficial.

Susan backed away, shaking her head. "I can't believe you're going to keep going."

"Look, I've disinfected it, and I don't think I need stitches. So why should I stop now?"

Having said this, I felt calmer.

At that moment, the autopsy assistant appeared with new pairs of gloves, which he handed to me. He looked worried.

"Besides," I added, "nothing would show up tonight."

And so, after drying my hands, I regloved and slowly returned to the autopsy table. The room seemed ominously quiet, a stillness I pierced with the switch of the handsaw. The blade spun and hummed, then shrieked as it bit into the skull. As I pressed it harder against the bone the screeching yielded to a drone. The sound was a lot less disturbing than Susan's worried prattle and the globs of blood and bone dust spraying against the biohazard bags enclosing the head and my saw. After sawing through the skullcap, I inserted a steel wedge in the cut. With a twist, I cracked the skull open to reveal the atrophic walnutlike brain in its shell. Several critical cuts later, I slipped the brain out, as I had hundreds before it, and cradled it in my hands.

Even without wiping off the blood, without cutting the brain to peer inside, I could feel its eerie softness. Every rampant thought inside me was now still as I examined the frightening destruction the virus had wrought. Necrotic, cottage-cheese-like matter oozed from a nick, probably the result of severe PML (progressive multifocal leukoencephalopathy), a viral illness that destroys the brain's white matter and its cells. I wouldn't know for sure for several more days, until the brain had been fixed in formalin long enough to be successfully sectioned and viewed under my microscope. I concluded the autopsy by attaching a piece of string to the brain's basilar artery and then slowly lowered it into a bucket of formalin. As it submerged, blood on the brain spread like a sunburst.

As I was putting the lid on the bucket, I could hear the autopsy assistant coming forward. His job was to slip the man inside a bag, zip it up, and then move it onto the gurney to await the arrival of the funeral home attendants. Now, without his brain, the man would be borne back to his family.

I peeled off my multiple layers of gloves, the sweaty face shield, and the space suit, then shoved everything into the bright red waste bag that warned of infectious disease. Then, without a word, I started out the open door of the autopsy suite.

Susan chased after me, following me down the hallway. "Jesus, Mahlon, go get your hand checked."

The Occupational Health Clinic was closed. "I will. I will. Tomorrow," I said.

"Don't blow this off," she said. "Make sure you do."

A few moments later I was out in the darkness, walking through the driving, chilling rain. As I trudged back across the campus, I thought about how deep the bloody scalpel had gone and knew I would worry about it. I was drenched by the time I reached the large, gothic door of "Old North," the building that housed the pathology department. Its unmanned labs glowed dimly with fluorescent lamps. The other faculty members had gone home.

My office was dark except for a ray of a street lamp pooling on my desk. But I didn't turn on the lights, for somehow the darkness seemed to ease my fears about the accident. And yet the feeling of uncertainty was still there, and I needed to talk to someone. In the blackness I made my way to the phone and dialed Jim Stevens, one of the doctors who had wanted the autopsy.

When he answered, I could hear his children clamoring in the background. "Sounds like I'm getting you at a bad time," I said.

"No, no, it's fine. What's up?"

"Jim, I just cut myself on that AIDS autopsy."

There was silence—it seemed like a minute passed before he answered. "How bad?"

My stabbed thumb began to pulse again. "Pretty bad." Then I explained how deep the cut had gone and that my hands had been covered with the corpse's blood. "Do you think I should start AZT right away?"

"Mahlon . . ." Jim began. I sensed he was trying to choose his words carefully. "There's really no evidence that AZT does any good at this point. It's up to you, but I guess I probably wouldn't."

Of course I knew that Stevens was right: in 1992 there was no definitive data suggesting that AZT would block an infection in someone exposed to HIV. There'd even been reports of nurses, stuck by HIV-contaminated needles, who had become infected despite immediate treatment with AZT. At this point, if virus had entered my blood, all I could do was hope that my immune system could stop it. But I couldn't stand the thought of doing nothing, of just watching and waiting for my error to explode into a nightmare.

As my thoughts drifted, Jim brought me back. "So, are you okay?"

I told him that I was a little spooked.

"Of course you are."

"I know I won't necessarily get infected. I just thought I'd check to see if there's anything I could be doing to protect myself."

"You want to come over and talk?"

I shrank away from the idea of disturbing him any further. I'd called him out of fear—a fear that only time and testing could allay—and now I felt embarrassed. "No. I'm fine. I'm sorry I bothered you at home."

A child came close to the phone and began speaking to Stevens. "Just a minute," he said gently, to me as well as to the child. I listened to them negotiating over a bedtime, and finally Stevens came back on the line. "Mahlon, I'm sorry."

With a pang of envy, I realized that I could barely picture his life—was his home well lit, warm on this clammy night, with children padding around in what—pajamas at this hour?—his wife perhaps turning down the beds? Feeling like a boor for disrupting his domestic comfort, I reassured him that I was fine. I wanted to get off the phone.

It was almost eleven when I got home. In those days I lived in a seventy-year-old stone cottage in Green Hills, a quiet residential enclave populated mostly by young families. At my back door was an old rusted bell, which I often rang when I came home, even though no one was there, like a lonely child who makes up an imaginary friend. When the bell was working, its dull buzz sounded friendly, like a grunting welcome from the old house. That night I rang it and was rewarded with its greeting. The back door windowpanes rattled as I entered the kitchen.

My home had been empty since my breakup with my fiancée, Alexis. That relationship—my only romantic connection in five years—had sputtered out in less than a year because Alexis had been a research wonk like I was, too driven by the grueling demands of academic science to enjoy a personal life. In the nine months since she had left, I had regressed to my "lab rat" ways— grabbing dinner at the office, taking call most weekends, lost in the solitary but satisfying riddles of my work. I'd always been a loner, with few close friends and lovers. I was used to being alone. Yet that night I felt acutely and painfully isolated.

I took refuge in my nightly rituals—preparing a tuna fish sandwich, my bedtime snack since childhood, and eating it standing at the kitchen counter, listening to the news on public radio. Finally, at one A.M., too agitated to climb into bed, I went into the living room and lay down on my soft leather sofa. There I thrashed around, trying to calm myself with the thought that the odds were with me: only 0.37 percent of health care workers who had accidents, 1 out of 270 people, ever became infected with HIV. But the familiar numbers didn't comfort me. I picked up an unfinished issue of *Science* magazine and read until I fell asleep.

CHAPTER 2

⧜

ACCORDING TO MY mother, I'd always been a fighter. In fact, my life began with a battle for survival, for during the final days of her pregnancy, my mother developed abruptio placentae, a condition in which the placenta slowly separates from the womb. Although confined to bed by her doctors, she went into early labor, and I was born six weeks prematurely, weighing just four pounds.

From the beginning it was clear that something was wrong with me. I gasped for air without a cry, seemingly unable to breathe. The doctor put me in a special oxygenated incubator, but I didn't seem to respond; and so, fearing the worst, he went to speak to my mother in her room. As my mother tells it: "Mahlon, he said, 'I'm sorry, he would've been a boy.' Can you believe it? He'd given up on you. I knew he was wrong, and I was furious. I told him, 'You keep him in that incubator. He'll be fine. You just keep him there!' ''

As it turned out, my mother's intuition proved better than medical opinion. To everyone's amazement but hers, I grew stronger. Word spread throughout the hospital that I was actually thriving, and the staff came to visit the "miracle baby" they had nearly abandoned. After five weeks I was discharged. The only vestige of my eventful birth seemed to be some scarring of my vocal cords, which left me with a soft and slightly raspy voice.

My mother named me for her grandfather, Mahlon Heinbaugh, a horse-and-buggy country doctor living in the mountains of western Maryland. In those days—early in this century—and in that part of the country, doctors were scarce and the demand for them consumed their lives. This was particularly true of my great-grandfather, who, in his single-minded devotion to patients, braved fierce snowstorms to deliver babies and to attend to children stricken with rheumatic fever. Considered to be one of the finest doctors in the area, he was eventually asked to head a sanitarium, a rural hospital for patients with prolonged illnesses.

He was a tall and magnanimous but shy man, a gentleman farmer who raised corn and cows, made cream and butter. And he had a special affection for his granddaughter; my mother often spent the entire summer with him and his wife. On long walks he would tell her stories about favorite patients and old friends. When she was old enough, he gave her a pony. She was out riding the pony on the humid evening when she found her grandfather lying in an orchard, stricken by a heart attack. Leaning against her and the pony, he was able to hobble back to the house.

The attack was attributed to overwork, but Mahlon Heinbaugh refused to let his health stand in the way of his caregiving. He continued working as hard as ever, until the morning in 1945 when he died of a heart attack while ministering to one of his patients.

Mahlon Heinbaugh had always encouraged my mother to pursue her love of music. And so, upon his death, she redoubled her efforts to become a cellist, no easy feat in her isolated mountain community. For a while, she studied with an excellent cellist who eventually married and moved away, leaving Mother to continue on alone. She did, and by age seventeen gained admittance to the prestigious Oberlin Conservatory of Music. It was there that she met and fell in love with an aspiring organist, my father.

My earliest memories are of music, the sonorous melodies of my mother's cello, and the grandeur of Dad's church organs. Life was Saint-Saëns and Bach. When I was big enough to reach, I would turn pages for my father as he played. Standing on the organ bench, I would always peer nervously at the rows of foot pedals down below, fearful of slipping and creating a cacophony of terrible sounds.

When my older sister, Becky, and I were very young, my family moved to Boston. My father pursued a doctorate in music education at Boston University while working as a music director at a Cambridge church. Mother studied part-time at Juilliard and gave private lessons on the cello. Becky and I took piano lessons, and then I branched out to the vibraphone while Becky tackled the flute. Both of us sang in my father's church choir. There's a picture of me singing a solo at one of his Christmas concerts, a small boy with shaggy blond hair, draped in a purple robe and holding up a candle.

My parents were two bullheaded individuals who certainly loved us but who each yearned to pursue an artistic career. Having to sustain our family, both of them had to forfeit certain ambitions, and those sacrifices began to strain their marriage. By the time I was five, they decided to separate, and my father moved out of our small ranch house in the suburb of Lexington to a city apartment on Beacon Hill. Becky and I, straddling their two worlds, were exposed to many rich experiences. On Saturdays my father played the organ at a reformed Jewish temple, magical services I would sit through with wonder. In the summers he would take us to nearby Marblehead to visit a family friend, a grand and matriarchal cellist named Lady Theobald, who was like a grandmother to us. Becky and I would often stay at her old whaler's house on the ocean, sleeping upstairs in the attic rooms and waking to the morning cries of wheeling seagulls dropping clams on her back patio. During the day I'd climb around the rock pools, observing sea life and popping seaweed for hours.

The simple marine creatures that washed up on the Marblehead shore engendered in me an abiding interest in biology. I'd walk the rocky coast searching for beached crabs with bulging eyes. I loved to pry open the shells of dead mussels, to rinse their shriveled valves with salt water, and every so often I'd find some sea creature still struggling to survive. Once, on Revere Beach, I spotted a jellyfish ailing from a gash, put it in my plastic pail, and brought it home—much to the horror of my mother. But after two days of my tender care and large dollops of tropical fish food, the jellyfish died. Curious about its wound and afraid I'd made it worse, I tried to examine the sticky blob. And then I buried it in the backyard and put up a wooden cross that I inscribed with orange crayon. I guess this was my first autopsy.

Those happy summers ended when my father, who had always

felt that church music shackled his creativity, decided to seek re-training as a choral conductor in Europe. Still freelancing as a cellist, Mother took on more private students to make ends meet. By then she had established her reputation as a cellist of such great refinement that she was often urged to audition for the Boston Symphony. The symphony might have paid her handsomely, but she would have had to tour extensively for concerts. Now that she was raising children as a single parent, she couldn't pursue the opportunity.

I missed my father, as any child would miss a parent, but I wasn't desolated by his leaving. Always an independent child, I grew even more self-sufficient, even fancied myself taking on his protective role. From a very early age I saw myself as a caretaker, not someone who was taken care of.

I remember that once my mother fell victim to a rogue deliv-eryman. "Weisman's" delivered baked goods from door to door and had a nervy habit of trying to foist unsolicited cakes and cook-ies on its customers. So one day we came home to find, along with our order of white bread, a box of cupcakes we couldn't afford. Becky and I hoped that the cupcakes were a gift, but knowing better, my mother left them out with a note. The next day a man drove up in a Weisman's truck and demanded payment for the returned cupcakes. Shocked at his audacity, my mother refused, but the man was insistent, even menacing. Finally, I stepped between my mother and the towering deliveryman to upbraid him for "tak-ing advantage of a family without a father." He looked at me, appalled, and then stalked back to his truck and drove away. By age nine, I had already made myself a pact to rescue my mother from such injustices.

After the deliveryman drove away, my mother swooped down on me and gave me a hug. She thanked me for standing up for her. "But," she added, "I think we do okay without a father."

Though financially pinched, we were culturally rich. My mother's house had become a center for chamber music sessions that drew an unusual mix of Boston's medical and musical luminaries. Among them were Clemens Benda, a German immigrant who became one of the titans of American neuropathology, and his Harvard colleague, the world-renowned neurologist Paul Yakovlev. Like many of that era's academic physicians, they were Renaissance men. Benda published poetry and for a while tried his hand at cello.

Benda's interest in my mother's music came to extend to me, already enraptured by medicine. Benda was the first person to tell me about neuroscience, about the mysteries of the brain. He would take me for rides in his sleek black Thunderbird, trying to explain the brain's basic functions and how they'd go awry. To my young mind, the workings of the mind, of personality, of creativity, seemed profoundly magical.

We lived in Boston until 1964, when my mother was offered a two-year teaching stint at Oberlin. That led to a permanent teaching position at the University of Tennessee at Knoxville, a middle-class, semiindustrial college town on the Tennessee River at the foot of the Smoky Mountains. My mother quickly became one of the most popular teachers at UT; her music appreciation classes were always filled to capacity. However, despite her accolades as a cellist and various teaching awards, her salary was paltry and she got short shrift on raises and promotions from the exclusively male review committees. Even her office was worse than most, the size of a closet. In those days, sex discrimination was so common that she could only view these iniquities as the trade-off for a stable job.

My mother never burdened us with her struggles, financial or emotional. She remained stoical even after my father returned to North America, married another woman, and eventually fathered two more children. We saw him only sporadically, usually when his conducting stints for various orchestras and ballet companies brought him to our area. If there was one obvious lesson Becky and I drew from our parents' lives—from my father's need to leave us to pursue artistic fulfillment, and from my mother's sacrifices to support herself in music—it was that work is a primary source of personal satisfaction.

To my mother, playing the cello was a calling, not a job. For long months before each concert she would practice relentlessly, in solitude, perfecting her art. By example, she taught us that a meaningful life required commitment to a worthy profession and the discipline to excel in it.

Still, having grown up watching our pennies, Becky and I would both eschew the "starving artist" life for careers that promised a better measure of financial security—computer technology for her and medicine for me. And I think we both remained a bit wary of marriage, which could be tenuous and could permanently derail a professional life.

I entered medical school in 1977 and was immediately captivated by pathology. My solitary nature inclined me more toward microscopic analysis of disease than toward witnessing the sufferings disease caused. And I liked the idea of playing Elliot Ness: pathologists are sleuths armed with microscopes who examine wounded tissues and analyze fluids for clues about the perpetrators of the crime of disease. Careful study of cellular changes could wring confessions of "Who did it?" and "How?" even from recalcitrant suspects. And within pathology, the most fascinating detective work, to me, was occurring in the realm that Clemens Benda had introduced me to years before—neuropathology, the study of the brain. In the 1970s, neuropathologists were trying to apprehend a master class of criminals—those that caused such diseases as multiple sclerosis, Alzheimer's and Parkinson's—by identifying the cells involved and genetic changes they bore. Tracing the modus operandi of such cunning malefactors, in the hope of finding ways to stop them, seemed an irresistibly magnetic challenge.

It was during my last year of medical school, in 1981, that a new disease, soon to be known as AIDS, was first reported in the June and July issues of *Morbidity and Mortality Weekly Report.* Initially, I didn't pay much attention to the illness taking hold in San Francisco and New York; for in those days it still wasn't clear whether AIDS would remain a medical curiosity or become an epidemic. Early descriptions said little about the involvement of the nervous system. And it was only in 1983 that the first autopsy studies on AIDS were even published from the National Institutes of Health.

A year later, in 1984, I started a residency in pathology/ neuropathology at Vanderbilt University in Nashville. Initially I was assigned to the "dead man's service," doing autopsies day and night. I rarely even saw the little room I had rented in an old stone boardinghouse near the hospital. Then, three months after I'd moved in, the bellicose landlady sued her "drunken bum" husband for a divorce and sold the boardinghouse.

My meager budget would make it hard to find another room, I knew. And since I was working fourteen-to-sixteen-hour days, I was already showering in the morgue and eating at the hospital—in effect, I was already living there. All I needed was a place to store my things and lay my head. Then an idea came to me: I'd get a truck!

I soon found a promising ad in the *Nashville Banner:* "White Chevy Step Van, 1976, 20hp generator, bubble top, good condition."

The owner was a narcoleptic ex-cop turned wholesale florist who'd used the van for deliveries before going retail. The white elephant got only eight miles to the gallon, but its air horn was pleasingly deafening and it had very little rust. On its maiden voyage the van made it all the way around the block without stalling. I was captivated.

I sold my old Volkswagen and, three days later, drove off in my new backfiring, wide-turning home that barely fit in one traffic lane. In a matter of days I'd risen from a fledgling neuropathologist to a real-life trucker. But the excitement was short-lived, for it was already late October and hard freezes were only a few weeks away. I had to find a parking space right away and then insulate my truck for the winter.

Neither Vanderbilt nor the VA hospital police let me park in their lots, so I found a spot under a streetlight on a stretch between the VA and a Vanderbilt dorm. The street's slight incline allowed rainwater to drain off the top rather than pool up and leak through the cracks I later discovered in the van's moon roof. Better yet, the VA police liked to perch in their cars on the hillside above me, perhaps ogling the sliding-glass-door balconies of the coeds who rarely used their curtains. So I was secure—throughout the twenty months I lived in the van, there was never a break-in.

My mother, horrified when I described my new home, immediately came from Knoxville laden with a down sleeping bag, comforters, and pillows.

"Oh, Mahlon," she fussed, "whatever possessed you to buy something like this?"

"Thrift," I explained. "Pure and simple."

"What are you going to do in the wintertime?"

I told her about the generator.

"Please be careful," she admonished me. "And make sure you lock the doors at night." She scrutinized the van's locks and door bars to make sure that I would be safe.

I scribbled down my new address for her with the name my colleagues had dubbed my new home:

> Mahlon Johnson
> c/o The Bread Truck
> 24th Avenue (third streetlight from the corner)
> Nashville, Tennessee.

As the weather got colder the generator died. But my mother's blankets and comforters kept me warm. On frigid nights my shoes actually froze to the plywood that I had laid down over the van's metal floor. But this was only a minor inconvenience, less troublesome than the stifling summer heat that turned my home into a baker's oven without an off switch.

But my new lifestyle proved quite efficient. I could leave work at midnight, jump the VA fence, and be home by 12:05. I could do my bedtime reading by flashlight (journals, of course). And every night was like camping out in the cold, crisp air.

The truck, as it turned out, was directly below the flight path of the medevac helicopters servicing medical emergencies in remote areas. In the evening I'd see them flying over like dragonflies with bodies in their claws. And at night I'd hear them hovering, chopper blades thrumming, as if to warn me what was coming my way.

I was living in the truck on the night I got called to do my first AIDS autopsy. The man was from California, the first of all those skeletal faces with staring eyes and skin stuck to bone. He was clearly a young man whose disease had aged him prematurely.

That first encounter with the ''plague'' was harrowing. When the autopsy was over I peeled off my garb with a dark paranoia. I knew that HIV had been swimming everywhere, in blood, in spinal fluid, spilling over my gloves. I took a long shower in the moldy cold of the autopsy dressing room, lathering my body several times. And yet even after showering I was still afraid that somewhere the virus had penetrated my armor, slipped in some crease of skin in my elbow or hand, waiting to get a foothold through a crack in my skin. For the first time, an unnerving fear of contagion had entered my life. This fear was different from the fear of, say, getting hepatitis, an illness you had a chance of surviving. But HIV was a more absolute threat, which raised a deep and primordial dread of dying.

In time, the danger would come to seem a necessary hazard of my profession, but no one could approach this lethal new disease without a realistic and human sense of unease.

I lived in the truck for twenty months, until the summer of 1986. Then, one night as I trudged home, wondering how I was going to stand another sweltering August in my makeshift home, I noticed some unfamiliar shadows on the sidewalk. There, to my amazement, standing in the dim orange glow of the street lamp, was a row of parking meters. The city of Nashville was installing meters on my street. Half a block more and the armless tax collectors would reach my sacred parking space. I was about to become part of the high-rent district (fifty cents per hour, to be exact).

The very next day, as luck would have it, the chairman of the pathology department offered me an instructorship at the university. In doing so, however, he made it quite clear that my colleagues didn't think it appropriate for someone in my position to be living in a truck. Looking back on it, I realize that the chairman was trying benevolently to temper my eccentricities.

And so, a week later, I found a small condo with high ceilings, windows, and light. Eventually I sold the truck to a housepainter who was greatly amused by the fact that I'd lived in it. But the experiment in truck living had lost its charm for me. I couldn't help but revel in my new home, equipped with such twentieth-century miracles as running water, electricity, a microwave, and (happily) air-conditioning.

IN FEBRUARY 1991, I received a call from Jim Stevens explaining that he was putting together a protocol to study brain lesions in AIDS patients. He wanted to evaluate whether positron emission tomography (PET) scans could be used to distinguish brain infections from tumors in AIDS patients. If they could, then patients could be rapidly diagnosed and treated without the need for a brain biopsy. Brain autopsies and biopsies were currently needed to determine which specific diseases were creating which images on the scans. For example, a common brain mass in AIDS patients is caused by the protozoa *Toxoplasma,* which produces abscesses mimicking common brain tumors, particularly lymphoma. Standard brain scans couldn't reliably tell them apart. It was hoped that PET scans would.

The most efficient means of getting the data Stevens needed was through a brain biopsy, drilling a tiny hole in the skull of the living patient, then inserting a small needle to ensnare a smidgen of tissue. But he explained that some surgeons were reluctant to biopsy AIDS patients who were destined to die anyway in a matter of months. A few felt it would be inhumane to subject such sick patients to the procedure; others worried about operative risks, such as bleeding in the brain or their own risk of exposure. Nonetheless, their risks were minor compared to the exposure a pathologist faced in removing an entire bloody brain.

"So we'll have to get autopsies to confirm what the patients had," he told me. "My question to you is basically, would you be willing to do them?"

If I undertook this assignment, time and again I would have to saw through the skullcaps of deceased AIDS patients, unleashing floods of virus-riddled blood and cerebrospinal fluid. I was aware of the danger, of course, but the pathology was so intriguing. Patients with AIDS develop rare brain infections that I seldom saw. Identifying them would be a tremendous intellectual challenge, a chance to learn. Beyond this, the lessons I could glean from the dead—the diagnosis of treatable conditions—would have immediate benefits for living patients. It was a chance to make a real contribution to the war on AIDS.

"What can I say, Jim? They make me nervous. But sure, I'll do them."

I quelled my stray fears by invoking the scientific mantra, the indisputable statistics: only 0.37 percent—1 in 270—of health care workers who stuck themselves with needles containing AIDS blood ever got infected. Besides, at that time there had been no well-documented case of a pathologist such as myself acquiring HIV from an autopsy.

C H A P T E R   3

Occupational Health, which evaluated work injuries, was at the end of a narrow corridor cluttered with movable carts and EKG machines. It was the sort of place where the phone is constantly ringing. An administrator was handing out requisition forms to a couple of fidgeting employees awaiting their turns. From among this gathering I was finally singled out and shown to a room, and told to sit on an examining table covered in crinkly white paper. I could barely remember the last time I'd sat like a patient, and the momentary feeling of discomfort and imagined indignity made me swing off the table and sit in the plastic chair next to the desk. Despite my accident, I was still a pathologist—a stalker, not a victim, of disease.

I was waiting to have my blood drawn for an HIV ELISA, the crude standard test that detects whether or not there are any antibodies against HIV present in the blood. If the ELISA detects any antibodies, then a more definitive technique called the Western Blot is used to show whether the blood contains specific antibodies targeting some of the different proteins that make up the HIV virus. These specific antibodies appear as bands on the test results. A rare false-positive ELISA would reveal only one antibody band, usually the one called the p24 band. A true HIV-positive blood sample would yield multiple (usually four to eight) bands of antibodies specific to four to eight different components of the virus.

At that point, I knew I would test negative. Viral activity, if any, would be impossible to pick up so soon after my accident. And I'd tested negative a year and a half before when Alexis, my fiancée, urged me to get screened since I was doing AIDS autopsies.

After a few minutes I was greeted by an attractive blond nurse practitioner who smiled coolly at me. She read the accident report with a look of concern. "You sure sound calm about all this," she said. "Some of the nurses I've seen come in here after a needle stick were hysterical."

"Well, the odds are pretty high that I won't get infected."

Without further comment, she pulled on a pair of rubber gloves, found a vein in my arm, and drew blood for the baseline HIV ELISA. She then handed me a schedule for HIV testing—once every six weeks for the next six months—and looked at me sternly. "Safe sex must be practiced during this period."

"Don't worry. I broke up with my fiancée a year ago. I'm still not up to anything heavy."

I assured her that I'd been abstinent for over a year and that currently there wasn't anyone on the horizon. "But even if there were, I plan to remain celibate until the tests prove that I'm all right.''

At this point I couldn't imagine dating someone without explaining my ''sexual limbo,'' even if it put a damper on a budding relationship. Any potential lover had the right to know. And I'd rather have the news come from me than from the inevitable rumors spawned by the accident.

Indeed, as I sat in the examining room, Susan was spreading word of my accident throughout the pathology department. Talking about it no doubt helped her master her anxiety, but her confessions made those first few days awkward. Everywhere I went I was greeted by concerned stares and stammered inquiries from friends and colleagues. One colleague who saw me coming down the hallway even lowered his head and veered into a snack bar as if to avoid me. Everyone seemed haunted by a vague unease: If this kind of accident had happened to an experienced person, then what about the rest of them? What would happen if somebody less seasoned than I were forced to remove the brain of a person who had died of AIDS? Everybody in Pathology was relieved when an infectious disease expert consulted on the matter made a broad pronouncement that there was nothing to worry about, that the risk of infection was minimal. And everybody wanted to believe him, including me—especially me.

As expected, my tests came back negative two days later, and I made an appointment for the next test, six weeks hence. That test, at the end of October, would be a critical one, for if there had been any exposure to virus, my body would probably have begun to mount a detectable immune response. And so, over the next six weeks, I found myself keeping a closer vigil over my health, on the lookout for the dreaded flulike illness that heralds seroconversion. I continued to run and lift weights as I had done for the previous twenty-eight years. To assure others I was healthy I started using a tanning bed that I had purchased during my residency.

In those days I was always inside, and quite pale as a consequence. Usually I didn't notice. But one day after doing an autopsy, I went to shower and caught a glimpse of myself in the mirror. "You look worse than that corpse," I told myself aloud. In fact, I had become the prototypical medical geek, a pasty-faced lab rat. After finishing my residency I tried to correct this (without having to stop work), by acquiring a tanning bed. And, using it cautiously, I was able to restore a measure of color to my hide.

As the day approached for the next test, I couldn't shake my feelings of uneasiness.

"Johnson!" Like a grade school principal, a portly, middle-aged woman summoned me from the waiting room into an examining room whose walls were filled with children's crayon drawings. Below the artwork stood a row of chairs. I sat down and rolled up my sleeve, trying to look indifferent as she busied herself with some test tubes with rubber stoppers. There was a firm politeness to her manner that bordered on officiousness. Under her stern gaze I found myself wondering if she could be afraid of drawing my blood, a thought I quickly quashed as my own projection. To the phlebotomist this was just another blood collection. It was only for me that this was a critical test, a defining moment.

I felt the needle sink in. "A little stick," she murmured with a grin, and it was over.

Two days passed before the results were in. When I called to get them, I was put on hold. Finally, the receptionist came back on and explained that I would have to get the verdict from Dr. Jane Davis of the Occupational Health Clinic.

"Then let me talk to her," I said.

"I'm sorry, she's preparing for a meeting. We'll have her call you later."

Frustrated, I hung up the phone, resigned to a nerve-racking wait. As a consulting pathologist I could always get access to test information relevant to my cases. But my own test results—those had to go through "my doctor," and so like any other patient I could do nothing but stew. Finally, at five-thirty my beeper went off, displaying Dr. Davis's phone number. I called back and this time she answered.

With false cheer I said, "Hello, Jane, I just wanted to find out about my ELISA."

The silence on her end of the phone was sobering.

"Mahlon," she said at last, "they couldn't give you the information at the office because . . . well, the HIV-1 ELISA was weakly positive, so we ran the Western Blot. It has a p24 band. It's probably a false positive . . . but . . ."

"Positive" was all I heard. There's a cliché that at the brink of death a person's life passes before his eyes, but strangely, at that moment, a mural of my future unfurled before me and splintered. Half a century of a life I'd all but taken for granted—marriage, children, seniority, retirement, security for my mother—all snipped to pieces.

Davis was still talking, so I tried to tune back in. She saying something about discussing the situation with other colleagues, something about people she'd seen with positive ELISAs and p24 bands. "It's a common false positive, Mahlon," she said.

I explained that my previous HIV ELISAs had been completely negative. "Doesn't it seem a little funny," I asked, "that I've suddenly changed to positive six weeks after the accident? That's perfect for an early infection."

"Not necessarily," she said. "Now, please don't jump to any conclusions. We're going to monitor this very carefully from here on in."

"Okay, thanks," I murmured, needing to end the discussion. My mind was flooding with dire thoughts.

As a pathologist I knew what AIDS truly was. Clinicians saw the wasting patients, but they never saw the destruction that AIDS wreaked inside the body—the transmogrification of lungs into bags of blood and brains into cottage cheese.

Shaken by these images, I hung up the phone and, to flee them, left my office.

In the hallway I heard somebody call out, "Mahlon!"

It was Harry Brown, a hulking infectious disease specialist whose natural frown lent him a formidable presence. Only a year older than I, Harry had already established a successful AIDS research program, as well as a national reputation as a researcher. As Harry kept advancing, he began to frown.

"Jane called me about your results."

I was taken aback. I had only just gotten the news myself. "She did? Already?"

"Are you feeling okay?" he asked.

I'd never felt better, I told him. I was even working out at the gym as much as I ever had. Then I forced myself to ask him, "So what do you think of all this?"

"We'll have to wait and see," he said, his voice sounding cluttered with thoughts that he wasn't expressing. "I sure hope it's nothing. But as I told Jane, and now I'll tell you too, I watched another medical school turn its back on an occupationally infected staff physician. They treated him badly.''

''What happened?'' I asked.

A resident at a premier medical school became infected from a needle stick while drawing the blood of a child who had contracted AIDS from a transfusion. Denying responsibility, the school refused to help the resident with medical costs until he and his family took legal action.

Up until that point, I had never imagined that the hospital would abandon me. But now it struck me that I, too, could become a pariah. Would a possible infection influence the clinicians I worked with, making them reluctant to send me their consult cases? Worse yet, would the administration try to discredit me somehow to escape liability?

''Look, I have a meeting to get to,'' Harry was saying. ''But I just want to warn you to keep a paper trail. You need to document all your previous tests as well as the ones that you have from here on in. Just in case. Our lab can help.'' With that, he shook my hand and wished me well.

Two weeks later, on November 15, my blood was tested again. This time the news was better. Though the level of antibodies was somewhat higher than normal, technically, I was still negative. What remained was a fourth, ten-week follow-up negative ELISA result to prove, with reasonable assurance, that I was not infected.

On November 30, 1992, I returned.

''Johnson!'' my named echoed from the next room. There stood the same pudgy middle-aged woman who had drawn my blood previously. As I sat down in the chair, she threw me the same grim look, and this time I knew I wasn't imagining her disdain. Did she think I was gay? Was she judging me, trying to inflict a shame that no one deserves to feel? Without a word, she pulled her gloves on slowly, reluctantly, as though she now dreaded contact with me, as though I were a leper. She leaned toward me, tied the rubber tourniquet, and, without the usual polite warning, plunged the syringe into my arm. Her brash needle hit a nerve, and pain rocketed up my arm. But somehow I managed not to flinch and to hold still while my blood squirted into the glass vacucontainer.

"Here, hold this!" she ordered, pressing a cotton swab over the stick site. Then she slapped a Band-Aid on the site and turned away.

I sat there, stupefied, angry, and the anger ripened. Kindness required no more effort than rudeness, and it would have been a gift for an uneasy patient like me. Too enraged to speak, I hurried out of the lab.

In the corridor, I encountered Beth Ann Jamison, Stevens's partner in the AIDS brain study, the one who had requested the now-infamous autopsy. She was a handsome, small-boned woman with a sculptured face, a radiant smile, and a childlike laugh. But now she looked concerned.

"You seem rattled," she said.

I told her about my encounter with the phlebotomist.

"I mean, what if I was a guy whose lover was dying of AIDS and I came in to get a blood test? That's not the way to treat people, especially patients."

She let me fume for a while before she broke in.

"Look," she said, "I'm not trying to defend this lady, God knows. Maybe, for all we know, she *was* judging you. Maybe she was having a bad day. But, as you know, most of the techs are pros.''

"It's not easy to be a patient," I muttered.

Beth Ann nodded sympathetically. Then she tapped my shoulder. "But how are you otherwise?"

I shrugged.

"Was that the big one, the definitive test?"

I nodded and held up two sets of crossed fingers. "If this one's negative . . ."

"I'm pulling for you," she said. "Call me as soon as you know."

TWO DAYS LATER Jane Davis informed me that my ELISA test was once again positive and that the Western Blot still had a p24 band. Her voice trembled as she broke the news. "However," she said, "I still think you're probably a false positive."

Even though I wanted to believe her—and I appreciated her reassurance—I knew that she was trying to bolster herself as well as me, to avoid acknowledging the horrible possibility of HIV in a fellow physician. I knew that people actually threatened by a disease could often face it more readily than those who watched helplessly. And there was scientific truth behind her words—my Western Blot was still showing only one band, not the four that would brand me HIV positive—but the uncertainty of my HIV status was upsetting me as much as the prospect of being positive. It was time to seek definitive answers.

"Let's not keep doing ELISAs," I told Jane. "I think I'd like to try PCR." PCR, polymerase chain reaction, a test measuring viral genes in blood, was state-of-the-art in viral detection. At this point, I knew, PCR would be more effective, because after the first few months of an HIV infection, the level of HIV in the blood can temporarily drop. The virus can retreat into the shadows of the lymph system, where it may hide from the searchlights of blood cultures while slowly continuing its destruction of the immune system.

Jane agreed that I should try PCR, which would have to be processed at a specialty lab in California. I would be in limbo for another two to three weeks, the soonest I could expect the results.

It was almost an eerie glimpse of the new world I was entering when, later that very day, I got a call from the university's Anatomic Donation Service. They knew I did AIDS autopsies, and they hoped I could solve a problem. A patient who had donated his body to Anatomy had died in a small town about two hours away from Nashville, but since he had AIDS the medical school couldn't accept it. Apparently the man's wife was hysterical and needed advice. Normally I would have referred the case to an AIDS social worker, but the call was just too timely to pass along. With AIDS hovering over my life, I was developing a fearful fascination with it; I couldn't help but identify with the caller's distress. I jotted down the name, Mrs. Hargrave, and the number, then called her back myself, thinking that this was my initiation rite into the living world of AIDS.

She answered the phone sobbing. She told me that she had checked his breathing and pulse. "He's just lying there, staring," she said.

"Why don't you call an ambulance?" I asked gently. "Or call the police?"

"I can't do that!" she cried. "The ambulance people will tell the whole town. Nobody 'round here knows that Mac had AIDS. If they find out, they'll burn the house down."

Flashing back to the ignorant scorn of my phlebotomist—a supposedly enlightened professional at a major urban medical center—I hated to imagine the virulent fear of a rural town. As I murmured words of comfort, Mrs. Hargrave told me more of her story, a tragedy compounded by prejudice.

Mac had gotten a blood transfusion in 1982, and in 1989 came down with pneumonia, which led to a diagnosis of AIDS. He had sought treatment two hours away at Vanderbilt in part to conceal his condition from the community. Eventually, Mrs. Hargrave decided that her husband's decline could no longer be hidden from their children, who by necessity became accomplices in the dark family secret. And so they explained his pneumonia as "a cold," his crippling fatigue as the result of his being "overworked." There had been no one in the community she could turn to, and now even a burial in her husband's hometown would be out of the question.

Mrs. Hargrave couldn't bear for the children to see their father's dead body, so Mac would have to be moved soon. In Tennessee it is illegal to move a dead body until that body is released by the proper authorities—the loose-lipped sheriff, the emergency medical service, or a distant medical examiner. Obviously, Mrs. Hargrave couldn't call any of them.

Touched by her suffering, I had a strong impulse to get into my car and drive the two hours to help her. But I was on call. Then I got an idea. I asked her how much her husband weighed. She said that he had been down to eighty pounds just before he died.

"Do you think you can carry him to your car?"

"I think so."

I suggested that she put Mac in the back of the car and drive him to the emergency room at a hospital in Murfreesboro, which was closer to where she lived than Nashville. There, she could play dumb and explain that he'd been suffering from respiratory distress and she thought he'd gone into a coma; they might buy that and not necessarily assume he had AIDS. Once he was pronounced dead, then she could make funeral arrangements in a town where she and her husband were not known.

Mrs. Hargrave embraced the idea tearfully, thanking me. As I hung up the phone, I imagined her walking into the room where her husband lay dead and staring, lifting him—perhaps in a fireman's carry—and bearing him out to the car. What if some neighbor saw her? What would she say: that he'd had some kind of collapse? But she had no alternative. I silently wished her the nerve to pull it off.

When I called her the next morning, she sounded a bit more cheerful. My plan, she said, had worked. Though her children were distraught, she claimed the family was grateful for the time they were granted with Mac. When she told me this, I couldn't help but think of my mother and sister, wondering how they would cope if I were dealt a similar fate. Long ago, I'd assumed the role of the family patriarch, the protector. If some catastrophic illness were to weaken me, how would they deal with this reversal, how would they manage without me?

CHAPTER 4

———— ⧗ ————

WHAT A COLD, stark December that was! The winter rains laid siege to Nashville, stripping the few remaining leaves from the wizened hackberry outside my window. An empty bird's nest lay knocked off its perch, feathers and sticks strewn like rubble. As usual, I signed on for Christmas call, since I was single, unlike most of my colleagues, who would want to spend the holidays with their spouses and children. Being on call also gave me an excuse to avoid the enforced revelry of holiday parties, which made me feel awkward and uncomfortably conscious of being unattached. I knew that by purposely sequestering myself out of shyness I was only increasing my sense of isolation, but that year I welcomed the solitude of my tiny office. As a child I had believed that I could avoid ill fate, real or perceived, by lying low. And now, as I awaited my PCR results, I fell back on that old superstition.

One night toward the middle of December, I arrived home to find a tall cardboard box bedecked with UPS stickers leaning up against my back door like an unwelcome visitor. It was a Christmas gift sent by my mother despite my pleas that she save her money that year. "Send me some daffodil bulbs," I'd told her a few weeks before when I'd gone down to Knoxville for my monthly neuropath consultation at the University of Tennessee. But I knew she wouldn't listen.

I brought the box inside and opened it to find a mass of green, the leaves of a silk ficus tree. My mother knew that I loved plants and missed the lushness of my garden in the bleak of winter. Though I was moved by her thoughtfulness, her generosity saddened me. All I could think of were the ten Boston winters when she'd worn the same coat, a hand-me-down from her sister, while Becky and I wore new winter clothes. Behind this carefully chosen, too-expensive gift lay a spate of small sacrifices, I knew. It filled me with sadness to think how bereft she would feel if I grew ill.

That night I even dreamed about the sorrow I would cause her. I dreamed she was in her old practice studio in Boston, cradling her cello, looking forlorn. It was a cloudless winter night, and the moonlight shone on her, making her look stooped and old. I was in the room with her, and she was playing, but I was at the end of life, and as I withered, the songs kept shortening. In the dream it was painfully obvious to me that when I was gone, she would stop playing and that silence would spread over the room like a fine layer of permanent dust.

To amuse my mother I always asked to talk to her dogs when I called. So when I phoned her the next morning, I told her to put on Orpheus, her Great Dane and her favorite of the three dogs she owned. "Oh, Mahlon," she said, as she always did, "he's just had his breakfast and he's sleeping. He can't come to the phone right now."

"Ah, just get him for me."

"I don't want to wake him up," she said. "Be grateful he's sleeping."

Then I sighed and said, "Mom, it's a beautiful tree. But it worries me that you sent it."

She went silent. We'd played this scene often enough before, Mom stubbornly trying to spoil me while I guiltily tried to spare her the expense. It was a ritualistic exchange of guilt, guilt on her part that she hadn't provided enough for her children and guilt from us that we'd been unable to repay her devotion. But torn by my new anxieties and fears, I escalated the familiar battle. Too forcefully, I insisted on sending back the tree.

"Why are you saying that?"

"Because I can tell it's really expensive, too expensive for your budget. I'm going to send it back to you."

"No you don't, buster," she snapped, stung by my adamance. "If you send it back I wash my hands of you."

My mother said she could spend her money any way she wanted. I argued that she had to think about her retirement, which would be more expensive than she realized. Beneath my scolding tone, I knew, lay the competing urges to confide in her and to shield her from my worries. Still, I kept pushing. "What will happen if I'm not around to take care of you?"

She hung up on me.

Though I was sorry I'd provoked her, I didn't call her back, unsure of what I wanted to say. I knew that she would seek out her cello in her dark, empty studio, play for a few furious moments, then stop and reflect. She always did that. And then she'd call me back.

She reached me a half hour later at my office. "There's something wrong, isn't there? What do you mean, if you're not around?"

I'd gone too far down the road to turn back, and I realized that I wanted her reassurance. Besides, the news wasn't definitive; it wasn't as though I were dropping a bomb. "Mom," I began, "I haven't told you this, but . . . well, I cut myself a few months ago during one of those AIDS autopsies. It was just a scalpel wound, but it's been worrying me."

"Oh no!" she said. "Does that mean you're infected? Ever since you first told me about that study, I've been worried. Why should you have to take all the risks?"

"No," I reassured her. "I'm okay. My test after the accident was negative. It's just that this week's follow-up test was a little funny."

"What do you mean, a little funny?"

"The test is indeterminate. I guess it got me a little spooked. This whole thing is probably a fluke. But it did get me thinking about your retirement. I keep worrying that if anything happens to me all you'll have is your retirement and my measly life insurance."

"I don't care about your damned life insurance," my mother insisted. "I care about you."

I told her about the PCR and viral co-cultures that might be the definitive tests in regard to my questionable HIV status. She asked me when the results would be back, and I explained I would probably get the verdict within three weeks. "Will you promise to tell me what happens?" she asked.

As I assured her that I would, I heard her dog Orpheus, his resonating sentry bark from downstairs. "I guess he just woke up," I said.

"Hush!" she told him. Then to me, "I really wish you were coming home for Christmas."

"I wish I was, too." Indeed, now that she knew what was going on, I regretted having put myself on call, indulging for a moment in the fantasy of a carefree family Christmas.

"Well, think about it, okay? Maybe you can rearrange things," she said.

"Okay," I said. But I knew I wouldn't.

ONCE MY BLOOD was flown to California, it somehow vanished into the labyrinth of a medical laboratory, where my name was unknown and where no one cared how long I waited for results. Again, I chafed at the helplessness of being a patient, at having to suffer with uncertainty as the weeks passed without a word. After several tries, I finally managed to reach the laboratory supervisor— only to hear that the lab technician running the tests had fallen ill and would probably not return until the New Year. By mid-January, however, there was still no news. My pestering phone calls drew only vague accounts of backlogs. As the time dragged on, my anxious state mutated into a bleak depression.

One Saturday afternoon when I was running an errand in downtown Nashville I happened to pass an Army-Navy store. I had a spare moment, so I wandered through the aisles, passing cluttered racks of olive-green pants and camouflage rain parkas. The rows of fishing rods and bobbers brought me back to my childhood summers on the ocean.

Finally, I stood in front of a peeling side wall beneath a bug-eyed deer head, with ears erect, watching over the store. On the wall was a rack of neatly displayed rifles fronted by a glass display case filled with handguns. I spied a large Luger, the kind of gun Nazis used in old war movies, nestled among black revolvers, loose bullets, and clips. It looked too heavy to pick up.

The thought came to me that perhaps, if I got really ill, I would need a gun.

Even for a doctor, drugs that can guarantee a quick and painless death are hard to get. Painkillers such as morphine and Demerol are strictly monitored in hospitals, and I would never want to burden my physician friends with the knowledge that they'd prescribed the drugs I used to end my life. Then, too, it was easy to botch a suicide attempt with drugs or carbon monoxide and wind up alive and in agony. A gun might offer me a swifter and more certain way out.

"You lookin' for somethin'?"

The question came from a burly salesman with a shaved head. He was seated behind a counter, hunched over a comic book.

"Do you have any small handguns?" I found myself asking. He looked at me doubtfully. "It's for home security," I explained.

He squinted at me. I felt like a pipsqueak in my white shirt and tie. Then, flexing his chest like a big bear, he lumbered over to the gun case and towered over me.

"A house nearby was broken into recently," I told him. This was actually the truth, although the burglars had turned out to be rich kids stealing CDs.

The man gestured toward the guns with a scarred, meaty hand. "So, what can I get you?" he said.

Pointing to a "Lady" Smith and Wesson .38, I asked, "How much is that?"

He gave the gun a withering glance. "Three hundred fifty dollars."

"Do you have anything smaller?"

He sighed with exasperation. "No."

Opening the glass case, he drew out the gun. It looked like a toy in his big palm.

"Is that the kind of gun people would get for basic protection?"

"Why, you want it?" he challenged.

Before I could answer, a phone rang on the back wall. He returned the gun to the cabinet and locked it with a dull click. Suddenly, I lost my nerve.

As soon as he turned his back, I slipped out of the store.

Outside, in the cold air, I recognized my notion of suicide for what it was: a morbid fantasy. The suspense of waiting for news had plunged me into a despair that I now willed myself to shake off.

THE FOLLOWING MONDAY, my long-overdue PCR results finally came in, results that left me too elated and hopeful to dwell on the outrage of waiting. It was "negative."

CHAPTER 5

BETWEEN JANUARY AND April, my life seemed almost normal as the fear of infection slowly relinquished its hold. But there was still one more hurdle, seemingly a formality now, that I had to clear to be pronounced "negative." It was well established that in some people the antibody response to HIV could be delayed and consequently would not show up until six months after the exposure. And so, wanting to establish my good health once and for all, I went to have blood drawn one more time, seven months after the accident. Whether out of irony or perversity, I timed it so that the results would be available to me on April 14, 1993, my thirty-ninth birthday.

On that day, I was at my office when my pager went off, reading out a number that was unfamiliar. I called and got the office of Dr. Carlson, an infectious disease expert affiliated with Occupational Health.

"Mahlon, your immune system is giving us fits," Carlson said the moment he came on the line. "We need to talk. Can you come over here right now?"

He was off the phone before I could ask anything. But I didn't need to. Something scary was going on. And with that thought, I turned and ran out of the office.

I rushed down the hallway, rounded the corner, and entered the stairwell, hoping desperately that my instincts were wrong. But deep within me there was a fearful sense that my life was about to change.

I skipped steps as I flew down the staircase, nearly colliding with two secretaries standing in the doorway. "Dr. Johnson!" one of them yelled at me. "What is wrong?" I didn't pause to answer.

Carlson, a muscular middle-aged Swede with close-cropped hair and round-rimmed glasses, was sitting on the edge of his office desk. Up until this time I had had little contact with him. In recent years he'd been doing more research though still consulted on infectious disease problems.

Carlson shook my hand and then asked me to sit down. "As I was saying, you have a very weird immune system that is causing us fits. Your HIV Western Blot is now showing five bands, although some are fairly faint. But don't panic. What all this means is not yet clear."

"What it probably means is that I've gotten infected," I said, sensing his uneasiness, his reluctance to face this new reality.

"Let's not jump to conclusions." Carlson turned away to find the report. "Remember you never got the flulike illness."

I stared at him with surprise. He knew as well as I that the "flulike illness" did not herald every HIV case and that the appearance of four or more bands was considered definitive evidence of HIV. I had five bands.* Was Carlson grasping at straws?

"Perhaps," I said finally. "But I had consistently negative HIV ELISAs until six weeks after the accident. How do you explain that?"

"Mahlon, we're still looking at the tests. Still sorting it all out. Until we figure things out, you might want to keep this to yourself. There's no point in scaring anyone who cares about you until there are some definitive answers."

It had been an endless ride: positive, negative, positive, negative—and then, almost as an afterthought, positive. Although I had yearned for the truth, when it finally came I couldn't quite accept it. "In the meanwhile I'll get the tests rerun," I said, allowing myself a last shred of optimism.

I left Carlson and went back to my office wanting to think things over. As the shock of the news wore off, I felt strangely neutral, as if possessed by dueling demons: denial and hope. As an outsider, even before facing HIV, I had always felt that break-throughs were long overdue. It almost defied imagination that after a decade of aggressive research by science's best minds something hadn't been found. Indeed, I was sure that something would be found—and if it were found within the next five to seven years, I might have a good chance of surviving. After all, many infected people lived a good ten years before they developed symptoms for AIDS.

And, I told myself, there was a powerful weapon that I could use to fight this disease—my training in scientific research. I had

---

* Eventually I fully seroconverted, showing seven bands.

two doctorates, I hadn't read a novel or taken a vacation in years— my whole life was medicine. Surely at a major medical center such as Vanderbilt, with its towering new library and research programs, I could uncover news of every promising new treatment the moment it was developed. As a doctor, I could get access to the best new drugs and, at the very least, stay healthy until the breakthroughs came. With a strange adrenaline rush, I told myself that I was embarking on the "ultimate experiment"—the battle for my life.

Fired up by these thoughts, I barely noticed the telephone ringing. I picked it up. "Happy Birthday," said a familiar voice— my father's. "I'm looking forward to seeing you tonight."

Astonishingly, with everything that had been going on, I'd forgotten about my father's imminent arrival.

"I just wanted to give you my flight information."

I glanced at my calendar and saw the date marked. Damn, I said to myself.

Dad had his own medical problems. During my annual Christmas call I'd suggested he get a blood test for prostate cancer. It came back positive. The doctors at the University of Texas, where he currently taught music, were suggesting radiation. Weeks before, I had urged him to fly to Nashville to consult a urologist colleague of mine about possibly having surgery instead. I couldn't believe the timing.

As you enter Nashville's airport, you're greeted by a giant multicolored banjo, a symbol of the city's country music heritage. The music business centers around "Music Row" on Seventeenth Street, lined by office towers of major labels squeezed among the old recording studio bungalows that gave birth to country's early stars. Four blocks away stands Vanderbilt University, a venerable Southern school and medical center that boasts, among other things, one of the National Cancer Institute's designated cancer centers in the United States. Thus, two cultures are juxtaposed, one celebrating love, sin, and hard work; the other struggling to undo the damage that such lifestyles have wrought. The duality struck me as I stood there waiting for Father's plane to arrive. Though I was filled with foreboding, the absurd midair banjo made me smile.

While awaiting his arrival I experienced my usual flip-flop of ambivalent feelings about my father. Although I cared deeply about him and felt some responsibility for his health, we had drifted far apart, separated by distance and by lives that chased different dreams. I had long since stopped thinking of him as a paternal influence in my life. Mother was the only person I associated with any kind of parental role. Father was more like a special uncle who visited from time to time.

Yet from my vantage point, I could understand why he had been pulled away from us. Being a church organist, directing religious choral music, had hardly been a challenge for a man with a doctorate and a great love of classical music and opera. Back when Becky and I were still children, and after my parents got divorced, my father trained as a conductor at opera houses in Sweden and Denmark before settling for a time in Vienna. There, he studied with the famous Swarowsky, who had been the teacher of Zubin Mehta. Along the way, he also managed to give organ concerts in some of Europe's most prominent cathedrals. Once, after a long absence, he sent me a postcard of Saint Paul's in London, where he'd played a recital. I remember admiring what he was doing but feeling that he was very removed from my life. For the past few years he'd been a choral conductor in Texas.

It had been several years since I'd last seen my sixty-five-year-old father. In the back of my mind was a terrible fear that he would disembark his plane and recognize me before I could recognize him. But I quickly spotted him and was surprised at how gray he'd become. He pumped my hand vigorously, his eyes dewy with emotion. It seemed that he wanted to be more affectionate but was afraid to because, no matter what I told him, he believed that I resented him for having left us, his family. He didn't want to push it.

As we headed back to Nashville, he chattered nervously, praising my perseverance in neuropathology and what in his mind were the accomplishments of someone such as myself, who wanted to dedicate his life to medicine.

I looked over at him, at his craggy, still-handsome face. He had put on some weight since I'd last seen him; his belly was pressing against the seat belt. "Mahlon," he said, "you're my number-one son. I hope you know that."

I shrugged. "You don't have to say that."

"I say it because it's true." He assured me that his other two sons were aware of his definitive feeling for me. "I wish we could get together more . . . we're really not that far away. You and Becky, why are the two of you so distant?"

What a sad question, I thought to myself. Hard to deal with at this particular moment. "We're not distant from you, Dad," I said. "We just went on with our lives. We had to, didn't we?"

He suddenly went suspiciously quiet and remained like that for a while. "Mahlon," he said finally, "what's going to happen to me?"

"What do you mean?"

"Could this possibly get me?"

I almost laughed at the irony of his question. The mixed emotions I felt were too overwhelming to express. But it really was a lot easier to focus on his problems.

"Dad." I tried to be reassuring. "This is basically a slow-growing cancer. You could've gone for years without it being detected on a rectal exam. Luckily we did the test. Even if you opt only for radiation you should be essentially cured."

"Well, I want surgery!" he said emphatically.

I reminded him how delicate the surgical procedure could be, that it could damage the nerves that governed urination and sexual function.

"I'll take that chance," he said with false bravado. His tone of voice brought back memories of long ago, when, in my childhood, he'd grow strident whenever he felt uncertain. I was just the opposite—whenever I felt uncertain I tended to withdraw into myself to try to figure things out. I wondered if my reticence was a reaction to my father's occasional bravura. "If I can only just get through this," he said, "there are a lot of things that I still want to do, things I should've done. I wish that I had spent more time with you."

"Dad, you'll get plenty of chances to spend more time with me—if you want. Trust me, this is not the end."

I sounded so certain, so confident, as though I'd contained my own fear of the future. And yet, sitting next to my father, I realized this was what I'd been doing my whole life, bottling my concerns and pressing forward until I could find a concrete means of addressing them.

"I just want you to understand one thing, Mahlon," he said.

"That I do have regrets. That I truly believe I have made a lot of mistakes."

The sky of downtown Nashville was just coming into view, in particular the menacing, Darth Vader–like tower of the Bell South Building. We drove to the Med Center Inn, lugged in my father's bulging cloth suitcase, and registered him. His mood plummeted as I escorted him down the drably carpeted hallway toward his room. He threw me a few doleful looks, as if regretting his decision to stay there, wondering why I hadn't offered him my spare bedroom. But even in the best of times, I would have found my father's sudden presence in my house disorienting. We weren't used to one another. And it would be especially awkward for me now, haunted by the harrowing thought that Dad, even with his prostate cancer, would probably outlive me.

Yet it was clear to me that I couldn't tell my father what was going on. He would get terribly upset when, just then, he had enough to deal with. Besides, there was nothing he could do to help me.

Still, when I got home and settled on my couch, it was hard to still my pangs of guilt. How could I relax in the comfort of my home, eating my nightly tuna fish sandwich, while my father was holed up in a hotel? Was he right? On some level, did Becky and I still blame him for leaving us? And yet, there I was, thirty-nine years old and single. How could I fault my father for the choices he'd made so long before when I'd been living my life the same way that he had, pursuing a career at a personal cost? And now came the crashing realization that I probably would not have children, would never have a chance to become "the good father."

The following morning, after dropping off my father at his appointment with the urologist, I was paged to yet another strange phone number. It was Jane Davis, calling from a lab. "So, I guess I'm in big trouble," I joked when I finally got her on the phone.

She didn't reply for a moment, and when she did her voice quivered. "Mahlon, I didn't mention it but we went ahead and did an HIV immunofluorescence test on your blood."

This elicited a chuckle from me. The hospital, formerly so nonplussed, was now scrambling to find out if I were truly infected. "And?" I asked.

"It's positive," she said.

"Well, that seals my fate then." I hesitated and then forced myself to say, "You just can't explain away that many positive tests."

"I'm afraid you're right. I'm very sorry, Mahlon."

There was a finality to this exchange that I hadn't felt in the one with Dr. Carlson. And I was surprised that my initial reaction was not devastation—but rather relief that the ordeal of waiting and testing was finally over, the evidence in, the proof incontrovertible. The simple sober truth made me realize that slowly, over the last few months, I'd been accepting that my diagnosis would be positive. In fact, I could now admit to myself that I'd never quite believed the reassurances of my colleagues, that the scientist in me had suspected the truth all along.

Meanwhile, my father, having charmed the urologist's staff, was meeting with Dr. Bruner, an affable, self-confident surgeon who was able to inspire trust in the most cynical of patients.

He paged me when he was done. On the drive to the airport, his mood seemed almost manic and he talked nonstop. When we were nearly there, he launched into a litany about his death and how he was trying to be philosophical about it.

I snapped at him, "Dad, I told you, you're not going to die!

You have a minuscule cancer that can barely be seen on the scans. The surgery will cure you, for God's sake!''

"Okay, okay,'' he said, surprised by my uncharacteristically sharp response, falling silent like a chastened schoolboy.

After a few moments of ruminative quiet, Dad dared to speak again, enumerating all the things he planned to do once he was cured. Among them, he wanted to visit Scotland, the land of his ancestors, a scenario far more appealing than my own. It seemed so ironic that after all the years apart, Dad and I would briefly reunite as a son who could help a father find a cure but probably couldn't cure himself. Surgery seemed such a godsend to contemplate in my circumstances. My father would fly back to Nashville within a few weeks, have his tumor out, and within a month could return to Texas most likely cured and carefree. In the meantime I'd begin the fight for my life.

CHAPTER 6

MY MOOD PLUMMETED when I was driving home from the airport, as if all the feelings I'd had to suppress to conceal them from my father were seeping poisonously into consciousness. As I was pulling into my driveway my pager went off. Grabbing it, I read the telephone number of a physician friend who, I knew, was calling to ask for research help. Normally I'd respond immediately, being compulsive, but now I felt too paralyzed to make the call. Dropping onto my couch, I stared at the fireplace. Then a wave of despair at what lay before me, the possible illness, the agonizing death, broke over me, and I burst into tears.

I grieved for my mother, my sister, for the work that— despite one serious relationship—had been the true emotional center of my life. I had been so inspired by medicine, so captivated, that for years I'd labored without vacations, or even many weekends off, to establish myself in neuropathology. Little by little my efforts had seemed to be paying off. Now I was forced to wonder exactly what I had achieved. A more thorough intellectual understanding of the mysteries of the brain, a handful of thorny puzzles solved, several dozen papers published? And with no hope for a future, where could my labors lead? What was the point of striving for professorship? In all probability I'd be dead in ten years. It was as if the floor had been kicked out from under me, the very foundation of my life rendered meaningless. Yet, even in my despair, I came to feel a strange glimmer of release from the psychic fortress that my work had become.

But even as I considered the once-preposterous idea of taking time off, the scope of my opportunities seemed vastly limited. It was a strange catch-22. If I could now afford to indulge myself, how would I do it? And with whom? For some time I had traveled down a solitary road that perhaps exacerbated my tendency toward self-containment, but now as I looked back on it, the terrain seemed unnervingly barren. But why would a woman want to be with me when I was carrying a communicable life-threatening disease—even if we did practice safe sex? How could I not be constantly conscious that there were still risks involved, that I carried within me the terrible power to inflict my fate on another? Improbable but fearsome scenarios floated through my head. What, for example, would happen if I were out on a date and got a nose bleed? What if the woman reached over with a handkerchief and, in the process of stanching my blood, exposed a nick on her finger? What if I fervently kissed a woman, and somehow, through some cut or scrape, my saliva managed to infect her? As a doctor, I knew that these scenarios were fairly unlikely, but my own infection had been a complete fluke too. If somehow my lover could become infected, how could I bear such a terrible responsibility?

Even if an HIV-negative woman were to accept me, I'd never be able to offer her a settled life with children. Worse yet, within a few years she might have to watch me die. Who would want to risk such an emotional scar? And if she did, what would happen to her after I was gone?

I realized that in the gay community HIV was viewed very differently. Safe sex was widely acknowledged as the only alternative to celibacy. The percentage of HIV-infected people in the gay community was so high that it was nearly impossible to guarantee absolutely that a potential lover might be HIV-negative and had been so for the previous six months. Also, within a gay relationship, there normally wasn't the issue of having children. And yet, despite a certain acceptance of HIV, I'd been told that within the gay community there existed a kind of viral apartheid, that many confirmed HIV negatives refused to have sex or get involved with someone they knew was HIV-positive. And, in the straight world, with vastly lower percentages of infected individuals, a woman could far more easily forgo involvement with anyone of dubious HIV status.

Clearly, the only solution was to find a healthy HIV-positive woman. I wasn't sure how—first of all, they were relatively scarce in Tennessee, and many who were infected would be IV drug users. No one I knew at the hospital would violate patient confidentiality to introduce me to someone. And I'd had little enough success finding a mate when I was uninfected. How could I do it with a red ribbon tied around my neck?

I sought refuge from these thoughts in my garden. Gardening

was how I'd gotten through the breakup with Alexis, my fiancée, with whom I had once shared the cottage. Because she loved to cook, I'd had contractors renovate my kitchen, though I couldn't really afford it, and I'd painted the rooms and put up blinds and shutters myself, hoping to make the place our haven from professional storms.

Alexis was as work obsessed as I was, an ambitious trainee in molecular physiology. At the time she was studying genes that cause the death of brain cells—as happens in Alzheimer's disease or AIDS. But the experiments she was asked to try were problematic, some nearly impossible to perform; and certain that her career was imperiled, she drove herself hard. Having been through such times myself, I really felt for her, and with my two doctorates and seven years of residency/fellowship, I had finally climbed to more secure ground. So I did my best to buoy her up. At night, while she worked late, I'd bring in a picnic basket full of homemade turkey sandwiches, as well as a crystal bowl filled with cut strawberries and kiwis. She eventually moved in with me, in part so that we could spend more time together.

But once we began living together, her career crises seemed to become worse. She'd come home at night so preoccupied she'd hardly even notice me. She began to speak in earnest about giving up molecular physiology and going back to school out of state. And I, in turn, grew increasingly frustrated. Finally, we were both so miserable that separation seemed like the only alternative.

Before the end we briefly saw a couple's therapist. He was, among other things, a proponent of shared hobbies like gardening, which I eventually continued on my own.

And so each Sunday became a pilgrimage to the nursery for another carload of plants: coreopsis, aster, veronica, sedum. I brought home truckloads of trees, hemlocks, Leyland cypresses, magnolias, not to mention shrub roses. I planted row upon row of tulips, hyacinths, daffodils, and lilies, and created islands of irises— purple and white, blue and yellow—in the backyard. After a day filled with malignant brain tumors and other killers, it was reassuring to see vibrant blooming life.

I was yanking weeds from my flower beds when a car pulled into my driveway. Carol, a friend from work, got out holding a huge spray of irises, which I assumed had come from her garden. Like me, Carol was an avid gardener, and we often traded tips.

Tall and slender with watery blue eyes, Carol had been raised in a strict Southern Baptist home, which she had rebelled against to become a "peacenik" liberal, love beads and all. Now, years later, she was more moderate, a sort of a walking compromise between her conservative rearing and activist youth. A cross now hung where beads had.

At the hospital, she worked as a research technician, running viral co-cultures on HIV-positive patients. The faceless tales of tragedy she read in her cultures inspired her to reach out to actual HIV sufferers: now she volunteered as support group counselor and as a guide on the Internet, advising and comforting people with AIDS.

She waved as she walked toward me, surveying what I was doing. "Looks like you've got a lot of work ahead of you."

"I've been kind of neglecting things lately."

She handed me the irises. "Maybe these will brighten your house until you can get yours in."

"Would you like to come in and see the place? Have some iced tea?" I asked.

"Sure," she said.

She'd never been to my house before, and I could guess why she was there. We went inside, and as I placed the irises in a vase, I asked, in a tone more demanding than I intended, "So, who told you?"

There was a pause. "Told me what?"

"I'm assuming you're here because somebody told you."

"Nobody told me. I assumed. I heard that you were running around the department earlier, looking worried."

"Well, I got some pretty upsetting news."

It wasn't that I wanted to hide the news from Carol, but I hadn't yet confided much to anyone. My feelings about my new status were still too raw and formless to discuss.

Carol tentatively approached me, unsure whether or not to hug me. "Oh, Mahlon," she said. "I'm so sorry."

I shrugged and led her to the living room, where she marveled at the white wool rugs that had been a gift from my sister, Becky. Then she got back to the point of her visit. "Tell me, is there anything I can do?" Carol said.

For a moment I suffered a flash of pride. I didn't want her to think of me in the same vein as the people she supported on the Internet. But I was touched that she'd taken the time to stop by, and even though I didn't feel ready to talk, I was grateful for her concern. Having enjoyed her company as a colleague, I appreciated her approaching me as a friend.

And so I found myself telling her, "Well, there is one thing . . ." I outlined what I had been thinking earlier, that I had realized how much I needed to meet a woman. And yet the idea of finding a companion seemed almost impossible now.

"Well, of course, there's the Internet," Carol said. "I'm plugged into a lot of people. But I guess there's no point in finding a woman who lives a thousand miles away."

"I don't suppose you know of anybody local?"

"Not really. There aren't that many, I guess."

"Right," I said.

Carol suddenly perked up. "I know what we can do. We can call Shannon." Shannon was a street-smart, sassy social worker who ran a support group for HIV-positive women.

"I doubt that she does matchmaking," I protested.

Carol frowned and waved her hands at me. "You don't need to stand on ceremony with Shannon. She's a compassionate woman. I'm sure she'll be delighted to help you."

CHAPTER 7

─────── ∞ ───────

SHORTLY AFTER MY seroconversion, I received a phone call from
the Tennessee Health Department, the local reporting arm of the
Centers for Disease Control and Prevention. Although reporting an
occupationally acquired HIV infection was voluntary in Tennessee, I
had done so thinking my situation should be shared because the risk
of HIV infection in health care workers seemed grossly underesti-
mated. Now a nurse assigned to the HIV epidemiology division
wanted to interview me.

She was a willowy woman with a round face who introduced
herself as Ms. Parker. No more than twenty-five, she reminded me
of a Shirley Temple who'd grown too tall too quickly. "We need to
find a quiet place to talk," she informed me with a strained smile,
clutching her file of papers protectively to her chest. I led her
through the sanitized hallways of the hospital's medical offices to a

faculty conference room with bright lights and white display boards upon which were scrawled the remnants of biological equations. We sat down at a large rectangular table, as passersby glanced through the small window, wondering why we needed this kind of closed-door conference.

"Let me begin by saying that your HIV status and anything you tell me about sexual partners will be kept entirely confidential," Ms. Parker assured me.

"I guess I'm too trusting anyway," I told her. "But my life's an open book."

"My questions may be embarrassing," she warned.

"Let 'em rip." I tried to be lighthearted.

She opened her file and began poring over what looked like a series of typed questions. "So," she said, "explain to me about your HIV exposures."

"There was only one," I said, somewhat surprised that she'd ask this question after having been briefed. I told her about the scalpel cut.

"Are you absolutely sure that it's the only exposure to HIV you've ever had?" Her look of skepticism was unnerving.

"Yes, I'm sure."

"What about sexual partners? Have you ever had any male sexual encounters?"

"No. Never."

"How many female partners have you had in the last five years?"

"Only one," I told her, and I explained that I had gotten an HIV test when our involvement got serious, a year and a half before the accident. We'd separated nine months before I cut myself doing the autopsy.

Ms. Parker seemed to ignore this information. She had been well trained on how to proceed with these interrogations. "And where is your ex-girlfriend now?" she said.

"She's doing a fellowship in New York."

"Has she been tested?"

"Not to my knowledge." I was getting irritated. No other illness I knew of would prompt such a barrage of questions. "Look, she's a shy scientist, not a party girl," I said. "I'm sure she's negative."

"The CDC will want her to be tested," Ms. Parker said.

"Why test her if I was negative when we were together?"

"Well, her status is still a loose end."

"A loose end?" I was incredulous. "Not to her. She's never been at risk."

Ms. Parker stifled a comment and glared at me. I could see that nothing I said, no matter how convincing, would stop her assault—not even the fact that I was a physician. I felt as though my two doctoral degrees and my years of experience were being completely discounted.

The interrogation continued. "Does she know about this happening to you?"

"I would assume not."

"You mean, you didn't tell her?"

"We're not in touch," I said angrily. "I told you, I was negative when we were involved. I have the documentation."

"Perhaps you could ask her to get tested."

I shook my head. Somebody knocked on the door, and then it swung open. One of the residents I knew stuck his head in. He apologized and, sensing the tension, retreated.

I turned back to Ms. Parker and demanded, "Why should I

add more stress to her life? There's no logical reason for her to get tested."

"Well, it would be good to know from our standpoint."

Then I lost my temper. "You're dealing with people whose lives have been ruined. And all you care about is getting data which has no real bearing on anything."

Ms. Parker's cheeks began reddening. "We're just trying to be thorough," she pointed out, with less bravado.

"To the point of ruthlessness."

She took offense. "Excuse me!"

I placed both my hands on the table and slid them toward her. "Here you have a bona fide case and you're scrambling to find another one. Why don't you focus on the matter at hand?" My interviewer just stared at me vacantly. Then I continued. "You're just not listening to me. You don't want to believe me that this is an occupational infection. So, let's get this straight once and for all. I didn't get this from sex, okay? I got it from a scalpel."

At this point Ms. Parker stood abruptly and muttered something about showing herself out. I stood, too, as she left the room with a stack of photocopies, undoubtedly the paper trail of my seroconversion. It amazed me that despite all I'd said I hadn't managed to break through her wall of cynicism.

My interview reminded me of what had happened to Kimberly Bergalis, who had been infected by her Florida dentist, Dr. David Acer. The CDC, at first convinced that it was impossible for a patient to become infected during a dental procedure, subjected her to hours of interrogation that focused on possible drug use as well as sexual and dating habits. No matter what she told them, the CDC refused to believe that Kimberly was as naive as she claimed to be. Luckily, she was vindicated by new molecular biologic techniques that proved she had been infected with the same strain of HIV as her dentist.

AIDS was such a frightening disease that even certain people who had to deal with it professionally had difficulty viewing it in any other way than as a sexually transmitted infection—as if that gave them a reason to blame the victim.

NOW THAT MY occupational infection had been established, I had to choose a doctor to oversee my progress. Beth Ann Jamison set up a meeting with the Infectious Disease people to discuss my options. We gathered in the Infectious Disease conference room, the same place where we'd planned the study on AIDS brains. The bookshelves were lined with glossy AIDS journals, with photographs of bony-looking boys touting new treatments for opportunistic infections such as cytomegalovirus. Since the start of our study in 1991, AIDS had become a big business. Many treatments had been developed for fighting the opportunistic infections triggered by immunocompromise but few, if any, for fighting the virus itself.

When I entered the room, Harry Brown and Beth Ann were sitting at the conference table, conferring quietly, and across from them sat Dr. Carlson, distractedly thumbing through a folder. I looked around and was surprised at how inhospitable the room felt. It was difficult to accept that I had more in common with the emaciated models in the drug advertisements in the AIDS journals than I did with these doctors.

Beth Ann began. "How have you been sleeping?"

"Fine," I said.

"Have you been able to work okay?"

I knew she was probably concerned that I might be exhibiting early signs of depression. "I'll be all right. I just feel like I've been cut loose. I need to find my bearings and go on. I need a compass."

"Well, we're just concerned about how you're going to approach your care."

I nodded.

"First of all," Harry said, "the labs can't give you results directly."

"And you should try not to call them to get your test values either," Beth Ann added gently. "They always have to go through a physician."

I explained that I'd only called the labs to learn about the repeat HIV tests after experiencing some difficulty getting information from Occupational Health, which wouldn't give me the information over the phone. "All along I kept hoping that there'd been some kind of mistake—that's why I kept calling rather than bothering anyone. Besides, I shouldn't have to wait six days to find out a test result that's available in two."

"I absolutely agree with you," Harry said.

I was caught in the middle. My expectations as a patient were broad, but I also sympathized with what I knew was a beleaguered medical system. As a patient I wanted to know everything yesterday. As a physician I knew I couldn't.

"We'd like you to pick one doctor," Beth Ann went on.

I had a hunch that both Beth Ann and Harry wanted me to see an AIDS doctor in Nashville who was extremely aggressive. But I had other ideas.

"I'm going to see Jim Stevens," I said. "After all, I have a working relationship with him."

What I didn't say was that I hoped Jim Stevens would be more willing to let me do what I wanted vis-à-vis treatment. After all, he had designed the PET/autopsy study and probably felt a certain responsibility for my accident. I thought I might be able to use that as leverage for trying new therapies as they became available.

"I understand that, but Mahlon, you also need somebody you can talk to," Beth Ann said.

"Well, how about you?" I looked up and said.

A sad look flitted across her face. "Mahlon, you're a friend. I can't be objective."

"Well, then, Stevens is fine," I said. "Besides, I want to explore the idea of early therapy and get on new drugs as they become available. His connections should help."

Harry nodded. "Just don't get your hands on anything and start taking it without some good advice. We'd hate to have you make a terrible mistake."

I glanced over at the stacks of AIDS magazines. "And what, die two months earlier than I might otherwise?"

Both Beth Ann and Harry looked shocked.

At this point Carlson took over. "How many people have you told about your infection?" he asked.

I explained to him that I had no close friends outside of the medical community and that currently, as far as I knew, nobody beyond Vanderbilt knew about it.

"You might want to be careful about telling lots of people," he warned me.

The advice, undoubtedly an attempt to shield me from discrimination, was good. But it still made me momentarily angry. After all, a normal response to such disturbing news would be to tell one's closest allies and discuss the situation as a way of gaining control over one's fear.

Turning to Harry and Beth Ann, Carlson went on. "I'm afraid someone better speak to the dean about Mahlon. In case the story does leak, the dean has got to know." In fact, he went on to say, in case the story did leak, Vanderbilt's press office was preparing a release stating that a health care worker had become infected handling tissue, emphasizing, however, that this worker had had no patient contact.

Beth Ann looked bewildered.

Carlson explained that he'd been worried about barrages of hysterical phone calls and anxiety-ridden nurses lining up outside Occupational Health. "Luckily, this hasn't happened yet."

"What happens if it does?" I said.

"We'll deal with it as best we can. I would hope that it would just blow over." He turned to me. "And as for you, Mahlon, you've got to remember you have at least ten good years. That's a lot of time to find a cure."

I was grateful for the words of hope. Nonetheless, I could not forget the statistics. Many HIV-positive people developed AIDS in fewer than five years. And in my particular situation this scenario was a distinct possibility. After all, I had been infected with HIV present in a corpse. This was an infection from someone in the final stage of illness, someone whose virus had probably mutated into an AZT-resistant, powerful strain. Beyond this, several recent studies suggested that patients over the age of thirty-eight or forty progressed more rapidly to AIDS than the typical eight to twelve years in, for example, young healthy gay men. And there were no drugs in clinical trials that looked promising enough to reassure me.

Dr. Carlson resumed. "Mahlon, in the event your story does leak to the media—I do have to ask if your family knows."

Suddenly I realized, Oh, my God, that's right—I hadn't even

considered such a possibility. ''Optimally, I'd like to wait a couple of years to tell Mom. It's going to break her heart.''

Carlson began shuffling the papers that he'd laid out on the conference table. The meeting was clearly over. Then he peered at me. ''I think you'd better tell her now. So she doesn't hear it first on the news.''

CHAPTER 8

I WAITED ANOTHER two weeks before I went to see Stevens. Before discussing my future, I wanted to learn more about the disease's progression and to see if current research held any obscure treatment hope I could cling to. So I spent my nights in the Vanderbilt medical library. I logged on to Medline, a medical information service that presented the latest studies on HIV therapies. I photocopied them all. And then I began to read like my life depended on it.

HIV-1 is a small retrovirus composed of a small outer envelope and an inner core of genetic material, RNA, and three enzymes it needs to reproduce. Like all retroviruses, HIV can't reproduce on its own but must instead invade cells such as human T-helper lymphocytes (CD4 cells) and trick them into making the components for more virus. The invaded cells thus become agents of their own destruction.

In essence, HIV acts like an invading spaceship that attacks a space station, a human CD4 lymphocyte, by attaching itself to the space station's wall and sending in its invaders—viral RNA and the enzymes reverse transcriptase, integrase, and protease—to take over the space station. First, the invading reverse transcriptase transforms viral RNA into DNA that resembles human DNA, so the body won't recognize the stranger within the gates. Then, the invading integrase helps the masqueraded viral DNA infiltrate the crew, tricking them into making components for more viral space-ships. Finally, the protease enzyme, a master metalsmith, appears and assembles the ships. Eventually the new ships rupture out of the space station, destroying it, and set out to attack other space stations. In 1993 the only drugs we had to fight these invaders were AZT, DDC, and DDI, all of which were designed to inhibit the action of reverse transcriptase.

At that time, many scientists believed that, like herpes, HIV settled down in the body after a patient's initial seroconversion and remained relatively inactive for a time, more like a stowaway than a voracious pillager. But now I came across articles from Ashley Haase's lab in Minnesota and Giuseppe Pantaleo's lab at the National Institutes of Health suggesting that this was not true—that from the moment HIV invaded the body it began fiercely ravaging the CD4 cells. At least to me, these articles implied that there might be some benefit to slowing the invasion with such antiviral drugs as AZT, however weak they might be, early in the infection rather than waiting until the devastation had reached the threshold of AIDS.

The papers validated my initial, visceral urge to start treatment right after the accident; it had tormented me to stand by helplessly during the long months of testing.

Armed with my new knowledge, I went to see Dr. Stevens, resolved to convince him to take some action.

His office was located in the Travel and Infectious Disease Clinic, run in conjunction with the AIDS Clinical Trial Group (ACTG). Though Vanderbilt had a number of infectious disease experts such as Dr. Carlson and Beth Ann Jamison, people who consulted, it was actually Stevens who practiced primarily AIDS medicine and supervised all the clinical trials of new drugs. In all my years at Vanderbilt, I'd never actually been to this clinic. Most of my contact with Stevens had been by telephone or in conference rooms, areas removed from the war rooms of the battle against AIDS.

When I walked in I was struck by a large patchwork quilt with red-and-white geometric designs, cats, and Chinese figures, hanging on the waiting room wall. Even from a distance you could feel the poignant messages of its soft, handmade squares that paid homage to the dead. Beneath it was a small brass commemorative plaque. The clinic was run by a no-nonsense nurse named Madeline, the daughter of a dedicated public health physician, who conducted her business with the discipline of a drill sergeant. She explained the protocols, drew blood, and oversaw the drug trials. Despite her serious manner, she was part mother, part confidante to the patients of the clinic. With her encouragement, they fought the disease and endured the side effects of drugs and the debilitating infections that were forever cropping up. I would soon come to understand that, in many ways, Madeline was more vital to this clinic than the decision-making doctors, and I believe this is probably true in many AIDS clinics around the country.

Madeline greeted me warmly. She seemed to sense that I needed to be treated like a doctor and, for the moment, postponed any paperwork that needed to be done. Indeed, as I walked down the hallway to Stevens's office, I reminded myself that my relationship with Stevens had always been as doctor to doctor. I imagined that he probably had seen a glint of hope somewhere on the horizon, knew about some new drug or a risky treatment that would be worth trying. It was now my hope that he would be sympathetic to the idea of turning my HIV infection into an experiment rather than following it as a disease.

Stevens greeted me warmly, but his expression was worried. I could tell how awkward he felt.

"It's okay, I'm doing all right," I spoke up before he could say anything.

Thirty-seven years old, Stevens was tall and rangy, a patricianly handsome, fair-haired man with silver at the temples. On his small wooden desk, among stacks of reports and case files, was a semicircular configuration of photographs: a dark-haired wife and three golden-haired children. He was a kindly man, a devout Baptist, who I knew aspired to serve as a medical missionary in some remote corner of the world.

Stevens leaned back in his chair. "I had no idea your testing ordeal had lasted this long. Why didn't you call me and tell me what was going on?"

I shrugged and explained that I'd been preoccupied with my blood workups in Occupational Health and that my HIV status had only just then become definitive. I hadn't seen any reason to bother him until my tests were conclusive, even though my accident had occurred while I was autopsying one of the patients in his study. I said so.

"Of course, you can bother me. You know that. You could have called at any time."

"I just wanted to keep things to myself until I knew the truth."

Stevens nodded and then thought for a moment. "Now, which patient was it that you cut yourself on?"

I was taken aback, surprised he'd forgotten the fateful night. But I reminded myself that it had occurred seven months and hundreds of patients ago. I ended up mumbling the details until he remembered with what seemed like a flush of embarrassment.

"Anyway," I said, trying to lessen the unease, "I'd like to talk to you about my treatment options. I've been doing a lot of research, and I've come to the conclusion that I should start on something, even if it's AZT."

I went on to mention Pantaleo's and Haase's papers. Jim listened patiently. "Well, I've got to tell you, Mahlon, the studies are interesting but there still isn't much evidence that early treatment does any good. And as you know, the data from the Concorde Trial is just coming out now and it doesn't show any survival benefit to starting AZT early."

"But 'early' in that study meant treating patients three or four years after they'd become infected, maybe longer. I've been infected for less than a year. I haven't seen any data on treating this early. It's an experiment that needs to be done."

"But if you take AZT now, you could develop resistance," he protested. "Then when you really need it, it won't work."

Most people developed strains of HIV resistant to AZT in two to three years.

"I'm not saying it's a miracle drug, but AZT does do something, and these guys are saying you've got to slow the virus down."

At that time, my only other treatment choices were the antivirals DDI or DDC. Like AZT, both of these were weak inhibitors of HIV's reverse transcriptase, the enzyme that allowed it to synthesize viral DNA from RNA. But because they were thought to be less effective than AZT, they were usually prescribed for people who couldn't tolerate it.

Stevens was getting a bit agitated. "Are you sure you want the hassle of the side effects?"

He was referring to AZT's toxicity, which could cause headaches, diarrhea, and in some cases nausea that lasted for weeks or even months. Many people refused to take AZT at all on account of its side effects. "Why go through all that so early?"

"It seems a small price to pay," I said stubbornly, envisioning my lymph nodes under attack at that very moment. "I'm willing to risk it if AZT can help keep me healthy."

Stevens's view was still the prevailing one in 1993. It would take a while for the newer notions of Pantaleo, Haase, and others to be implemented as standard practice. And I could understand Stevens's caution. Throughout medical history, in the face of hopelessness, physicians and patients had all too often seized upon poorly proven potential "cures."

At the turn of the century, before antibiotics were discovered, Western Europe was ravaged by syphilis, which could cause dementia. A German psychiatrist named Wagner-Jurregg created a sensation when he reported dramatic improvements in syphilitic patients who were infected with malaria, his theory being that raging malarial fevers could "burn out" the venereal disease. And so, despite the looseness of Wagner-Jurregg's trials, "malariotherapy," which occasionally proved fatal, became an accepted treatment for syphilis. Wagner-Jurregg was even awarded the Nobel Prize for a treatment of unestablished efficacy, which within a few decades was supplanted by penicillin. Now that we were faced with a new untreatable sexually transmitted disease, it was hard to ignore the bitter lessons of the past.

Finally I said, "Jim, what would you do if you became infected?"

"I don't know. It would be a tough decision. I know I'd pray and ask for guidance."

"Of course," I said, not wanting to offend him. "But couldn't I at least try to get on something?"

"Mahlon, I'd like you to hold off for a little while and see what happens. I really think that's the best course right now."

I had expected Stevens to resist, but I hadn't thought that he'd shut the door on me. Being a physician and an AIDS researcher myself, theoretically I could get my hands on AZT. But I knew I needed to be monitored during treatment, and I wanted Stevens as my sounding board for current and future therapeutic strategies. There were also new drugs on the horizon, including "protease inhibitors," which sounded promising in the literature. If I wanted to be in a position to get these drugs in a timely way, I would have to go along with Stevens, at least for the time being.

CHAPTER 9

————— ∞ —————

DURING THE NEXT few weeks, I alternated between feeling resigned to the possibility of a foreshortened life and a fierce determination to fight the disease. In the daytime, preoccupied with work, I was less aware of my HIV infection. But at night, my trepidation at what was to come, along with a deeper sense of loneliness, haunted me.

Still, I felt too unsettled to call Carol's friend Shannon about meeting a woman from her support group. If she couldn't come up with anyone—or worse, if the person she recommended rejected me—I knew that I'd be crushed with disappointment.

Shannon and I were not total strangers; we'd seen each other around the hospital. So when I finally summoned up the nerve to phone, she felt free to tease me a little.

"It's high time you called me," Shannon said. "I was starting to give up on you."

"Well, it wasn't easy," I said.

"A phone call? Did you think I would just hang up?" She laughed.

"Well, this is kind of embarrassing. Especially because I don't really know you."

"Remember, Mahlon, this is my world, too. We're all in this together. Carol tells me that you're the independent type, but in our little community, we're very tight. People don't have to stand on ceremony."

"I'll try not to," I said.

She asked me how long I'd known about my seroconversion, and I told her several weeks; she said that this was the hard period, the time of acceptance and adjustment. A lot of people she knew had slid into depressions. I reassured her I was okay and was too busy with work to dwell on it.

Then, after hesitating, I forced myself to ask, "Do you know anyone who would want to meet an HIV-positive man?"

"Well, there's one thing you have to keep in mind," she said. "A lot of HIV-positive women are very distrustful of men."

In most of the cases she had seen, the men had contracted the virus from someone else and had transmitted it sexually to their girlfriends. The result, understandably, was a lot of anger and hostility.

I told Shannon that I understood, but that I hoped there might be a woman who would give me a chance.

"Well, my first choice would have been Jan. She's the backbone of the support group. But the problem is she's already got full-blown AIDS. She and her son even had to move back in with her parents. At this point, unfortunately, dating a man is probably the last thing on her mind—she's fighting to stay alive."

"Maybe she needs a friend."

"But there is another woman who's healthy, and she did say she'd like to meet somebody. But I've got to warn you, Mahlon—she's one of the most beautiful women I've ever seen."

"Really?" I said.

"Do you think you can handle a knockout?"

"I don't know. What is she like?"

Shannon chuckled. "Well, before I get your hopes up, I'd like to check back with her and make sure she's interested."

"Oh, sure. . . . May I ask how she was infected?"

"How else but by the man she was dating?"

"I see."

"But look, I'd love to help you if I can. Let me see what she says and call you back. How's that?"

I thanked her and hung up, a little rattled but proud that I had finally taken a first positive step. I'd never gone out on a blind date before, which was nerve-racking in itself, and it had been almost two years since I was with a woman. However, in this case, I'd be meeting someone who shared my fate, a secret that could not help but link us. So, for the first time since my diagnosis, I felt my mood lifting, thinking that recapturing life was the first step to prolonging it.

That night when I got home, I checked myself in the mirror.

"Good God," I said aloud. "You're as pale as a tuna. Why would some woman want to meet you?"

My tanning bed, which I hadn't used much, was located in the unfinished attic room next to the upstairs guest room. Now I impulsively took off my clothes, set the timer, and opened the lid, swatting away a moth. I climbed into the tanning bed, put on my goggles, and imagined myself on a beach in some exotic part of the world. Within moments, I was lulled to sleep by the hum of the tanning fans.

When a ringing phone awoke me, the house was completely black. Forgetting where I was, I jumped to grab the phone and, in my haste, I stepped between two cross beams. The next thing I knew I was clinging to the rafters with my feet dangling in midair. Recognizing the Dutch-blue rug of the downstairs bathroom, I realized I had crashed through the ceiling. I was just getting my bearings when the answering machine picked up. Still balancing myself on the rafters, I hung there motionless, waiting to hear who it was.

"Mahlon, hi, it's Becky. It's pretty late where you are . . . so, where are you? Give me a call."

Pulling myself up, I climbed back into the attic, found the light switch, and put on my clothes. Then I went to the phone to call Becky back.

We hadn't spoken for a few weeks, a relatively long time for us. Although she lived in Silicon Valley, we'd always been close— and especially so in the wake of our respective romantic tragedies: my shattered engagement and Becky's catastrophic divorce. We loved to laugh over our mother's various eccentric misadventures, usually involving her many animals. Being a typical little brother, I always teased Becky unmercifully, and despite herself, she always seemed to bite.

"Your phone call nearly crippled me," I said when she answered.

"What do you mean?"

"I just fell through the damn ceiling trying to answer it."

"What are you saying . . . how?" She sounded skeptical.

"I was up there in my tanning bed and the phone rang." I explained about stepping the wrong way, falling through, and holding on.

Now she sounded alarmed. "Oh, my God, are you okay?"

There was real concern in her voice, as well as relief. I suddenly thought of her, sitting alone in her apartment in California with the two greyhounds she'd rescued from the grueling world of the dog track. I thought of her having to bury me, and suddenly I couldn't speak. I kept trying, but my voice kept breaking. What came out was a bowing moan like a cello. "No," I said, and put my hand over the receiver.

"Mahlon, what's wrong?"

Crying now, I couldn't answer.

"Mahlon . . . have you had more tests done?"

"Hmmm," was all I could say.

"What's going on?" she said. "Please tell me."

I finally managed to control my voice, and said, "The tests look bad."

"What are you saying?"

"The Western Blot is positive now."

"But what does that mean?" Now Becky started to cry.

"It means that I'm infected," I told her.

"But what about those tests in December? The ones that were negative."

I explained that the viral co-cultures taken in December could have been negative at that point in the illness.

"Oh, Mahlon, I can't believe this. Have you told Mother yet?"

I said I hadn't and that I didn't know how I could do it, that it would break our mother's heart.

"But don't you think you should?"

Of course I did. "I've been trying to prepare for it slowly. Please don't say anything to her until I'm ready to break the news. Which has to be soon," I said, remembering Dr. Carlson's warning.

"Don't worry, I won't."

I knew that keeping the secret would be a terrible burden for Becky, since she spoke to our mother several times a week. After a long pause, Becky said softly, "I thought we were going to grow old together."

"I thought so too."

"Mahlon . . . how much time do we have?"

This was a painful question. After her divorce, Becky had told me that she was reconciled to being single for the rest of her life, to having no other family except for Mother and me. Even though I was the one in danger, I still felt responsible for leaving her so alone.

"I just don't know. We might even have ten more years. Maybe by then they'll have found some kind of cure." Becky had fallen silent. "Are you there?" I said.

"Yeah, I'm here," she said barely audibly.

"All we can do is hope."

"I know."

In the past, Becky had always leaned on Mom for solace, but now, I told her, she would have to be the strong one. "You really have no choice."

"Of course," she said. "I'll just have to . . . You can understand, even though I worried this might be coming, it's just such a terrible shock.''

''Come on,'' I joked. ''I've always said I never wanted to grow old.''

''Oh, Mahlon, don't say that.''

''But now I do. And you never know, Becky, I might slip up and live longer than the rest of you.''

CHAPTER 10

―――――― ∞ ――――――

EARLY ONE MORNING I was getting ready to catch a flight to give a lecture in Knoxville when Shannon called me to say that the woman in her support group had agreed to meet me.

"Great," I said. "So what's her name?"

"Her name is Dawn. And here's her phone number. However, if I were you I'd wait a few weeks before calling her. She's about to go out of town—she's taking her son somewhere."

Her son? "How old is her son?" I asked.

"I believe he's twelve."

"Twelve? How old is she?"

"She's younger than you, actually." Shannon laughed. "I hope that's okay with you, Mahlon," she said dryly.

·　　·　　·

DURING THE FORTY-FIVE-MINUTE flight to Knoxville, I kept thinking about this romantic possibility. It had been so long since I'd been out on a date, I was afraid I'd forgotten how to act. What would Dawn want to talk about? What were her interests? Would she be nonplussed by the fact that I did autopsies? I suddenly grew nervous, wishing I'd asked Shannon more about this woman—I didn't think to at the time because I was so delighted that she had actually consented to meet me. Then again, perhaps confidentiality issues prevented Shannon from telling me more.

From the Knoxville airport, I took a taxi along Alcoa Highway, a thoroughfare flanked by a series of car and mobile home dealerships that fly the orange-and-white University of Tennessee football banners. The early-morning traffic was light, and as the taxi sped along, I remembered Saturday mornings in the autumn, when Alcoa Highway became bumper-to-bumper traffic crawling toward the football stadium where 90,000 football fans, zealously clad in orange, cheered the home team.

My work at the University of Tennessee involved giving neuropathology conferences and reviewing the more inscrutable neuropathology cases. More often than not, it was a tiring day, but my Vanderbilt schedule made it difficult for me to spend the night. So I'd try to teach efficiently, hoping to finish at five o'clock and spend an hour with my mother before flying back to Nashville that same evening. But this time I arranged to finish work early so that I could have a meal with my mother. As Carlson had warned, I had to tell her of my infection in case the story hit the newspapers.

Late in the afternoon, Mom picked me up at the hospital with Orpheus, her Great Dane, who, from the backseat, put both his paws on my shoulders and started licking me. Mother's graying hair was swept back conservatively, and she wore a dark raincoat over a floor-length dress. She looked smart but seemed somewhat agitated. Although my birthday had passed a few weeks before, she announced that there was a surprise waiting for me at home.

Wondering if, despite herself, Becky had tipped Mom off, I asked about my sister. In fact, my mother said, she'd just heard from Becky, who was planning on a trip to Tennessee. "She's definitely coming either Thanksgiving or Christmas. She's still not quite sure which."

"That's still a long way off," I said. "Maybe you and I should try to fly out there for a few days."

"That'd be difficult for me, Mahlon." She explained that until the end of the year she was scheduled to play at least two recitals per month.

"I'm glad you've been doing so much performing," I said. "It's a credit to your perseverance."

"Well, they're not the most spectacular venues in the world," she pointed out. "But they keep me on my toes."

After music, my mother's second great love was animals. Besides the Great Dane, she had two "American retrievers" (i.e., mutts) and a cat, but these were only her house pets. She had also dedicated her wooded half acre to the local birds. What had started as a hobby—hanging up a few bird feeders—had evolved into a massive undertaking, as my mother acquired perhaps a dozen more feeders and converted an old door into an avian buffet table. If you were to drop by the house at dawn, you'd see a stooped gray-haired figure going out into the backyard lugging forty-pound bags of sunflower seed for what, in the birds' minds, must have become "Ma's Avian Diner." Their chirping and cawing would begin at dawn, and with the noise came droppings that peppered the yard.

Once I started medical school, I was appalled to learn of the fungal spores that bird droppings could harbor and spread. Armed with these facts, I tried to explain to Mom the health hazards presented by this measure of her humanity. I cited infections such as cryptococcus and histoplasma—even in those days, with what I believed was my unassailable immune system, I was nervous about coming in contact with all that guano. I urged her to take precautions, even exaggerating the risks to make sure I could effect change. After years of nagging, I finally convinced her to wear boots when she walked around the yard and to take them off before going into the house. She also said she'd wear rubber gloves and a mask whenever she cleaned the bird feeders. Whether she actually did or not, I never knew; interacting with Mom always reminded me of where my stubbornness came from. Nevertheless, the birds were beautiful, and her love for them was touching.

The moment we arrived home, Poppy, one of the "American retrievers" Mom had adopted as a stray, greeted us as best she could while dragging a huge bone she was unwilling to relinquish with Orpheus around. She was joined by the part collie, Poohbear, another stray recently entrusted to Mom by our vet. Jasmine, the cat, rubbed against my leg, eyeing Poohbear, whom she didn't completely trust. I felt appropriately welcomed.

Mom bustled into the house behind me, her long, kimono-like dress whispering as she moved. I smelled cooking and then realized what the surprise was. She'd made me my favorite dish, a Turkish casserole with chicken and rice.

"Smells great," I said.

"Good . . . we can have a little celebration now, just the two of us . . . if we're lucky," she added, casting a wary glance over her collection of four-legged "gourmets."

The house, where I'd spent most of my adolescence, was

filled with furniture that my mother had bought back in the days when she was teaching at Oberlin. I could still remember the three of us going to an "antique store" (really a junk shop) in town, where we found some old Victorian furniture that had seen better years but nonetheless retained some sense of refinement. We'd brought home a dining table, which once had a built-in centerpiece that was now missing, and ornate scrolled chairs.

She'd set the table with two places, and I went and sat down in the chair I'd been occupying since junior high school. Although the dining table was beginning to look worn and ramshackle, it was reassuring to once again sit in "my place," where I'd eaten so many meals and joked around with my mother and sister. In those days my greatest concern was fighting off the dogs to eat my dinner. I wasn't worried about fighting off a virus or staying alive or even about my mother's retirement. Sitting there now, I felt as though I'd crossed over into an irrevocable state of anxiety.

At the end of January, to end my mother's worry, I'd oversold the negative findings of the PCR and viral cultures. I knew they weren't definitive and that my seven-month ELISA would be the final word, and yet I so much wanted to allay her fears. But now I regretted my impulse, afraid that news of my infection would hit her even harder.

I ate two helpings of Turkish casserole, and my mother commented that she hadn't seen me eat that much since I'd been in college. There was a momentary lull, but as I marshaled the strength to tell her my news, Mom turned the conversation to my father. "How is your father doing, Mahlon?" she asked. "Has he figured out what he wants to do about his cancer?"

I explained that he had opted for surgery and would soon be returning to Nashville.

"So, is he going to be okay?"

"The prognosis is good."

"There's no real danger, is there?"

I shook my head, aware of the terrible weight of my own danger.

"I'm glad," she said. "As you know, I don't wish your father ill."

"I know you don't."

"I mean, the family has had some hard times, but things have turned out okay, haven't they?"

I looked up at her, admiring her strength and feeling even more anguished about the subject at hand. I was fighting tears and vainly hoped that she wouldn't notice. But she did, and I saw a flicker of alarm in her expression. But all she said was, "You look tired, Mahlon, are you working too hard?"

"Same as always."

"Well, I hope you're doing more than just work. . . . Have you met anybody? Is there anybody you're interested in?"

I felt momentarily relieved. "Actually, some friends of mine are trying to set me up with somebody."

"Oh . . . really? That's good. What do you know about her?"

"She works. She has a son. I hear she's really beautiful."

"Well, I hope the two of you get along. I want you to be happy."

I glanced at my watch. It was already five. My plane was leaving in forty-five minutes, and we were fifteen to thirty minutes from the airport, depending on the traffic. I told her that we probably should leave, figuring that I had no choice but to break my news on the way. She wouldn't let me clear the plates.

She grabbed her coat and car keys and called Orpheus to come for the ride.

Traffic on Alcoa Highway was worse than usual, as if backed up by a car wreck miles ahead. As far ahead as I could see, cars were mired in a slow-moving grid, their bumpers and hoods glazed by the low sun's glare. And Mom was a slow driver who missed many opportunities to maneuver the car through the traffic. To the west the sky was darkening, threatening rain, and I wondered if the plane would be delayed by weather. At the rate we were going I hoped so—I didn't want to miss it, the last flight back to Nashville.

We edged past Knoxville's U.S. Marine outpost, with its covered trucks and camouflaged jeeps, that abutted the Tennessee River. Against the horizon of the Smoky Mountains stood a park crammed with mobile homes. As I cast about in my mind for the right words, I was suddenly gripped with fear that I'd miss the plane. Then my mother and I would be thrown together for the evening, with me trying to act as though my seroconversion were not a death sentence and watching her reach for empty words of comfort. What a nightmare that would be.

At last, the traffic began to ease up; however, Mom continued at a snail's pace, as if reluctant to see me leave. I managed to resist telling her to drive faster. But then she said, "So, if you miss the plane it's not the end of the world. You can stay over and get an early one tomorrow."

Filled with dread, I blurted out, "Mom, just keep driving. Because I can't spend the night."

There was a moment of surprise. "Why not?"

"You know I've always been giving you a hard time about the birds."

"So?"

"Just that the droppings carry a lot of diseases, fungal spores which are easily brought in the house by the dogs and the cat."

"So, what does that have to do with anything?"

I shook my head. Why couldn't I just say it directly?

"Mom, I have to be careful about my health now. I have to avoid exposure to fungi now."

I saw her whole body stiffen. Eyes riveted to the road, she gripped the steering wheel so tightly her arms were shaking.

"Mom, some of my tests were funny again," I said.

"What tests?" she sputtered.

"My latest ELISAs—seven months."

She blinked as she tried to take in what I was saying. "But, Mahlon, I thought this was all cleared up. You said—"

"I know, I reassured you everything was okay. And I shouldn't have done that. God knows I shouldn't have. But I thought everything was okay, too. Until I went to get my seven-month test."

"So, you mean you're not negative?"

"Not anymore."

"So, are you infected?"

"I'm afraid this is for real now, Mom. These latest tests are conclusive."

There was a terrible pause. We were passing a huge excavation of red earth. The bulldozers that had created it formed a senseless configuration around a Quonset hut. The huge yellow insectlike machines were unmanned; no doubt the drivers had left for the day. I looked beyond the excavation toward the distant ridges of the Smoky Mountains, nestled against a dense cottony bank of clouds.

Suddenly, my mother spat out, "What an unbelievable waste!

I never wanted you to do that AIDS study. It wasn't worth your life.''

"Mom, it was my job. Part of it, anyway.''

"No, that's above and beyond what you should be expected to do.''

I disagreed. And then I launched into a well-rehearsed discussion of my health and the promise of new treatments that were in clinical trials. That this was an opportunity to be a guinea pig for new treatments, to contribute to the important research being done. Even though I wanted to believe this myself, the words, as I uttered them, sounded hollow.

My mother seemed to sense my feeling of helplessness and drove on without speaking for a while, trying to piece her thoughts together. Orpheus began rubbing himself against the backseat, and she reached her hand back to still his movements. Determined to give her some measure of reassurance, I now mentioned my plans to establish a trust fund for her, explaining that there would be enough money so that she wouldn't have to worry, that both she and my sister would be well taken care of financially.

"Well, that's very kind of you, Mahlon, but it's hard for me to hear that right now.''

"Well, I guess it's no comfort to know I'm worth more dead than alive,'' I joked.

She didn't laugh. Instead, she stepped on the accelerator, now seeming determined to get me to the airport in time; and, in fact, we pulled up to the curb of the terminal with minutes to spare.

"I'm sorry I dropped this on you as I was leaving,'' I said to her. "I didn't know when I should tell you.''

"It wouldn't have mattered,'' she reassured me. "There was no good time to break the news.''

I leaned over to kiss my mother good-bye and saw that she flinched.

"You can't get AIDS from a kiss on the cheek," I informed her, immediately feeling foolish for doing so.

She looked at me as though I were insane. "I don't give a damn about catching AIDS and dying myself. I lived most of my life. I've done what I've wanted. But it just breaks my heart that it might be happening to you."

"Maybe it'll be okay." I was searching for any positive note I could find to reassure her. "I'm going to try and get on AZT and anything promising as soon as I can. We don't know what happens if you treat this early. At least it might buy me time."

She seized on the note of hope, as I knew she would. She grabbed my hand and pulled it to her. "Mahlon," she said urgently, "I always believed you'd survive as a preemie. During those first few days I remember how you fought to live. Even when the doctors gave up hope, I never did. You proved them wrong then and you'll do it now. That is what I believe."

I embraced her once more and watched her grimacing to fight back tears as she drove away. Orpheus planted his paws on top of the passenger seat and, probably sensing Mom's sorrow, inched his way over so that he could sit next to her. I watched how she turned to speak to him, something comforting perhaps, and then once again set her eyes on the road.

CHAPTER 11

⎯⎯⎯⎯ ∞ ⎯⎯⎯⎯

ALL THROUGHOUT THAT first infected summer, I dreamed of surviving, I worried about dying, but most of all I tried to believe that Dawn would become the companion who would face it all with me. As I waited for her to get back to town, I nurtured the fantasy of being with her until this unknown woman, Dawn, came to seem like my salvation—my one chance to recapture an emotional life.

On the telephone, her voice sounded soft and vulnerable, hesitant, and yet, she said she was pleased to hear from me. Listening to her working-class diction, I was intrigued, even relieved, since my previous engagement had succumbed to the professional conflicts of two similarly driven, ambitious people. Perhaps, I thought, a less career-obsessed companion could help me temper my workaholic bent, learn to relax and have fun. Already smitten by the end of our conversation, I asked Dawn to dinner, but she preferred lunch first. For our inaugural date, I deliberately chose September 14, the anniversary of my accident, as if meeting Dawn would usher my life into a new, hopeful phase.

We were to meet in Vanderbilt's rotunda-like hospital lobby. I got there first and stood to one side, watching patients and their families file through. Before long, I noticed a tall, lovely blonde stroll in and look around timidly. She wore a clinging knit sweater and a wraparound denim skirt. Her fine, bluntly cut hair swept back and forth as luxuriantly as a curtain of beads. She was unattainably beautiful, and I began to panic at the thought that this might be Dawn. Shannon had said she was a knockout, but I hadn't expected her to be intimidatingly so.

The blonde kept standing around, clearly searching for someone. At last, taking a deep breath, I forced myself to cross the lobby floor to where she stood. I couldn't even bring myself to look at her until I was right in front of her.

"Dawn?" I managed to ask.

She smiled shyly and nodded. "You must be Mahlon."

We shook hands and then she dug into her purse and nervously fished out a Bic lighter and a Newport menthol. "I'm dying for a cigarette . . . do you mind if I smoke?"

I told her that, unfortunately, she couldn't. "Hospital rules . . . but let's go outside, where it doesn't matter."

She lit up as soon as we got outside and continued smoking all the way to the parking garage. "So where are we going for lunch?" she asked warily once we'd climbed into my car.

"I thought we'd go to Faisons."

She nodded vaguely, as though she hadn't heard of the restaurant. "Am I dressed okay for it?" she asked me apprehensively. "I didn't know what to wear."

I was touched by her self-consciousness and her need for reassurance.

"Don't worry, you look great," I said. "This place is casual anyway."

As we drove, I tried to relax by concentrating on the scenery. It was the perfect afternoon for a first rendezvous: sharp sunlight, a cloudless sky, and a splash of yellow in the leaves, as Tennessee inched toward the cold of winter.

"I never get to this part of town very much," Dawn was saying, "unless I come for a doctor's appointment."

Her doctor was a local infectious disease specialist affiliated with Vanderbilt, a good friend of Jim Stevens. Feeling connected through our physicians, I imagined us as two souls fighting a wily enemy from the same trench. And yet, I worried about how to broach the subject of this very private knowledge I had of her, of the dark, painful reality that we both were hiding from the world. Our common fate had brought us together, yet inevitably it was terribly awkward for two people, having barely met, to be cognizant of each other's most intimate secret. Then, too, I got tongue-tied with women even in less emotionally fraught situations.

We had reached the restaurant, and as we headed up the stone walkway, Dawn stumbled and muttered something deprecating to herself. I started to reach for her hand but drew back, afraid that my gesture might seem too forward. Turning to me, she said, "I'm sorry, Mahlon, I can't seem to do anything right."

Here was a soul as shy as I was, I thought, and my heart went out to her. I hardly dared to think that this dazzling woman might possibly be nonplussed by me.

Faisons, situated in an old Victorian house, had converted its stone porch to an intimate dining area filled with trees and potted palms. An hour earlier the place might have been hopping with the business lunch crowd, but it was empty now. We decided to sit outside in a quiet corner next to the street, away from the ears of waitresses. Dawn kept smoking, lighting one cigarette from the butt of the last. Though sensitive to smoke, I sympathized with her anxiety too much to ask her to stop. As soon as we ordered, I decided to take the bull by the horns. Leaning toward Dawn, I said, "I'm sorry about what's happened to you. I don't know the details, but I can only assume it has been a nightmare."

She sighed and stabbed out her cigarette. "Well, Mahlon, it's still difficult. I still can't believe it. I still can't believe that someone I trusted would do this to me."

"That's what makes it all the worse," I agreed.

"And now he's taken my life away."

"Where is he?" I asked.

"He's with his parents. He's already sick, very sick. I can't even bear to see him now."

The waitress arrived with our glasses of minted iced tea. Dawn reached for two packets of Nutrasweet, then went on. "Shannon didn't tell you the story?"

"No, of course not," I said, reminding her that her story was considered confidential.

"Well," she said, lighting up another cigarette, "Carl actually knew about his HIV status."

"What do you mean?"

"He knew he was HIV-positive for over a year but never bothered to tell me."

I stared at her. "How could he do that to you?"

Dawn blew out a plume of smoke. "That's a good question, one I've asked myself and him many times." She shook her head.

"What was the answer?"

"He claims he didn't know at first, and then after he did, he was waiting for the right time to tell me. But for a year some of his friends knew he was HIV-positive and no one bothered to tell me."

"How did you find out?"

"Believe it or not, the Red Cross told me when I gave my yearly blood donation. Just think, if I wasn't trying to be a good citizen I probably still wouldn't know."

I tried to murmur words of comfort but inwardly writhed at the thought of such a profound and callous betrayal. Looking at me fixedly, Dawn said, "A woman would never do such a thing to a man."

There was blame in her gaze, and I flinched, suspecting that she was right. I couldn't imagine how, if I were in her shoes, I could possibly overcome my bitterness. Remembering Shannon's warning about the deep-seated ambivalence many HIV-positive women had about men, I wondered what it would take for me to establish any kind of trust with this wounded soul.

She paused, looking through the fronds of a huge fern sprouting up next to her. "Sometimes I wonder if I don't deserve this."

"What? Nobody deserves this," I said.

"No, I had a really wild life once upon a time, I admit it. I've done a lot of things I'm not proud of."

"Come on," I said. "Who hasn't? And you've also done a lot of good things—Shannon tells me that you're great in the women's support group and that you're a wonderful mother."

Dawn hazarded a smile. "That's kind of her. My son, Howie, is the only good thing in my life, the only thing I've done right."

"How has he handled all of this?"

Dawn shook her head and looked dismal. "He used to be such a confident, happy kid. Now he's afraid I'm going to get sick any minute. He wakes up in the middle of the night with bad dreams about me dying some horrible death. Luckily, none of his friends have found out anything yet."

"But your parents know, right?"

Dawn grunted. "Daddy can't even talk about it. He'll start crying at just the mention of Carl's name, and Mom just gets angry. They both hated Carl. Daddy probably would've killed him, but by the time he found out, Carl had moved to Memphis. But the thing is, Mahlon, my parents basically think I'm a disaster, especially in comparison to my sister, who has a great job and a great husband. Compared to me, she's a princess."

"You're being too hard on yourself," I said. Dawn's mood was spiraling into darkness, and I reflected that one of the chief problems in people with HIV is depression. "Hey," I joked, "I have a glass slipper at home that you should try on."

Dawn laughed weakly. "God, here I am going on about myself. I'm sorry. So, tell me about you."

I told her about the AIDS study and my scalpel wound. "In fact, today's my anniversary," I added.

She looked perplexed. "Your anniversary?"

"The anniversary of my accident, the beginning of my HIV infection. One year ago." I didn't mention to her that I had purposely planned the date to coincide with it.

Dawn said, "Just a year ago . . . wow." Then she frowned. "But a scalpel cut—isn't that just one of the risks of your job?"

At first her remark stunned me because it sounded so unsympathetic. But I rationalized it with the recognition that, after all, our situations were different—that no one had caused my infection, that no one had done anything to me. Unlike Dawn, I was not the victim of a deception.

The check arrived, and as we walked to the car, my mind strayed to a neuropathology book chapter I'd planned to start writing. There you go again, I scolded myself. You get a little uncomfortable and right away you want to get back to work. I had promised myself that, this time around, I wasn't going to fall back on those old defenses. I knew that Dawn had the afternoon off, so there was no reason not to prolong our date, to take the time to really get to know her. So I said to Dawn, "Hey, you want to go for a ride? There's a place I'd like to show you."

"Sure, why not?" she said.

I drove her to Radner Lake, one of Nashville's most beautiful parks, surrounded by a majestic forest—a quiet, romantic place. When we arrived, I ran around to Dawn's side of the car and opened the door. I was determined to try to break through her dark mood. "Come on," I said. "I'll give you a piggyback ride. All the way to the lake."

"Oh, no," she said. "I'm too heavy for that."

"What do you mean? I can carry you. I lift weights every day."

Dawn laughed nervously. "Mahlon, I'm pretty happy to walk."

"Come on," I said. "Climb on. I used to do this all the time. I won't take no for an answer."

Dawn giggled, seemingly flattered to be wooed in such a harmless way. Finally, she climbed on, and with her on my back, I ran, whipping down the steep path to the water.

"I can't watch, I can't watch," she cried, putting her hands over her eyes.

At the bottom of the path, we collapsed, rolling over each other and laughing. But then with a sudden shyness, Dawn drew back, and awkwardly, I did too. Without looking at each other, we dusted ourselves off and, chatting idly without touching, headed back to the car.

On the way back, I took a detour through Bellmeade, the affluent section of Nashville. We drove along its narrow lanes, admiring the perfectly manicured lawns and the elegant turn-of-the-century mansions built of cut stone and painted brick. I had only lived with one woman before, Alexis, my fiancée, and now I found myself fantasizing about living with Dawn and taking care of her. Before I was infected I never would have contemplated such a commitment as early as a first date. But it seemed that Dawn was awakening new stirrings of longing and hope in me.

"What are you thinking about?" I asked her as we neared the medical center's parking garage.

"I don't know. I guess I'm wondering about how sick I'm going to get."

I was a little stung by her words. I had enjoyed our excursion to the park and hoped that it had cheered her.

"Don't do that," I said. "You're obviously doing fine."

"I'd just like to see my son finish high school."

I reminded her that many people remained asymptomatic for five to ten years. "I'll bet you'll be okay for a long time," I said. "And there will be better therapies coming that will keep all of us healthy longer."

"I don't know, Mahlon." Dawn frowned. "I always seem to have such bad luck."

I insisted on driving Dawn to her car and made a great show of hopping out and opening the door for her. As she got out, she giggled and then, surprising me, leaned forward and gave me an inspiring hug. "I'm sorry if I sounded down," she said. "I promise you that I'll be more fun the next time."

"You were fine," I told her. "Don't worry, I had a great time."

And as I watched her drive off, I thought that already she had enriched my life immeasurably.

CHAPTER 12

———— ∞ ————

OCTOBER 1993.

My CD4 counts were already falling, a strange and disturbing development in someone barely a year into an HIV infection.

The CD4 count is the measure of the T-helper lymphocytes in the blood. T-helpers are like field commanders that, in response to foreign invaders, strategize an immune response. They do this in part by releasing cytokines, special delivery battle plans, to the fighting units—the macrophages, B lymphocytes, and other T-lymphocyte populations. The AIDS virus kills off these field commanders and the result is catastrophic: a well-organized military force disintegrates into anarchy.

A CD4 count measures the number of CD4 lymphocytes per milliliter of blood and the percentage of CD4s relative to the total number of T and B lymphocytes in the blood. Both the absolute number and the percentage are important indirect measures of how the immune system is holding up against HIV's attack. CD4 concentrations also vary somewhat from month to month.

Most laboratories consider a CD4 count between 600 and 1,200 to be normal. When people contract HIV, their CD4s often rise temporarily and then sink to around 90 percent of their pre-infection normal range. But as the infection progresses, the virus kills off CD4 cells faster than the body can make them, and so the CD4 counts keep dropping. A count of 200 (14 percent) is the laboratory definition of AIDS.

In some 70 percent of people with HIV, it takes eight to twelve years for the virus to drive their counts down to 200. In 1 to 5 percent of HIV-infected people the virus reaches a standoff with the CD4 lymphocytes and so their counts remain stable. These lucky few are called "long-term nonprogressors." And then there are the most unfortunate souls, whose counts plummet to 200 within three to five years of infection. They are on a steep slope, a seemingly unstoppable slide into the fire. These are referred to as the "rapid progressors."

Almost immediately after my seroconversion in April, my counts had dropped from 821 CD4s per milliliter of blood (45 percent of the lymphocytes being CD4s) down to 590 (39 percent) on July 20, down to 520 (37 percent) on September 21—just a few days after I'd met Dawn. After the results of September 21, I discussed the decline with Jim Stevens, who suggested that my 800 count in April might have been a little high and that my "normal" range could very easily be in the 700s. This would mean that a drop to 500 was not that significant. But my next test, taken only six days later, brought even more sobering results. My CD4 count had now dropped to 460.

Jim completely discounted the drop of 60 cells, pointing out that the percentages of CD4s from the new test were slightly higher than the previous ones. He reminded me of how hard I'd been working on grant proposals and that stress might very well account for the decline. "It would be highly unlikely that your counts would drop that quickly in so short a time," he told me. "Not to mention so soon into an HIV infection. I'm sure normal range for you is somewhere between six hundred and seven hundred."

Then he chided me for getting this last test so soon. Unlike nearly every other asymptomatic HIV-infected person, who would be having blood counts done biannually, I was having mine analyzed constantly—sometimes as often as twice a month. Such frequent testing, he told me, would pick up more fluctuation. "Mahlon," he said, "if you continue to monitor yourself too closely you could end up destroying your own morale."

Still, I had to keep checking. I just had to have a concrete sense of how my immune system was fighting the disease. Having my counts done as often as I wanted gave me a sense, however false it might be, that by monitoring my condition I was taking some measure of control over my fate—and ultimately, treatment. As a researcher, I also hoped that by careful documentation of my own early infection, through frequent CD4 counts and intermittent banking of my blood, I might contribute to our understanding of early HIV infection. And so I constructed a table of my blood work, methodically adding the data as it came in. It reminded me of charting a sea course for a vessel with a broken rudder.

SEVERAL WEEKS LATER, unwilling to accept my count of 460, I got tested again. Results of Western Blot tests, since they documented HIV infections, were kept confidential and never fed into the hospital's computer, but CD4 counts, offering a more general picture of the immune system, were accessible to any doctor who had a password. So I had gotten into the habit of logging on to check my counts myself, rather than waiting to be notified, a habit that was no doubt irritating to Jim Stevens. This time, my hands trembled as I entered the precise codes that would access my results. They rolled down the screen like a wave crashing onto sand. When I saw the figure I went numb with shock: I had dropped to 380.

The rate of the decline was devastating. In just a few short months, my counts had plummeted by more than 200. Only a year into the infection, I was 180 away from AIDS.

Could I be a rapid progressor? The thought was terrifying.

I called Stevens but his line was busy, so I hurried over to his office. Still on the phone, he motioned me in, then hung up the phone with a quizzical frown. "You look very worried, Mahlon," he said.

"I just got my latest counts."

"I just got them myself. Once again, you beat me to the punch."

"Jim, I'm at three-eighty. I'd really like to start on something," I insisted. "I think it's time to get on AZT."

Jim trotted out all his old arguments about the Concorde study, and once again I countered them. Then I pressed him about other drugs, especially the new protease inhibitors, which I'd read that Mike Saag was testing at the University of Alabama. In Saag's study, patients on protease inhibitors showed big rises in their CD4 counts, but only temporarily, for it seemed that the virus quickly developed resistance to the drugs. However, there was one patient whose counts rose and stayed high—heartening evidence that the drugs held great promise. Unfortunately, according to Hoffman La Roche, one manufacturer, protease inhibitors were very hard to make and the supply was limited. But I asked Stevens if there was some way we could get them.

"Mahlon," he said, "it's an early study, and only one patient did that well. From my point of view, AZT is still the best drug we've got. And we're going to need it later if you get sick."

"Jim, I'm telling you I'd rather go for broke now, try to slow down the virus now and gamble that better treatments will be out there by the time AZT quits working. I don't want treatment when I've got AIDS. What's the point then? I won't be able to work. I won't be able to do anything. If there's no good treatment by that time, I might as well go on and die."

Stevens was stirred. "Well, that's a bit extreme, don't you think?"

"If I'm unlucky, at least I'll have died trying."

Jim glanced away, frowning for a moment. "Mahlon, I want you to live. That's my first priority as your physician. So I don't want to do anything wrong. If we make a mistake now, it's still my responsibility—"

"No, it's my responsibility," I said. "Because I'm the one who's pushing for this."

"If something happens to you, I know I'll carry it with me for the rest of my life."

"But Jim," I said, "something *is* going to happen to me— that much we know. And if it's up to me, I'd rather have my health destroyed by a drug than by the virus. It's as simple as that."

Stevens shook his head. "It amazes me how certain you are about this."

"I've got nothing to lose."

I knew as well as Stevens did that there wasn't strong scientific evidence to support my desire for treatment. I was going on gut instinct, driven as much by my compulsion to act and to regain control of my life as by the available data. But if AZT was the only weapon I had, I was determined to use it and hope that the gun wouldn't blow up in my face.

Finally, Jim said, "Mahlon, can I ask you to wait just one more month? That's all, I promise. Wait until the end of November, early December. See how your counts are, see if they bounce back at all. If they're still the same, I promise we'll put you on AZT without any more discussion."

I left Stevens's office disappointed not to have the prescription in my hands but relieved that at least I'd pinned him down to a date. I reasoned that one month more wouldn't make too much difference; at least I wouldn't have to fight him all over again.

I wasn't back in my office five minutes when I got the idea to have my counts done one more time. I knew I was getting obsessive about the numbers, but I had to make sure that the 380 wasn't just a fluke. As I was leaving for the phlebotomy lab, Carol called, and I told her what I was doing. "Whoa," she said, "if you're going through some kind of infection, don't you think you should at least wait a few more days?"

"But I'm not sick now," I protested. "Besides, I just want to make sure this one wasn't a mistake. It's thirty dollars for peace of mind."

"Go ahead, but just realize that you're going to get another low count. And that might depress you even more."

"I know. But if my body has cleared whatever it was fighting, I might have already bounced back."

"I certainly hope so."

"I'm barely a year out—I can't believe it," I said. "I must've gotten infected by some terribly virulent strain."

"Don't be so sure," she reassured me. "Watching the virus as closely as you are will definitely show you many more fluctuations, good and bad."

At Carol's urging, I held off for two more days before getting my counts done again. This time they scrolled down my computer screen at 390, an insignificant change. All I could do was stare at the number, paralyzed, trying to get my panic under control. Only one more month, I told myself, one more month and I could begin trying to reverse the fall.

CHAPTER 13

———— ∞ ————

TONIGHT WOULD BE my fourth date with Dawn in six weeks. Although she lived only twenty minutes away from me, she'd seemed more comfortable getting acquainted by talking on the phone, which we did frequently, sometimes for an hour or more. In these conversations we were relatively candid about our lives and our histories, but I found myself skirting the subjects of my CD4 tests and my crusade for early treatment. Though I had dreamed of finding an HIV-positive companion who could share the fears and uncertainties of the infection, my budding relationship with Dawn seemed too fragile to burden with the sobering news of my falling counts.

After our lunch at Faisons, Dawn and I had gone out for meals and then to the movies—she loved good restaurants and sappy romantic comedies. For our fourth date, I wanted to do something special, so I was delighted to get invited to a country music benefit for AIDS and cancer research at the Starwood Amphitheater. Dawn was thrilled, too, for country music was her favorite; and she loved Alabama and Diamond Rio, the bands that were performing.

Then, after the concert, she was coming to see my house for the first time. I'd planned the evening carefully, right down to the flowers. I brought Autumn Joy, Blue Mist, and mums from my garden into my old stone garage and plunged them into cold water. I'd swept the fireplace, stacked wood, and placed several romantic guitar CDs by Segovia in the player. Ransacking my closet, I'd searched among the rows of jackets and dress pants I never wore for just the right combination of jeans and a dress shirt. I was excited when I went to pick her up.

This was my first visit to Dawn's home, too, for we'd always met at restaurants. Heading down busy Murfreesboro Road, I strained to find her side street among the discount stores, car repair shops, and occasional stripped-down automobiles on cinder blocks. Finally I found it, a lane of wall-to-wall matchbox houses with barren dirt yards. Dawn's was a white clapboard, modest but clean, its mailbox guarded by an amputated old tree.

Dawn came to the door wearing a sweater and jeans and greeted me with a hug. "My friends are so jealous that I'm going to this concert," she gushed.

I was pleased. She led me into the house through a cluttered hallway that ended in a room lit only by the blue screen of a TV. I could barely make out the figure sitting in front of it, zombielike. "I want you to meet Howie," Dawn said, not bothering to switch on the light.

I moved closer, so I could see him more clearly, extending my hand in greeting. "Hello," he said, keeping his own hands at his sides. He had darker hair than his mother and was at least twenty pounds overweight. Remembering what Dawn had told me about his nightmares and depressions over her illness, I wondered if it troubled him to see his mother go out on a date.

I asked Dawn as we were driving to Starwood. No, she said, explaining that Howie's mood was just a reflection of her own.

"I've been railing on and on about my job ever since I got home," she told me. "I probably shouldn't do it in front of him because he takes it to heart."

"What's wrong at work?" I asked.

According to Dawn, a new boss was more lenient with her than some of the other receptionists, who resented it and accused her of using her sex appeal to gain favors.

"I'm the only young one there," Dawn pointed out. "The rest of them are a bunch of old biddies who think they own the place."

"What are they objecting to, specifically?"

"That I come in late, that I leave early, and he's cool about it. They claim that I flirt with him, but I don't. I'm just really nice, and in return, he's nice to me."

"They're probably just jealous of your boss's interest—and because you're younger and so attractive."

Dawn shrugged. "I don't know . . . I guess."

Again, I could see Dawn sinking into depression. Determined to counterbalance it, I reached over and gently stroked her shoulder. "Hey," I said.

But she kept obsessing. "Being attractive to men has always gotten me in trouble. I've relied on it a lot . . . I guess I still rely on it, much as I don't want to." She paused for a moment. "Believe it or not, I used to like the thought of being a high-priced call girl, you know, having men shower money and gifts on me. But now all I can think is that being pretty has ruined my life. I don't want to be pretty."

"Well," I said, trying to shift her mood but not sure how to do it, "you can't help being gorgeous. Don't let those women ruin this evening for you. The concert is going to be wonderful."

She squeezed my hand. "Okay, you're right. Let's go and have a great time."

A sea of bobbing cowboy hats separated us from the entrance to the Starwood Amphitheater. Somewhere on the other side of them was the side gate for contributors with special passes, which I possessed. But going through these gates seemed about as safe as going through a herd of horses in a thunderstorm. I could smell the beer and sense the restlessness. Uneasy about this mass of cowboys, I pushed forward toward the special gate with Dawn behind me, her ring-laden fingers gripping my hand.

"This would be a lot easier if we just held up a bloody finger and started yelling 'AIDS,' " I said.

Dawn laughed, trying to stick close to me. Angling forward, we reached one of the side gates and were admitted, stumbling through a seam in the crowd. Eventually we found our seats amid a mass of milling fans. Dawn dug into her denim-covered purse and fished out a cigarette as a group of tipsy girls in front of us began screaming for Diamond Rio.

When the band jogged out onto the stage, a salvo of screams went up, followed by a thunder of clapping. Then the music started and the crowd settled down.

Dawn seemed to know the words to every song and sang along to herself. I tried to enjoy what I was hearing, but as a classical music lover, I found the melodies too simple and predictable. Then again I could hardly listen because I was getting so distracted by the sadness Dawn was radiating. Figuring her mind was still on the women at work, I put my arm around her, and she in turn rested her head on my shoulder. "This may be the last time I ever see this band," she said wistfully, blowing out a plume of smoke.

"No, we'll see them again if you want."

"That's not what I mean," she said. I knew she was tormenting herself again about AIDS. She and I did seem to be an island in the middle of a lake of carefree people who were healthy, not haunted by uncertainty and fear of death. For Dawn, those fears were never far below the surface.

Finally, she disengaged herself from me, placing her hands on the small of her back. "Mahlon," she said, "believe it or not, I don't know if I can sit here much longer."

"How come?"

"My back and legs are killing me."

"Why didn't you say something?"

She smiled wanly. "Because I really wanted to come— you know that. And, I'm sure you realize that I complain too much as it is."

"Let's go, then," I said, happy for the excuse to leave. "You certainly won't feel any better sitting like this." Dawn agreed, and we squeezed our way out of the orchestra row.

"Would you like me to take you home?" I asked as we drove out of the parking lot.

"No. I really want to see your house. I've been looking forward to that, too."

"Are you sure?"

"Really, let's just go there." Dawn frowned. "You know

. . . I'm so sorry . . . two out of four dates I've wimped out on you," she said.

"Don't worry about it. I'm sorry about your back. Maybe I can give you a back rub . . ." I paused, "I'm trying to help Shannon learn massage techniques to use on her patients. It's therapeutic."

"Are you going to show her how?" Dawn surprised me with what seemed like a pang of jealousy.

"That would be a little awkward since she's married. I'm just loaning her some of my massage books."

"Oh, so you're an expert."

"Not really, but I've tried to learn."

We arrived at my house and entered through the back door, which opened up into the cozy kitchen that I'd remodeled for Alexis. A small marble lamp in the corner cast a warm glow on the Dutch blue-and-white tiles. But the highlight of the room was the handmade wooden cabinets.

Dawn stepped in and looked around quietly, hands clasped together, while I opened some champagne and fetched a pair of tulip wineglasses. After filling her glass, I put on one of the Segovia CDs and gave Dawn a tour of the living room with its broad stone fireplace, the upstairs bedrooms, and the master bathroom, whose ceiling I'd now repaired. I was proud of how the place looked and hoped that Dawn would be impressed. When we finally settled in the living room, I knelt and started a fire. Dawn sat down next to me on the fleecelike wool rug.

"You obviously care a lot about this place."

I told her I loved it. She didn't respond.

"How are you feeling now?" I said, putting my hand on her back.

"A little better. But it still hurts, and my legs, too."

"Should I give you a massage?" I asked, unable to hide my nervousness.

She looked at me suspiciously.

"Look, I promise to behave. I'll just work on your legs and back. Why don't you go into the bathroom and change into my robe?"

"Okay," she said, "but could we have some different music?"

I reeled off what I had and she chose Mary Chapin Carpenter. When she returned, swaddled in navy blue terry cloth, she looked sheepish, so I encouraged her to lie on her stomach on the rug and propped her head on a pillow. "I love this CD," she said as the music came on.

I started to massage her legs and back, and slowly I could feel the tension leave her. I marveled at the softness of her skin, feeling grateful that I could touch her at all. She had been so ambivalent about physical contact, sometimes impulsively hugging me, sometimes welcoming my arm around her shoulders, but often, unpredictably, she would shrink from my touch. Now she sighed deeply. "I can't believe how good this feels," she said.

I was beginning to get excited, but couldn't and wouldn't betray the brittle gift of Dawn's trust. It was clear how scarred she was, how unable to separate her sexuality from the infection. It would take a long time, and a lot of patience on my part, to ease her emotional wounds enough to let sex become part of the equation between us. Then, too, there was the issue of safe sex, which I felt we'd have to practice scrupulously, for mixing our strains of virus could be devastating in our fragile state of health.

For now, massage was the only way that I could be physically close and giving to Dawn without being threatening. And, frustrating as massage might ultimately prove, for now I relished the warmth.

But then suddenly Dawn caught her breath and went completely rigid.

"What's wrong?" I asked. "I'm sorry. Did I scare you?"

My hands had strayed closer than they should have to her buttocks.

"It's not your fault. It's me," she said. "I just—" And then she burst into tears.

Feeling terrible, I moved up and touched my forehead to her shoulder. I didn't know what to say. She pushed me away and yanked at my bathrobe. I helped her pull it back over her legs.

Safely shrouded in the robe, she sat up. "It's not what you're thinking," she said tearfully. "You didn't do anything wrong. I just realized how much of my life has been taken away from me. This is the first time in years—since I found out I was infected—that I've felt at all like a woman."

CHAPTER 14

A FEW DAYS after the Diamond Rio concert, Shannon called and asked how my romance was going.

"I'm sure you know more about it than I do," I said, suspecting that I'd become the talk of Dawn's support group.

"I know it all, lover boy," Shannon shot back. "Not just me and the girls in the group, but all the AIDS nurses at Vanderbilt are rooting for you, too."

"What?" I said, embarrassed. Shannon liked to tease me about being shy, and I never knew if she was kidding.

"Come on, Mahlon. All we see is sickness. Be generous and give us something good to talk about."

"Well," I spluttered.

Shannon started laughing. "I'm not serious," she said. "And

I'm glad things are working out with Dawn. But that's not why I called. We need your help.''

"We" referred to herself and Carol and also to an emergency technician named Bart, a tightly knit triumvirate I'd nicknamed "the Archangels." Each of them had been touched in some way by the plight of HIV sufferers and now dedicated whatever free time and personal resources they could muster to provide aid and comfort. They were the selfless, unsung heroes of the war on AIDS.

Once they learned of my falling counts, the Archangels had adopted me, calling me often to see how I was doing and to encourage me. My natural inclination had been to hole up with my work, to hide my wounds in private, but they kept reaching out, refusing to let me isolate myself in the anxieties of my illness. At first their ministrations made me a little uncomfortable, although I was grateful for their concern. Now I had come to cherish their support and to acknowledge, grudgingly, that HIV had yielded one benefit to me, the gift of friendship.

Recently, the Archangels had begun to recruit for their missions helping people with AIDS. Today, for example, somebody had made a donation to Nashville Cares, the local support organization for people with AIDS. Bart needed me to help him move furniture to a vacant apartment that would soon be occupied by someone living with AIDS. Checking my schedule, I told Shannon that I could help after five in the afternoon.

Shannon had been following the AIDS epidemic from the beginning, and the moment an AIDS clinic was established at Vanderbilt in the mid-eighties, she applied for a job there. She was married to a liberal Protestant minister who went out of his way to invite gay members into his church. He had attracted a barrage of criticism from the church hierarchy for performing ''same-sex covenants,'' but he remained committed to dignifying all loving relationships, especially in an era when one indiscriminate sexual act could be a fatal mistake. The congregation had formed hospice groups to care for those dying of AIDS. Over the years, Shannon had sat for countless death vigils and recorded the news of those lost to the disease on her personal ''honor roll,'' a typed, single-spaced list that now ran to four pages in length. To watch someone die of AIDS was terrible, she told me, yet it was a privilege to be able to offer solace.

Often the dying left poignant legacies. One sick parishioner had gone into Shannon's fallow, neglected backyard and created a beautiful garden. He spent his last lucid hours patiently explaining the wonders of horticulture to Shannon, who as a result became a rabidly devoted gardener.

Carol, my tech friend, who had been raised as a Southern Baptist, once told me that when she first began to culture the blood of HIV patients she didn't feel comfortable being around any homosexual. But every time she visited the Vanderbilt clinic to pick up vials of blood, she ended up talking to the patients, many of them gay men, and started to grow attached to them.

Eventually she became involved in an on-line support network for people with HIV—and again, most of her contacts turned out to be gay men. Married and a mother, Carol would arise long before the rest of her family, often at four in the morning, to log on to her computer and chat with AIDS-afflicted people waiting for her ''I'm here'' message to flash across their computer screens. Some needed information about the illness or treatments, others were suffering from ostracism and loneliness. Carol gave these

"PWAs" solace and encouragement on a daily basis. And whenever she couldn't reach them, she'd begin to worry and would call local contacts who had access to these patients. Sometimes word came back that the person had gone into the hospital for treatment; more often she was told he or she had died. Carol grieved for every one of these people. And it wasn't beyond her to drive halfway across the country to console the lover or the bereaved family of someone she'd corresponded with but had never met. She was blessed with a great empathy that was linked to a terrible tragedy in her own life. Her eldest son had been killed in a freak accident.

And then there was Bart, a gay man who spent much of his time driving the road trucks of country music stars and who opened his home to homeless AIDS patients. He lived in a small bungalow a few blocks away from the medical complex at Vanderbilt. When I arrived at his house at around five P.M. as planned, he was in the process of retaping an IV line running into the arm of a fair-haired, gaunt-looking man lying on his bed. Bart was a muscular man in his late forties who looked more like an old-time wrestler than an emergency medical technician. He was having trouble restarting the IV of his squirming patient. "Need some help?" I gently offered.

"Hell no," Bart said in his gravelly voice. "He's actually a doctor," he told his patient, who laughed. "But I think this will help," he said, fishing a filterless Pall Mall out of a pack resting on the table next to the IV pole. He lit the cigarette, took a hefty drag, and then reinserted the needle. Turning to me, he chortled, "Who said smoking was bad for you?"

Once he finished taping the arm, Bart said to me, "I got a pickup truck. You ready to haul?"

Because Bart drove country music band trucks for a living, driving came second nature to him. As we sped along Hillsboro Road in the direction of Green Hills, my neighborhood, he talked about where he'd gone on his last road trip and that his truck had nearly fishtailed off the road during a freak snowstorm. As he spoke to me, his eyes kept leaving the road, which I found unnerving.

I asked him about the gaunt young man. Was he a lover or a former lover, since he was sleeping in Bart's bed? Bart shook his head and said that no, he'd only met him for the first time a few weeks before and that he had moved in the day Bart returned from a road trip. And since Bart knew he'd be gone a lot on many road trips over the next few weeks, he'd invited the patient to stay in his bedroom.

"It's like this," he said to me, "when you first meet a person, sure, you don't know them. But after having them living in your house for a while and taking care of them, you get to know them pretty well, maybe even better than some of your friends."

We eventually arrived at the condominium of a corpulent Mediterranean-looking man who was fretting that we hadn't arrived earlier. Apparently his wife was coming home in forty-five minutes and he'd promised her that all the furniture would be out by then. They were expecting a new delivery of furniture any minute.

"Well, I'm sorry I couldn't get here until now," Bart said. "But I couldn't do it myself. I needed help." He pointed to me. "I was so frantic I had to call my doctor to help me."

The disgruntled man turned toward me with sudden reverence. "Oh, my goodness," he said. "Did I take you away from your patients?"

Before I could say anything Bart interjected, "Na, just a couple of dead people. He's a pathologist. But I guess they can wait, right, Mahlon?" He hefted one corner of a sleeper sofa and stood waiting for me to man the other side. "Get ready," he warned. "This sucker is heavy."

Between the two of us, we managed to angle the sofa around the corners of the condominium hallways and down its flights of cement stairs, mushing our fingers on the stucco walls. After that, the rest of the move was easy, but more so for Bart than for me, with my weight-trained muscles that were used to a rest every five minutes. Once we got everything into the back of the pickup truck, Bart turned to me with a cynical look and said, "You think this little 'donation' is about altruism? It's about getting free haulage."

At that moment the "altruist" came out to the railing on the walkway above us and waved a frantic good-bye as though he were glad to be rid of us. Perhaps he assumed that both Bart and I had AIDS.

Maybe it was because we'd sweated together, moving the furniture, that I finally felt emboldened to ask Bart what had happened on the night I'd first met him, a couple of years before. Our first meeting took place in the emergency room, where, amid the cacophony of ambulances and the confusion of gurneys and stretchers, he had appeared out of nowhere with a woman to sign an autopsy permit for a young man who had died in his house. Bart had struck me as remarkably edgy, not subdued or relieved that a loved one's ordeal was over, and he seemed awkward with the woman—at the time, I had assumed they were a couple. When I'd asked Bart the routine questions to complete my paperwork, his answers were evasive and he couldn't meet my eye. Something had been tormenting him.

"Who was that young man in the emergency room?" I asked him now.

"You should know," Bart said tersely, with pain in his voice. "You took out his brain."

"Well, if I remember correctly, he was suffering from cryptococcal meningitis."

Bart nodded. "Yeah. That's what you said it was."

I waited, knowing whatever Bart had to tell me was not easy for him. "Well, we were very close," he said finally. "He told me that he didn't want to suffer and asked me to help him die when it was time."

"Oh. What a burden."

"Don't I know it," Bart agreed. "It was a hard thing to do and it ended up being a lot worse than I expected. And that's why I was so nervous around you. Because you were the one who might figure out what I'd done."

Years before, at a truck stop in Arkansas, Bart had met a twenty-six-year-old hitchhiker who was looking for a ride to Nashville. The guy was drunk and Bart filled him with coffee, trying to sober him up. They talked the entire way back to Nashville, and Bart learned that Hank had just left his wife and child in Texas and was traveling around, trying to figure out what he wanted to do with his life. Hank ended up staying at Bart's house and getting involved with him.

"It lasted for six months, and I became very emotionally attached to Hank. But then one day I came home from being out on the road, from driving fifteen hundred miles, to find this blond stripper sleeping in my bed. Hank had moved her in. She was shooting drugs when nobody was around, I later found out. I was nice and let her stay a few days, but when I asked her to leave,

Hank got riled up and left also. Never saw him after that. I found out that he went back to Texas, begged his wife to take him in, and then sometime later they moved with their kid back to Nashville. He never bothered to tell me that he was here.

"Then, a couple years later, I'm standing in line at the Department of Motor Vehicles, waiting to get my license renewed, when I see this man who looks familiar but I can't place him. Something about the eyes I recognize, but the rest of him, his body, his body language, doesn't ring a bell. It was only after I'd left and had driven a mile away that I realized it was Hank. I rushed back to the DMV, but he was gone."

"But how come you didn't recognize him?" I asked, thinking this was odd after the two had lived together for six months.

"Well, by then he'd changed. Physically, emotionally. He'd already come down with pneumocystis, told his wife he was positive; she and the kid had left him, and then he lost his house and job. He was in dire straits—it obviously took its toll on the way he looked.

"Then another year goes by and I get this call from a social worker at Nashville Cares, who tells me he's interviewing this homeless AIDS patient and when he mentions there's a trucker who takes in sick people, the guy asks if it's me. It was Hank. They had him staying at some fly-by-night hotel, and I just called him and said of course I wanted to see him. I went right over to where he was and we held each other and cried. 'I didn't think you'd want to see me,' he kept saying. 'I didn't think you'd come.' And then I told him I wanted him to come back, and he came back and lived with me. Until the end."

The pickup truck had pulled into the parking lot of the building where the empty apartment was located. We had come to a halt, though neither of us made a move to get out of the cab. Bart continued, "So, he was well for a while, and while he was well we had this talk about my helping him die. I agreed to do it if he seemed to be suffering. Pretty soon after we talked, he started to get sick again. The typical horrors: his mind started to go, and his lungs got bad, and finally he couldn't really talk. He seemed generally pretty miserable. It was getting close to the time when we had to decide what we were going to do, and I spoke to a hospice nurse who managed to get me a prescription for Roxanol. When I picked up the bottle, I took it and lay on the bed with him. I explained that it was a really strong narcotic, that if I gave him enough of it he'd stop breathing. 'You don't appear to be comfortable, Hank,' I said. 'You appear to be in some kind of pain. I wish you could tell me what you want me to do.' He got this big tear in his eye and it rolled down his cheek. Then I took the Roxanols, and gave him the whole bottle orally. And at the time that I did that, I never realized they wouldn't be enough. He was only thirty years old, and he had a very strong heart.

"Then it got awful. His respiration slowed down to, like, once a minute and was really erratic. And he stayed like that, taking these long gasping breaths, and really seemed to be struggling. I was getting frantic. So I called the hospice nurse back, told her right up front that I'd given him the whole bottle and that he was still in pain—those were the exact words I used—and I needed another bottle. She was very kind; she knew what was going on and didn't question me about it, and managed to get the doctor Hank had seen to call in a prescription. Then I asked the woman you saw me with at the hospital to get it. Unfortunately, this was all happening at rush hour and she was taking a long time getting back, and watching him gasping for breath like he was really got to me. At one point it became so unbearable to watch that I took a pillow and held it over his face.'' Bart paused, his voice cracking. ''I'm not proud of this, Mahlon, but I was just trying to get him to stop gasping. But then in the midst of doing that I suddenly remembered him telling me he didn't want to suffocate. So I took the pillow away. . . . He was staring at me, wide-eyed. I held him and apologized for what I'd done and then, knowing I had to do something, I went and got the rest of his pain medication, all his Percocets and Demerols, and I crushed them up and mixed them with saline and gave him an injection in his arm. And that finally ended it for him a few minutes later.''

And so when I had begun to question Bart about Hank, he'd assumed the worst.

''I just figured you found out that I'd OD'd him. And that it would be just a matter of time before the police came and arrested me.''

Now Bart opened his door, got out of the pickup truck, and went around to the rear to unload the furniture. I followed him, and as he popped the tailgate, I said, ''My questions, as I remember, were minor administrative ones.''

Bart snorted. ''Yeah, but who knew what you'd be able to tell from my answers?''

''Well, I can certainly understand why you did what you did. It probably seemed like the only humane thing to do.''

Bart looked at me, his eyes glistening. ''Well, thank you, I guess,'' he said.

''By the way,'' I told him, ''a mild overdose of a narcotic wouldn't necessarily be detected in the autopsy of an AIDS patient with a reasonable cause of death who was already on high doses of pain medication.''

"Oh, well," Bart said wryly, "I'll keep that in mind for the next time.''

Three years before, from my perch in the ivory tower of academic medicine, I might have been shocked by Bart's story. But now I could see how the lofty concepts of "preserving human dignity" and "ending suffering" could, in the real world of AIDS, come down to a deathbed grapple with a soul in pain begging for release. I wondered how many similar autopsies I'd done not suspecting that death had come through an act of mercy, and what I would choose when the end came for me. If the healer's commitment to the living seemed a profound responsibility, the commitment of people like the Archangels to those who were beyond healing now seemed to border on a sacred trust.

When we arrived back at Bart's apartment, we found his guest standing in the kitchen, looking disoriented. He'd been mixing a bowl of tuna salad when a jar of mayonnaise had fallen to the floor and fractured into gooey shards. He began apologizing profusely, saying that when the accident first happened he'd tried to bend down to wipe up the mess but had gotten dizzy and had to go lie down. Now he'd come back in for another attempt. He stood there, gazing at us vacantly. Bart asked me to take the fellow into the bedroom while he cleaned the floor. I offered my arm, and the young man leaned on me as we walked. The moment I got him comfortably situated on the bed, he began crying.

When I tried to comfort him, he turned to me glassy-eyed and said in a small, breaking voice, "Are they going to find something? You're a doctor, you can tell me.''

I told him that I prayed for this, both as a doctor and as a patient. He looked at me strangely and then I explained about myself. And as I told him my story, I noticed on the far wall a bulletin board plastered with photographs: all the AIDS patients Bart had cared for during the last few years, a collage of mostly youthful faces of the dead.

CHAPTER 15

ALTHOUGH THE ARCHANGELS were giving me, perhaps for the first time, the sense that I belonged to a community, the true emotional center of my life was Dawn. Since the night of the concert, when she'd first trusted me to massage her, I'd made it my mission to convince her that I deserved her faith. In trying to prove that I was too caring and giving ever to betray her, I kept our relationship focused entirely on Dawn, on fulfilling what I perceived to be her needs—never confiding the fact of my falling counts or that I would soon begin taking AZT. I knew that even thinking about HIV depressed Dawn, and besides, I didn't want to worry her.

In late November, Dawn began having trouble with a tooth, and it turned out that she needed a root canal. I took her to the dentist, but she neglected to tell me that, on her previous visit, she had mentioned that she was HIV-positive, infected by a boyfriend. It was the responsible thing to do: to warn people who would be performing a medical procedure, but as we sat in the waiting room I was assailed by caustic stares from the receptionist and aides that I was hard-pressed to understand.

Once Dawn was taken inside, the receptionist banished me for an hour and a half, but when I returned, Dawn had still not emerged. I occupied myself with a stack of work-related paper, but as time dragged on, I began to worry. Another half hour went by, and I kept trying to make eye contact with the receptionist, who refused to look at me.

"Why is this taking so long?" I finally demanded.

"Sir, this is a root canal."

"I'm aware of that."

"Then you should know that it's a long procedure . . . this one is taking longer than usual."

"Do you know why?"

The woman glowered at me. "No, I don't."

After another interminable fifteen minutes, the woman closed the admitting window, preparing to leave for the night. "So what's going on?" I said.

"Somebody will be with you shortly," she replied.

"Somebody? What about Dawn?"

"I'm sorry, but I have to leave now," the receptionist said, breezing out the door.

I was flabbergasted. The office was closed and I was still waiting.

I stayed patient for a while, then knocked on the door to the inner offices, but no one answered. Telling myself I'd wait another fifteen minutes before barging in, I sat back down. The time had nearly elapsed when at last the door opened and, white-faced, out came Dawn.

I hurried over to her. "What happened? Are you okay?"

She stood there, whimpering, seemingly unsteady on her feet.

"He had trouble getting it," she muttered. "I don't know. Probably was afraid of me. I got scared."

A moment later the dental assistant emerged, turning a slick smile on me as though nothing were amiss. "Dawn had a little bit of a panic attack," she drawled. "But I think she's all right now, aren't you?" I felt her eyes snidely appraising me.

I was furious, but I didn't want to waste time on somebody so clearly unsympathetic. I helped Dawn check out so we could leave and discuss what had happened. Outside in the chilly late-November evening, I said gently, "So tell me, what got you so upset?"

Dawn grew tearful. "They were wearing so much stuff, all these gowns and masks, it was like they were going to the moon. They made me feel like I was a leper."

Once we got into the car, she began to sob openly. "Even with the Novocain it was hurting me," she cried. "I just can't stand pain."

Reaching over the stick shift to hug her, I reassured her. "Okay, it's over now. Everything will be all right."

"You don't understand, I'm petrified of pain. What am I going to do when I get sick?" Dawn started digging through her purse for a cigarette. "If I can't take a root canal, how will I be able to deal with this disease?"

"Don't think about that now. You're still incredibly healthy. Besides, everybody and their mother will take care of you. . . . I certainly will."

"It could happen so suddenly," Dawn said. "You know that. One day you're feeling great and the next day you wake up with . . . some horrible fungus growing in your mouth."

"Has that ever happened to you?"

"No, but it did to Jan, my friend from the support group. And it was so terrible. Everything burned when she tried to eat— even chocolate ice cream . . . in fact, now she's in the hospital."

"For what?"

"Retinitis."

"Oh, no. How long has she been there?"

"A few days."

"How is she doing?"

"I don't know. I haven't gone to see her. I just can't face it that she's going to die."

I tried to comfort Dawn by saying that retinitis, terrible as it was, didn't mean that Jan was on her deathbed. But Dawn kept obsessing about the fact that she couldn't stand the sight of illness, reproaching herself for abandoning her friend.

"How about if I go and see her?" I found myself offering. "Maybe bring her something from both of us?"

Dawn turned to me with tear-stained cheeks. "Would you do that? You wouldn't mind?"

"Maybe I could drop in at lunchtime."

"That would be so sweet. Thank you," Dawn said.

ON MY WAY to work the next morning, I detoured to the northern outskirts of Nashville, where I stopped off at the greenhouse of an old orchid grower. There I selected a cattleya with large lavender blooms and tied a purple bow around its terra-cotta pot. When

I delivered it to Jan, I found her half asleep in a room that was surprisingly barren. There were no other flowers or cards, no sign of visitors, and it struck me what an isolating disease AIDS could be, that it could keep family and friends away.

Dawn had told me that, the afternoon before, Jan had had laser surgery to reattach her retina, which I assumed had become detached as the result of a CMV infection.* She lay there with a stainless steel patch, like a miniature vegetable strainer, over her right eye. She had a thin, boyish face and short brown hair that, tragically, made her look very young.

"Jan?" I whispered.

She lifted her head and squinted, trying to identify me. For a moment she seemed a bit unnerved by the presence of a stranger.

"My name is Mahlon, I'm a friend of Dawn's."

"Oh, my God, Mahlon! You've come to see me?"

I told her that Dawn had spoken so much about her that I just wanted to come by.

"She's spoken a lot about you, too."

Standing there holding the pot, I suddenly realized the folly in bringing an orchid to a person who was virtually blind. Nevertheless, I told her what it was, and as I was setting it down on the table, she said, "Oh, bring it here and let me see."

I held the plant in front of Jan, and she sniffed the blossoms. "That's such a beautiful color. Never seen one like it before." I doubted that she could see a thing. Still, she was cheerful. "Where did you get it from?"

---

* Ravaging cytomegalovirus infections frequently occur in immunosuppressed patients. When they occur in the eye they can blind by causing detachment of the retina.

Dawn had already told me about Jan's incredible morale. Though the other women in the group would slump into depression when their CD4 counts dropped to 200, Jan managed to remain vibrant and unfazed with a CD4 count of only 60. According to Dawn, nothing daunted Jan—not her intermittent pneumonias, her oral thrush,* or even her progressive blindness from CMV retinitis.

I described the orchid greenhouse and then asked Jan how she was feeling. I knew that laser surgery on the retina could cause severe headaches. "I've still got this pain behind my eye," Jan replied with a dismissive wave. "But I'm okay."

"Do they have you on drugs?"

"They may try another infusion of foscarnet, since I sure can't take ganciclovir. It put me into renal failure, but I pulled out of it," she said with a grin.

And yet I knew that foscarnet was highly toxic, a last-ditch effort to control CMV retinitis. If Jan's kidneys failed on infusions of foscarnet, she'd have to risk direct injections into the eye or cease the treatment and go completely blind. Jan understood what she was up against. She seemed so incredibly brave.

"When do they think you can go home?" I asked.

"Not soon enough," she said. "My mother told me that my son has been neglecting his homework again."

"He's probably worried," I said.

"He'll be all right. I told him the operation was going to make me better, but of course he suspects the worst." I thought of Dawn's son worrying about her, about how crippling it must be for

---

* Oral thrush, a fungal infection of the mouth, is commonly seen in pre-AIDS and AIDS patients.

the children of HIV-positive women to have to contemplate their mothers' deaths.

Jan changed the subject. "So how's Dawn doing? Do you see her a lot? Everyone in the group is so excited for the two of you."

I shrugged and said, "It usually depends on Howie, if she can get somebody to stay with him. Sometimes he doesn't like her to go out at all."

"I got to hand it to Dawn," Jan said. "To try and get involved with a guy again. Myself, I couldn't. I can't fool with guys anymore."

"I'll bet there are a lot of HIV-positive guys out there who are looking," I said.

Jan laughed and then said sardonically, "I know. I used to date one."

She was clearly a fighter—and I marveled at the stoicism and unfailing optimism of this woman, besieged by so much pain and suffering. Thinking of Dawn's panic attack at the dentist's office, I wondered how she would ever find the will to face this illness. And I had to question my own mettle. Could I possibly face disability and imminent death with anything like the courage I saw in Jan?

"Mahlon, can you give me some advice?" Jan was saying.

She'd been thinking about selling off her life insurance policy. "I can get seventy percent of its face value from one of those companies. What do you think? That way I could take Matthew to Disneyworld, buy him a nice Walkman, maybe put the rest in a college fund."

I wasn't sure how to answer Jan. Cashing in her life insurance was tantamount to accepting that the end was near. So I treated the question as a straightforward business proposition.

"I'm sorry to have to ask you this, but if you cash in your policy now, will your son get substantially less after you die?"

"I guess he would get less."

"If I were you, I'd find out exactly how much less and then I'd make my decision based on that."

What I wanted to say was, "Don't cash it in. Keep fighting." But I didn't want to give her false hope. I wanted her to show me how to fight.

CHAPTER 16

To my dismay, Dawn never seemed to get around to having her CD4 counts checked. On one hand, she was preoccupied with HIV and her feeling of doom, but on the other she wasn't pursuing her own care. I saw this paradox as just one more manifestation of her depression, convinced that taking some action might lift her mood. And so I began gently suggesting that she get her blood work done, and offered to set her up with Madeline at the AIDS clinic at Vanderbilt in early December. To my great relief, she agreed.

My own status was still rocky. I got tested again on December 6, and then, frantically, kept logging on to check if the results were posted. Finally, twenty-four hours later, they were. My counts had gone up to 550—nearly normal again. I felt a surge of relief, though I knew I couldn't trust the number. I had been sliding too fast to believe I had truly rallied; and besides, my new counts would make it tough to insist that Stevens put me on AZT.

I'd waited, as he'd asked, haunted by visions of the virus ravaging my body unchecked. A higher count was only modest assurance that I was holding it at bay—and only for now. Hoping Stevens wouldn't give me too much of an argument, I headed over to the clinic. I found him at his desk, reading reports.

"I'm sorry to bother you," I said, "but today's the day I begin AZT."

Chuckling at my directness, he told me to come in. "Did you get your latest counts?"

I told him what they were.

"So, I guess my prudence paid off."

"I'm not so sure."

Stevens shook his head.

"Just don't forget that virus in my body is from a corpse that had end-stage AIDS. I'm sure there are relatively few cases where the virus has been transmitted at such a late period in the infection. Sure, my counts are better this time, but let's not forget that they've been falling steadily. It's only reasonable to worry that I'm a rapid progressor. I'd like to see if treating fairly early does anything. It's an experiment worth trying."

"My only concern," Stevens said, "is what if, through your stubbornness, you die?"

"Well," I replied. "At least I'd like to die trying to save my own life."

"I did promise you, so okay. I'll write you the script. Then we'll see how you do."

As Stevens reached for his prescription pad, I felt a tremendous sense of triumph. I carefully folded the prescription with the reverence I would have accorded a fat paycheck. I'd actually broken through, managed to pierce Stevens's caution, and I was ready to begin my "ultimate experiment."

Dawn had gotten her results back, too. That night, she called me, exuberant, to say that her count was 900, high normal.

"That's fantastic," I exclaimed, though I quailed at the thought that, though I'd been infected much more recently, I might well hit rock bottom before Dawn did.

Since she was cheerful for the first time in weeks, I ventured to share my good news—I'd received a prescription for AZT and was excited about starting "early" therapy. Dawn groaned when I told her.

"But why? Why are you taking it when you're perfectly fine?"

With great reluctance I now told her that, despite my recent reprieve of 550, my CD4 counts had been falling.

"How come you didn't tell me?" she said, very little inflection in her voice. I could sense that she took this news as a red flag.

"I didn't want to tell you till I was sure what was going on. There was no reason to scare you."

"Carl's counts fell really quickly, too."

"Well, by taking AZT and hopefully some new drugs as early as I am, I'm hoping I can stabilize them."

"AZT . . . that's hardly going to save your life."

"Well, it slows the progression of the virus."

"But what about the side effects?"

"I'll just have to deal with them."

"But what about Christmas?" Dawn said, sounding deflated. "If it makes you sick, as it probably will, you'll ruin your holiday."

"I don't care about holidays."

"Well, maybe I do. I thought we were going to spend some of the holiday together."

So much for being supportive, I thought to myself. But then I reasoned that since I'd waited so long already, another two-week delay wouldn't hurt me. And I had wanted the Christmas with Dawn to be special. I agreed to hold off.

Now Dawn told me that since her CD4 count was so high, her father was insisting she be retested for HIV. "My counts haven't fallen, so he thinks I could be negative." The AIDS nurse at Vanderbilt had told her not to get her hopes up, since she'd tested positive before and since Carl now had full-blown AIDS. "But I'm just going to do it to please him," Dawn said.

I hoped that Dawn was feeling as realistic as she sounded, not indulging in the luxury of imagining that she might have been a false positive. That would be wonderful, of course, but was extremely unlikely. Yet, once I hung up the phone, I wondered what would happen if, by some happy quirk of fate, Dawn had escaped infection. What if she tested negative this time and could once again return to the ranks of the normal?

I had a sudden vision of Dawn getting the good news and dropping the phone, racing in her Datsun to her son's school, running stop signs and shouting, "I'm negative, I'm negative." She'd even dash into the principal's office, crying, "I'm negative, I'm negative, where's Howie?" She'd fly down the hallway, tears streaming down her cheeks, hair tangling, until she reached her son's homeroom. And she'd stop, savoring the moment. Then she'd whisper through a crack in the door, "Howie!" And grabbing him in a bear hug, she'd tell him that she was negative, and Howie would cheer. Then, hand in hand, they'd leave the school together and would start a new life—a life that I could be no part of.

With this vision came the chill of fear. I just couldn't bear the idea of losing her, of being left again to face this disease alone.

CHAPTER 17

———— ∞ ————

WAS DAWN HIV-positive or not?

A week later, she called me at work. "Well, my ELISAs and Western Blot came back."

"And?"

"They're both positive again. . . . I knew they would be, in my heart I knew. I was just hoping against hope."

"I'm so sorry," I said.

She didn't respond. The possibility, however remote, of a misdiagnosis would make any HIV-positive person nurture a desperate, furtive hope that, after all the psychological anguish, life would be restored. "I was praying that at least for you this nightmare might end," I told Dawn.

I could almost feel her despondency leaking through the phone. "Let's put this in perspective," I said, trying to comfort her. "Your counts are great. You're holding steady. That's still really good news."

Silence greeted me.

Helplessly, I cast about in my mind for words that might make Dawn feel better. Then I had a flash of inspiration.

"I know what we should do. We should go out and celebrate the good part of this," I said.

"No, I don't feel like it. The whole thing's just a nightmare."

"Come on, I have this great idea. I want it to be a surprise. I promise you're going to love it."

Finally I convinced her to meet me on the curb outside her office. She climbed into my car with a downhearted look on her face and pecked me listlessly on the cheek. "So where are we going?" she asked suspiciously.

"Wait and see," I told her. "All I'll say is that I guarantee you a wonderful time."

"Come on, tell me . . ."

I kept stonewalling.

Finally we arrived, and luckily found a parking space right in front of our destination. As I pulled into it, Dawn started to catch on. "Oh, my God! You're kidding," she said. We were idling in front of McClure's, the fanciest clothing store in Nashville. "Mahlon, I've never been in here before."

"Well, I have, looking at stuff for you. But I didn't want to buy anything without your trying it on."

"I can't believe it!" she exclaimed.

McClure's was a high-ceilinged establishment with a marble entrance and a crystal chandelier. As we walked in, Dawn kept looking around in awe. Escorting her to the racks, I showed her some of the clothes that had originally caught my eye, and encouraged her to try them on. "Oh, Mahlon, really?" she asked. "Are you serious?"

Laughing at her childlike delight, I nodded.

Now, one of the salesladies came over, introduced herself, and began to pull out some other selections. I sat down to wait as she whisked Dawn off to the fitting room.

Bashfully, Dawn emerged to "model" each outfit. A few were very sexy. "Do you think this is too revealing?" she'd giggle. I was charmed by her giddiness and a bit aroused as we indulged in the flirtation of a normal couple. With a surge of regret, I had to remind myself that our teasing could only be in fun, that it could not raise any expectations. This was not, after all, a normal relationship.

"I'm trying to be a gentleman," I said finally. "So don't kill me."

Dawn laughed ruefully.

Just then, the saleslady approached me with an armful of dresses. "Oh, show them to her," I said, gesturing toward Dawn, who was already heading back to the fitting room. Leaving them to carry on, I went to look at shoes.

Dawn finally came to get me a half hour later. With the saleslady's help, she had put together four stunning outfits. Interlacing her hand with mine, she led me back to the counter where her selections lay, near the cash register.

"Wrap 'em up," I said in my best "big spender" voice.

Dawn giggled.

As she began tallying the bill, the saleslady summoned up the nerve to ask whether "the lady" was my fiancée.

"Nope. Just friends," I said, still playing the redneck oil tycoon.

Too embarrassed to wait for the total price to be revealed, Dawn excused herself, saying that she would wait for me outside.

As I settled the bill I was giddy. My sobersided pre-HIV self would never have embarked on such a devil-may-care spontaneous shopping spree. I felt expansive, gallant—and best of all, I'd cheered up Dawn.

That night as I sat by my fire, with Dawn leaning against me, I reflected that we had never been so relaxed with each other. We chatted about plans for the holidays, and then Dawn hinted that she would enjoy a massage. "Would you mind?" she asked.

"Of course not."

As usual, she went to the bathroom to change into my bathrobe, then positioned herself on her stomach with a pillow under her chin.

"So, where should I begin?"

"Back," she said.

Then she suddenly rose to her knees, shed my robe, and lay back down, clad only in her underwear. Trying to act nonchalant, I began the massage—so far our only intimate ritual—a bit unnerved. Was it possible that Dawn was trying to send me some kind of message?

I had been so careful, so disciplined, so determined to win her trust, that I feared blowing it all with one false move. So I kept my movements chaste and nonthreatening, in case I was misconstruing things. Sensing my confusion, Dawn half turned around and looked at me. "Let's quit fooling around," she said.

I stared at her, amazed.

"Mahlon," she said. "Come here."

.   .   .

WE HAD A date scheduled for the very next night, to attend an AIDS benefit that featured a silent auction and a fashion show. Wearing my best (and only) black suit, I picked up Dawn, who was dressed in one of her new sleek black outfits. "You look stunning," I said, and she smiled graciously, but she clearly seemed on edge. I tried to make small talk to put her at ease, scanning her face for a sign that she regretted our intimacy the night before. I couldn't tell.

So I was nervous when we arrived at the benefit. From the moment we walked in, it was clear that this was no typical Nashville event. It had a hip New York–style disco feeling—a kind of scene neither one of us had ever witnessed—and we felt stodgy and conservative next to a row of male bodybuilders wearing bikinis and posing on pedestals. Some of them, I noticed, had scleral inflammation in their eyes; others wore heavy makeup to hide the telltale lesions of Kaposi's sarcoma. Heterosexual as well as same-sex couples (both male and female) were dancing together in the disco area, their expressions fractured by the intense, syncopated strobe lights, in costumes ranging from formal wear to drag.

"I wonder who all these people are," Dawn said. "Where are all the people we know? Where's Shannon? I don't see anybody from my support group."

As we continued walking through the crowd, we passed men making amorous overtures to one another, and Dawn's clutch grew tighter on my arm. "I know I'm supposed to be accepting of all this," she said at last. "Especially because we're all in it together. But I still have trouble watching two guys. I'm sure they'd have trouble watching me be affectionate to you."

"I don't think so," I said. "After all, everywhere they go, they see heterosexuals smootching."

Coming directly toward us was a tall youth with pale eyes. He was leading an older, gaunt man wearing sunglasses and clutching a white cane. Obviously the older man was all but blind, probably suffering from CMV retinitis. I didn't want Dawn to see him, knowing he would remind her of Jan. Gently changing direction, I led her toward the fashion show.

"This isn't an AIDS benefit, it's a gay party," Dawn said finally. "I feel like we don't belong here. I think we should go."

Without waiting for me, she whirled around and headed for the door.

Once we got outside, I reminded Dawn that since AIDS was so pervasive in the gay community, it stood to reason that many people attending the benefit would be gay. "But, Mahlon," she said, "I felt so strange. Here we are, we're this white-bread couple—as Middle America as you can get. In that room it hit me that we can't even relate to the majority of people who have AIDS—that we're the outsiders."

Dawn had a point. For her and myself and others like us, I yearned for the solidarity that bonded HIV-infected people within the gay community. Sadly, among heterosexuals, it didn't seem to exist.

Dawn seemed to read my thoughts, for, as we reached my car, she turned to me and said, "Who do we have but each other?"

"It's true, that's all we have," I said.

"So I guess you're stuck with me."

"Thank God," I said, and meant it.

With these words, I allowed myself to dare imagine that perhaps the previous night had been a breakthrough in our relationship and that maybe Dawn would be the one after all. But as we settled into the car, with her usual quick downshift of mood, she grew sullen.

"Where to?" I asked, hoping that the cloud would pass. "Do you want to come over tonight?"

"No," she said. "Just take me home."

I was stung. I wondered if the gift of intimacy, the evening of trust and giving, had been too emotionally perilous for her. Perhaps her return to the old, preinfection Dawn, the Dawn comfortable and confident in her sexuality, had been only a momentary lapse. For she had once again retreated into her prison of mistrust and slammed the gate shut behind her.

CHAPTER 18

—————— ∞ ——————

I WAS IN my office working when Carol stopped by. I invited her to sit down, which she did, resting her head against the wall.

"I drove by your house yesterday," she said. "The yard looks overgrown."

"Well, it is December."

"I know. But it looked like this in the autumn, too. I can tell you really haven't been out there very much."

"It's true, I haven't."

"How come?"

"Just look around," I said, referring to the stacks of AIDS articles.

Carol didn't bother. "Come on, Mahlon, no matter how busy you've gotten, you've always made time for your plants. They used to bring you such pleasure."

"They still do."

"Don't tell me your life has narrowed to just your work and beating HIV?"

"And Dawn," I said.

"And Dawn," Carol repeated. "So how's that going?"

I shrugged. "Not great."

"Why? Doesn't Dawn like gardening?"

I laughed. "Not really. But that's not why I haven't been working in the garden much."

I hadn't told anyone, but now I confessed to Carol that I had been thinking of selling my house. "Maybe that's why I've been neglecting my garden," I added.

"But where will you live?"

I still owned the condo that I'd moved into after living in the bread truck. I had put the condo on the market several years before but so far had failed to sell it. And now that I was getting calls from realtors claiming to have buyers interested in my house, I thought I ought to explore the option.

"Realtors always say that," Carol pointed out. "I thought you planned to live in that house forever."

Well, I had, I told her. But recently one of the infectious disease doctors at Vanderbilt mentioned that an AIDS patient of his, who lived near me, got stuck selling his house for way below the market value because word of his illness got around. Apparently, in Nashville, the primordial fear of an infectious disease was taking its toll on real estate.

"Let's not forget that this is the Bible Belt," I reminded Carol.

Alarmed by the story I called back the realtors who had approached me about selling the house, and, in the guise of an AIDS researcher, asked if the disease would daunt prospective buyers. All of them told me that it was far better to sell before the news got out—that couples with children, especially, would be apprehensive about buying a home owned by someone with HIV. When I heard this, I had a vision of strangers edging their way through my beloved cottage, afraid to touch anything, afraid to use the bathroom, cautiously scanning the floors for drops of blood.

"So, you can understand why I'm tempted to sell now," I said to Carol.

"And what does Dawn think about your decision?"

"She doesn't know anything about it."

"Hmmm," Carol said, then softly asked, "So tell me, why isn't it going well with her?"

At this point, I'd barely formulated my reservations about Dawn in my own mind, reluctant as I was to have to face them. But when I started telling Carol, they seemed to crystallize: that Dawn wasn't a fighter, that she was depressed much of the time, and that, worst of all, she seemed ambivalent about me.

Hearing the sadness in my voice, Carol got upset. "I'm so sorry," she said. "I feel like I set you up for this disappointment."

"No, you didn't," I told her. "I asked you to help me find someone. And I don't know what I would do without Dawn."

Carol shook her head. "Oh, Mahlon," she said. "I don't think that a virus, even HIV, is enough to keep two people together."

"Come on, Carol, if you felt that way, why did you help set me up with an HIV-positive woman?"

Carol leaned forward in her chair. "The question is whether Dawn is the right HIV-positive woman."

"I don't have many alternatives. I wouldn't even know where to look for another woman. And I don't want to be alone for whatever's left of my life."

"Well, you're not exactly alone," Carol said gently, "you have your family and me and Bart and Shannon . . ."

"Thank you—I mean that—but you know it's not the same."

"The same as what? As being in love with someone who's too depressed to share your life or care for you? I hope it's not the same."

By now I was angry and defensive. "You just don't understand what it's like to be HIV-positive and straight," I said bitterly.

"Maybe not the way you do, Mahlon," she replied. "But I'm as close to it as I can get."

Sensing she'd touched a nerve, Carol backed off, inventing an excuse to leave my office. But she had raised disturbing doubts in me that I wanted to deny. I ended up taking a long walk around the Vanderbilt campus, passing all the places that had figured in the drama of my life over the last few years: the VA, the street where I'd lived in the truck. As I trudged along, I told myself that Carol was well-meaning but wrong. I somehow had to reach Dawn and make this relationship work.

I HAD ALREADY decided to introduce her to my family. When Becky arrived in Knoxville for her yearly visit, she and my mother drove up to Nashville for the big event. I was already a little nervous because Becky had been teasing me mercilessly about Dawn, so when they showed up early, it really rattled me. I was driving back from the grocery store when I saw them pull into the driveway. My house wasn't quite ready for visitors yet, especially not the muddy-pawed Orpheus, who greatly admired my fluffy white wool rugs.

I pulled in behind them, and I could hear Becky cry out, "Oh, my God, look who's here." Orpheus barked in greeting.

Becky jumped out of the car, ran over to my open window, and threw her arms around me. Her unruly mane of auburn hair was sun-kissed and lighter than I remembered. Orph followed closely behind, jumping up to give me a quick kiss before trotting over to one of the fallow flower beds to stake out his territory. Pulling back so I could get out of the car, Becky cast an appraising gaze over me. "So," she said hesitating, "you look fine. You feeling okay?"

"Of course he's feeling okay," my mother said as she came up to us, and I kissed her on the cheek.

"Yeah," I told Becky, "don't give up on me yet."

Looking irritated, my mother asked, "Do we have to launch into this right away?"

"Oh, Mom, don't worry about it," Becky said. "We're fine."

"By the way, you're a little early," I said to them both.

That was because there had been a change of plans. Instead of going out to breakfast at Nashville's famous Pancake Pantry, Becky had decided to make pancakes at my house. It would be a better place to get to know Dawn, she said.

It was just as well that we were eating at home, for Dawn arrived late. She was wearing one of the outfits that I had bought for her, a black cashmere sweater and gray wool pants. When I answered the door, she seemed apprehensive. "Do I look okay?" she asked.

"You look wonderful." Sensing her acute discomfort, I

touched her arm. "They've heard a lot of good things about you, so don't worry. They're going to love you."

She looked doubtful.

When I introduced Dawn to Becky, my sister began to exclaim over what she was wearing. Dawn was quick to announce that both the sweater and pants had been gifts from me. Moments later, my sister cornered me alone in the kitchen and said teasingly, "Hey, big spender!"

"Don't worry," I whispered wickedly. "There will be plenty left over for you when the time comes."

"Don't be cruel!" she chided me.

"Cruel what?" Mom said, coming into the kitchen.

"Nothing, he's being mean to his sister, again," Becky said as she began to gather ingredients for the pancake batter.

My mother went back into the living room, where I heard her trying to make conversation with Dawn. Dawn, in turn, gave staccato answers to the polite questions directed her way. Figuring I should go and rescue her, I wandered back into the room and found Dawn going on about Howie, how well he was doing in school, how he had applied to a program for gifted children.

"What are his areas of interest?" Mom asked.

"Well, he likes music, but science is what he's most interested in."

"Really," Mom said. "Has he talked much to Mahlon about medicine?"

"Well, to be honest, he and Mahlon don't really hit it off."

I was shocked, which must have shown in my face since my mother glanced at me inquisitively. Howie and I had had little contact; I'd hardly gotten to know him. I did notice, however, that Dawn seemed to keep us apart.

Sensing that she'd made an awkward remark, Dawn stood up and excused herself to go outside and smoke, in deference to my mother.

Once she was gone, my mother said, "I hope we didn't make her nervous."

"It's always stressful to meet somebody else's family. And she's been pretty depressed lately."

My mother fell silent for a moment, at which point Becky came into the room holding a marketing brochure that one of the realtors had sent me. "Mom says you're thinking of selling the house. Why? Does it have something to do with Dawn?"

No, I told her. Dawn had no idea of my plan. I explained the problem of my HIV status and told Becky that I had confided it to only one realtor, a woman named Lottie.

"But why did you have to tell her, Mahlon?" Mom complained.

"She has a right to know—particularly if it's my motivation for selling."

Dawn returned at this point and caught the tail end of the conversation. She turned to me. "Mahlon, you probably didn't have to tell the realtor. But, then again, you'd be surprised how many people seem to find out about these things anyway." She didn't even react to the news that I was selling the house.

She just listened as Mom and Becky and I discussed pros and cons of selling. I explained that I didn't want to saddle them with the responsibility of a property that might be hard to sell after I died.

"But, Mahlon, I still hate to see you sell a place you love," Becky said.

"You put so much work into it," Mom agreed.

"Yes, but just in case something happens to me, I don't want you to become a landlady," I told Mother. "You're really not in the position to do that. How, for example, would you make my house payments before my will was settled and the money released?"

Here Dawn butted in, "This house certainly seems like a lot to handle, especially the outside. Me, I try to get my dad to do my yard work. I've always thought that Mahlon should unload this house."

My mother and Becky were staring in dismay at Dawn. "I mean, it's old," she went on, then caught herself, sensing she'd said something inappropriate. "I'm sorry, that's just what I think. It's none of my business anyway." An awkward silence fell and persisted until Dawn looked at her watch and said, "Mahlon, you know, I've actually got a lot to do—with Christmas shopping and everything. I probably should get going."

"Don't you want something to eat?" Becky said.

"No, but thank you. The three of you probably want some time alone together anyway."

Figuring Dawn wanted to make an escape, I didn't protest. Dawn said good-bye to my mother and my sister and then I escorted her to the car, just to make sure everything was okay. As soon as we got outside, she lit up another cigarette and blew out a huge scarf of smoke. "I'm sorry I opened my mouth," she said. "What I said didn't seem to go very well with them."

"Don't worry. Everybody is entitled to their opinion."

"Yes, but I obviously upset them."

"Look, if they're upset they'll get over it." I had to admit to myself that I was a little upset, too, over Dawn's rather abrupt revelations that Howie resented me and that she didn't like my house. But wanting to move on, I said, "Now about Christmas Eve—what time do you want me to come over?"

Dawn was looking at me uncertainly, still concerned about her various faux pas. "I'll let you know," she said, and with only a quick good-bye kiss, got into her car.

When I came back into the house, I knew that my mother and Becky had been discussing Dawn.

Looking wounded, Becky said, "Doesn't she know how much this place means to you?"

"Oh, yeah, she does. I just don't think she likes old houses."

"She doesn't care enough about you," my mother said softly.

"How can you say that? You just met her. She was nervous." Becky anxiously changed the subject.

After brunch, we spent a few hours sitting by the fireplace, with Becky and me chatting about what was going on in our respective lives while Mom sat and listened contentedly. As the afternoon waned and they prepared to leave, I said, "By the way, I want you both to know that I finally got my script for AZT. I'm going to start taking it after the holidays."

"I just hope you can tolerate it okay," Becky said.

"He's going to be fine," Mom said with quiet conviction. "After all, he was the miracle baby."

We all fell silent for a few moments. "What if I moved up to Nashville?" Mom said out of the blue.

"And move in here?" I asked.

"I could look after the yard, cook for you when you felt bad. I'm sure I could find an accompanist over at Blair Music School."

I shrugged. "No, Mom . . . you have your own life. Besides, you never know, maybe I'll be okay for quite a while yet."

CHAPTER 19

⸺ ❧ ⸺

CHRISTMAS 1993.

I went out and bought a live spruce tree in a planter and spiraled tiny white Christmas lights among its delicate branches. Under the tree I arranged my gifts for Dawn, lots of small packages wrapped in embossed gold gift paper, each accompanied by its own little card, containing jewelry and silk scarves that I'd ordered from various museum catalogs.

I worked until nine on Christmas Eve, then met Dawn at her parents' house. I'd brought presents for them and Howie, and my two biggest gifts for Dawn, which I thought she could open with her family on Christmas morning. But when she saw the carefully wrapped packages, Dawn couldn't resist opening them. One of them was a sweater, the other a silk jacket, which she immediately put on and twirled around the room in, modeling. The spontaneous decision to open the presents seemed to displease Dawn's mother, but I didn't think much about it until the following afternoon when I went to pick her up.

Dawn was as gloomy as I'd ever seen her.

"My mom freaked out after you left," she said. "She called me selfish for opening my presents and taking all the attention away from Howie."

"Did Howie seem upset?" I asked, concerned.

"No, and when I asked him later, he said it was fine." Dawn lit up a cigarette. "But she wouldn't let up on me, not for a minute. She said I was showing off your generosity. . . . She just can't stand to see me happy. She doesn't think I deserve it."

"Really? Why?"

"Come on," Dawn said. "Why do you think?"

"HIV—are you sure?"

Dawn shrugged. "I don't know. Maybe it was because Howie's father wanted to stop by and I guess he felt a little awkward with you there."

"Well, nobody told me."

"Look, it's not your fault. . . ."

"Maybe I just should've given you all your presents today in private."

"No, I thought it was nice." Dawn's thoughts seemed to drift for a moment. "God, it depresses me for days when she lays into me like that."

"Try to forget about it. It's Christmas," I said. "The two of us will have a good time."

When we arrived at my house, Dawn plopped herself down on the couch, without mentioning the Christmas decorations or the tree, and, lighting a cigarette, stared miserably out the window. I'd seen her sink into such states before and sometimes had managed to distract her enough to stop the slide. I got some of her presents out from under the tree and arranged them on the coffee table in front of her. "Thank you, Mahlon," she said, but didn't make a move to open them.

Now what? I thought helplessly. Then I spied some water that had leaked out of the Christmas tree stand onto the wooden floor.

"Uh-oh, I'd better wipe that up," I said.

"Huh?" said Dawn, awakening from her fog.

"That puddle." I headed to the kitchen for a towel.

"Oh, Mahlon," Dawn was saying exasperatedly. "What difference does it make? It's just water." When I got back to the living room she added, crankily, "You always have to be so neat. How would anybody ever live with you? I know I couldn't stand it."

I was taken aback. We hadn't quite decided to move in together yet, but Dawn had repeatedly told me that she dreamed of living in a big modern house, presumably one that I might provide. Now it seemed that she was dismissing out of hand the prospect of our sharing a future. "I'm not as neat as you think," I said, lamely defending myself.

"Yes you are," she snapped. "Look at this place."

"I just wanted it to be nice for Christmas."

"Well, you didn't have to fix it up for me," she said. "I don't care!"

Unsettled by her outburst, I took the towel back to the kitchen, trying to compose myself. When I returned, Dawn was sitting on the rug, toying listlessly with her Christmas presents.

"Let's open them," I said, hoping to recover her goodwill. When she began to unwrap one, I took it as an encouraging sign that her mood had shifted. Flopping down to meet her on the rug, I nibbled playfully at her ear.

"Will you leave me alone?" she said sharply, pushing me away.

I drew back, stung and embarrassed. "Sorry, I was just trying to cheer you up."

Wordlessly, she handed me a brown paper bag, which held her gifts for me—two lumpy packages, clumsily wrapped. One contained rolled-up stonewashed jeans and the other eight pairs of white athletic socks. Worrying that Dawn felt self-conscious because her gifts were more modest than mine—I knew her budget was tight—I tried to reassure her that I liked them. But the chill Dawn was radiating seemed impenetrable, and it was clear that the holiday could not be salvaged. Neither of us said much as I drove her home.

Now the Christmas decorations that I'd hung with such enthusiastic hopes seemed to mock my belief that I could somehow win Dawn over, that my affection and patience could prevail over her depression and sense of repugnance toward me. Miserable though it made me, I had to consider that perhaps Carol and my mother and Becky were right—that Dawn might be beyond rescue, or at least rescue by me. Grimly, I collected the torn-off wrapping papers for the trash, mordantly reflecting that if only I had taken Christmas call as usual, I would have forestalled reaching this disastrous impasse with Dawn. Then it came to me that there was a hopeful step I could take to shake off my despair. I could begin taking AZT.

"You'd better make sure you've got plenty of empty buckets and garbage cans around the house," Carol had warned me. Headaches, nausea, vomiting, and diarrhea were just a few of the reported side effects of AZT. For some people, these side effects were fairly mild and tended to wane in a couple of weeks; for others, they persisted. But I knew that if I did suffer side effects, the worst wouldn't appear for at least twelve hours.

"Merry Christmas," I said to myself, and downed the first dose.

Two hours passed, then three. So far, so good.

That night, I drove to a supermarket to lay in the supplies I'd need. It was deserted because of the holiday. Thinking that two weeks would be a long time to spend in the bathroom, I bought two huge family packs of the softest toilet paper, blue to match my bathroom tiles (in case I died on the toilet and had to be found by outsiders?). By the time I arrived home, I had a mild headache, another common side effect of AZT. This might not be so bad after all, I told myself.

I was wrong. By morning, I was in the throes of the diarrhea, an explosive kind presaged by abdominal roiling. Sometimes the cramps were so severe that I imagined my stomach could actually burst. The gastrointestinal sirens and eruptions continued throughout that day and into the next, yet I was determined to continue going in to the office—luckily, my office wasn't too far from the toilet. By New Year's Day, the diarrhea had subsided, but nausea continued to plague me, a constant queasiness that made it impossible to eat.

Once the diarrhea abated enough so that I could go out in public, I started making nightly pilgrimages to the grocery store in pursuit of food that wouldn't revolt me. Light-headed from hunger, I spent what seemed like hours wandering the aisles and often returned home empty-handed. After a while, my circular migrations caught the attention of the store manager, who took to following me around to see if I was shoplifting. But eventually my perseverance was rewarded as I bit into an apple and my stomach wholeheartedly accepted it. Normal digestion seemed to kick in at last.

Carol had told Bart I'd gone on AZT, and so he called me from the road. "Through the grapevine I heard you found a magic food," he said. "Congratulations. Should I bring you back some grannies from California?"

"That's okay," I had to tell him. "Red delicious is the only kind that works for me."

"Well, excuse me!" Bart said, laughing.

Within a few days, as apple cores piled up in every trash can in my house and office, the nausea eased.

Once I was feeling a little better, I resumed making overtures to Dawn. When I called, she was inevitably lying on the couch with the television blaring, too depressed to go to work or even to shower.

"Can I come over and see you?" I'd ask.

"No," she'd reply.

"Is there anything I can bring you?"

"No, Mahlon, there isn't."

"Not even some chocolates?"

"No," she would say. "Now let me go. Thanks for calling."

I did manage to coax Dawn into calling the psychiatrist she'd been seeing on and off, and he increased her dose of antidepressants. But the medication didn't seem to improve her mood much, and it didn't improve the way she treated me. It was clear that she had nothing left to give me anymore and that I no longer had the right to ask anything of her. I had to face the desolating fact that, all along, there had probably been no room in Dawn's life for anyone but her son, Howie.

Then, as if I wasn't suffering enough anguish over the collapse of my relationship with Dawn, I soon was forced to confront another major loss. Lottie, my realtor, had gotten an offer on my house. Though the offer was slightly less than my asking price, she encouraged me to accept it, especially since the buyers could pay cash, so there was no worry about financing. "Forget it," I told her. "With everything I've put into the house I'd barely be breaking even."

This wasn't exactly true, but I hoped that by insisting on the asking price I could fend off the buyers. I wasn't ready to move yet. Indeed, just the night before I had taken my live spruce tree outside and planted it with the secret hope that I'd be around to watch it grow.

When Lottie and I hung up, I went out to the garden that I'd tended to so devotedly. The wind was rustling through the stands of evergreens that I had planted. I remembered coming home from work on oppressively hot summer nights to drench my baking plants by flashlight. Chipmunks and an occasional timid snake would flee my beam for the shadows. A skittish rabbit, who had taken up residence in the garden, would often be basking in the moonlight. So I'd stand quietly in the dark, spraying soft fans of water over my flowers and shrubs, hoping not to disturb him.

I spent the whole next day praying silently for the sale to fall through. To my relief, Lottie didn't call me at work. I returned home feeling cheered by the reprieve, only to be ambushed by a message from Lottie on my machine.

"Congratulations," she said. "They've come up with what you wanted. We can close in six weeks."

My first sensation was a numbing grief. It seemed that in losing first Dawn—whose depression had reached bottom and would soon land her in a psychiatric ward—and now the house, I was being stripped of the major keystones of my life. But then it struck me that perhaps the losses were fated, even necessary divestitures. Perhaps I was meant to be single-minded in my fight against HIV, and the attachments that I'd seen as comforts were only serving to distract me.

CHAPTER 20

APRIL 1994.

Rays of morning light slipped through the cream-colored Venetian blinds into the examining room, making me blink as I looked out over Twenty-first Avenue at the cars and students going by. Some ten years earlier, I'd arrived at this building to begin my residency, full of naive conviction that medicine was the pursuit of miracles. Now I wished I could recover that sense of hope.

In the four months that I'd been taking AZT, I'd seen negligible change in my CD4 blood counts. From a level of 550 in December 1993, my counts had slipped down to 430 by the end of January. In February and March they had risen slightly, but by April they were back down to 430. The AZT didn't seem to be working in me.

There was little on the therapeutic horizon except for a drug called Delavirdine, which blocked the same enzyme of HIV, reverse transcriptase, as AZT but used a different mechanism. With the help of Jim Stevens, I got into the Delavirdine trial.

Before its manufacturer can apply for FDA approval, a new drug must undergo a three-phase trial. In the first phase, a drug that has shown promise in laboratory animals is administered to healthy volunteers to see how humans metabolize it and whether it causes side effects. In the second phase, a few research centers get the drug to try out on volunteer patients, to see whether it works and to test a range of dosages. In the third phase, the drug is issued to university hospitals or clinics across the country for formal studies on large numbers of patients. Both the earlier one and phase three trials are usually conducted as so-called double-blind experiments, in which patients are randomly assigned either the real drug or an inactive placebo. Since the pills are assigned secret codes before they are shipped from the labs to the hospitals, no one participating in the trial—neither the doctors nor the patients—knows whether a given person has received the dummy or the real drug.

Vanderbilt is one of the academic hospitals that make up the AIDS Clinical Trial Group (ACTG), which over the past decade has run trials on anti-HIV drugs. For these trials, the hospitals advertise for HIV-infected volunteers who are then screened to see if they fit preestablished criteria. Often the criteria exclude patients with significant exposure to other drugs (such as AZT), against which the HIV virus might have mutated, or those with medical complications, such as opportunistic infections, requiring medications that might confound the response to the drug being tested. Drug trials, for the most part, are experiments, not attempts at therapy, though many volunteers do benefit from the treatments. But to benefit, a patient has to get lucky twice—lucky enough to be accepted into the trial in the first place and then lucky enough to get the drug and not the placebo.

Having cleared the first hurdle, I was now hoping my luck would hold.

There was a tap on the door and in walked a nurse named Zac. Middle-aged, with gray hair and dressed in a neat white lab coat, he had a distinguished air that was belied by his kindly, boyish face. Before the nightmare of my HIV infection, I had seen him around the hospital and wondered who he was. Eventually someone told me that he'd once been a successful businessman and that he'd lost so many of his friends to AIDS that he'd abandoned his lucrative job and joined the battle. Now, as a nurse, he was on the front lines.

Zac immediately got down to business, lining up bottles of what looked like horse pills, each neatly labeled with codes. I opened one and poured out a handful of unmarked, nondescript white tablets that to me looked more like the dreaded placebos than anything else.

"You should take one from each bottle three times a day," Zac said, showing me the bottles labeled "W," "X," "Y," and "Z." "Then take two AZT every eight hours."

"So there's no way of knowing whether I'm getting Delavirdine or placebo?"

"I'm afraid not. We get these blind."

"It's been a year and a half since my accident," I said irritably. "I don't have time to waste on placebos." I had hoped to get Delavirdine directly, on a compassionate-use basis, rather than have to roll the dice in the trial.

"I know. We talked about that," Zac said, trying to sound

reassuring. "But we'll probably be able to tell whether or not you're on the drug by following your CD4 counts and watching for side effects."

Since AZT alone had done little for my counts, if they changed now it would mean that I was on Delavirdine. But I hated to have to wait to find out, and I wished that Delavirdine wasn't my only hope.

"What have you heard about those new protease inhibitors?" I asked Zac.

"Whoa," he said. "One thing at a time."

"I know they're about to go into trials."

"Well, as far as I know there aren't any protease inhibitors being studied by the ACTG right now. Anyway, I doubt the guidelines of our trial would allow a protease inhibitor," he cautioned.

Zac seemed like a kindhearted guy, so I didn't want to vent my frustration on him. But I was starting to feel as though all of us HIV-positive patients were like cattle in a slaughterhouse. Some of us would be herded into chute A (excluded from the trial), some to chute B (AZT and placebo), and some to chute C (AZT and Delavirdine), but we were all marked for death. The only question was how long we would last.

USUALLY I WAS half asleep by the time I trudged into the bathroom to peel off my contacts for the night. But as I stood in front of the mirror, I noticed something frightening: red bumps, not on my face, but all over my neck—like a terrible shaving rash. I was now fourteen days into the Delavirdine trial.

For the past two weeks I'd been hoping that the anonymous white pills were, perhaps, Delavirdine, which, together with AZT, might slow my relentless progression toward AIDS. Yet I'd hardly felt any different than before, which made me worry that I'd received the placebo. This rash was the first indication that I'd actually been on Delavirdine, the drug I coveted. But, ironically, such an allergic reaction as this rash might require me to drop out of the trial. Carefully, I examined the bumps, praying to find evidence that they might represent contact dermatitis, caused by a new shirt or something, even an insect bite—anything but a drug-related rash. But as I pulled off my shirt I could see more bumps on my shoulders. Then I checked my legs, feet, and buttocks, which had not been exposed to my shirt, and the bumps were there, too. I even checked my penis—nothing there, at least so far. But a rash so widespread had to be drug-related.

By morning the rash was all over my chest and stomach. As a doctor I knew that the responsible course would be to report this adverse side effect, but as a patient I was tempted to stay on the drug and ride it out. Torn, I decided to skip my next dose.

But by the time I got to work, I had concluded that I had to confess. So I called Zac at the AIDS clinic, and he told me to come in. Later that day, as I sat on the examining table with my shirt off, I tried to think of a way that I could desensitize my immune system in order to keep taking Delavirdine—hoping, praying, I wouldn't be dropped from the study. Finally, Zac breezed in and examined the rash.

"So tell me again. When did you notice this?"

"Last night."

"Does it itch?"

"No. Not yet."

"Hmm," he said, looking at my back. "It sure looks like a drug rash. Someone else in the study got one, too."

Ceremoniously he took the reading glasses dangling from a chain around his neck and placed them on his nose, then opened the sacred Clinical Trial Notebook.

"Here we go," I said. "The bible."

"I know how you feel," Zac sympathized. "Some little rule in here is going to determine your fate. Terrible, isn't it?"

"Yes, it is."

"Well," Zac said. "It says here that if a rash develops the patient should discontinue the drug immediately. The patient may then be placed on antipuretics until the rash clears up and may then be restarted on Delavirdine."

"Good! So I can stay in the study?"

"Well, I think so," Zac said, more optimistic now. To be sure, he called one of the infectious disease doctors, who told him that the other patient who'd gotten a rash had stayed on Delavirdine. His rash had slowly gone away in about a week.

"Apparently, the itch was awful, but he got through it," Zac reported to me as he put down the telephone. "If I were you I'd go back on the drug and try to tough it out."

Surely the itch couldn't be that bad, I thought, if that other patient had gotten through it. So I took my next doses of Delavirdine, and by the following morning the rash had started spreading. The itching was so intense on my buttocks and back that sitting at my desk became pure torture. At first, I tried to ignore the itch, but every little movement I made sent a shock wave to my brain, goading me to scratch. I knew I shouldn't succumb to the urge because scratching would release histamines that would only make the itching worse. But for a moment I gave in, and the relief I felt was exquisite.

Just as I was about to indulge in another bout of scratching, Carol walked into my office.

"What happened to you?" she asked. "That rash looks awful. Is it poison ivy?"

I explained as Carol scrutinized my arms and neck. "Poor baby," she said, chuckling. "So that's why I haven't seen you."

"It's not funny. It's starting to itch like hell."

"I'm sorry, but you just look so funny and stiff."

"Thanks a lot."

As we talked, I got up, unobtrusively, I thought, to press my burning butt against the wall. "What are you doing?" Carol accused, as she spied my furtive rubs. "Stop that scratching!" she said.

I could tell by the amused look on her face that Carol was already considering how to slant my story for her many friends on the Internet. Indeed, a few days later, I started getting cards from HIV-infected strangers all over the country, advising on itch management. Some of Carol's gay computer friends even offered to come up and help me scratch. The one woman on-line just wanted to know if the rash got worse with an erection.

Over the next few days the rash began to roar. Miserable though I was—and suspecting that working out would only increase the itching—I finally decided to head over to the gym to try to get my mind off the discomfort. Once I started lifting weights, however, the urge to scratch in certain places became unbearable, and I couldn't seem to find a discreet way to do it among the co-eds in their skimpy gym shorts and the medical students who knew me as a teacher. Fortunately, the weight room had a square support column in the center of the room. It was a good place to rest between sets.

After about five days the rash began to recede and the itching lessened. By then I had discovered that cold packs helped immensely, reducing the raging itch to a less-distracting frozen ache. Colds packs were to Delavirdine what apples were to AZT. Unfortunately, the packs leaked, creating embarrassing wet spots on my clothing. At least once a day, Carol stopped by my office to scold me for scratching, whether I had or not.

After one month on Delavirdine, I got my routine check of my CD4s. The blood sample was sent directly to the ACTG lab, so again I had an irritating wait for official word. Finally, I got the phone call from Zac, and the news was tremendously buoying. "Congratulations," he said. "Your CD4s are now over six hundred."

CHAPTER 21

―――――――――∞―――――――――

BUT THE TRIUMPH was short-lived. By the following month my counts had dropped back down into the 440 range. Zac gave me the bad news early one morning. "Couldn't that count be a mistake, couldn't it be someone else's?" I agonized. Zac was sure. Dejected, I decided to take a walk, and grabbed an article on new AIDS drug combinations with the idea of dropping it with Jim Stevens and getting his thoughts on my apparent setback. As I approached the back door to the building, I saw Madeline leaning up against the entrance, smoking a cigarette.

"Hey, how's life on the front?" I asked.

She smiled. "Oh, you know, we keep getting small advances here and there, so we can't give up hope. I keep thinking that in another six months, another year, we're bound to find something, some new treatment that can make a difference. I feel so hopeful about that, though maybe I'm just an incurable optimist."

"Well, you've got to be. That's what your patients need."

"So how are you doing?" she asked me.

I told her about my counts.

"I know," she said. She took a long draw on her cigarette.

"So, that little speech was for me, huh?"

"Partly. But it's also what I believe to be true. We can't stop hoping. So I'm praying that you can keep up your morale, kiddo."

Though I knew Madeline was trying to cheer me up, I was touched and inspired by her words. But now that I had apparently struck out with Delavirdine, I would be excluded from enrolling in many AIDS Clinical Trial Group studies of future drugs, since they usually accepted only "drug-naive" patients, either with low CD4 counts or advanced disease. I realized I might have to go outside clinical trials to try something new. Beyond monitoring on-line services for news of promising treatments, I had to talk to people, contact drug companies testing new treatments. At this point I even contemplated trying theoretically promising drugs that had yet to be tested and proven.

I certainly would not be the first physician to experiment on himself. As far back as 1777, Dr. James Nooth, surgeon to the Duke of Kent, inserted cancerous tissues into a small incision in his arm to see if the illness could be communicated. Fortunately, nothing happened. Louis Pasteur injected himself with the first experimental rabies vaccine. And, right here at Vanderbilt, early in the century, a physician named Thomas E. Brittingham had believed there might be a difference between the antigens produced on normal white blood cells and on leukemic cells. To test this, he injected himself with leukemic cells, and his body reacted violently. He nearly died, but the reaction supported his theory.

The treatment of leukemia had come a long way since Brittingham, especially after it was discovered that simultaneous treatment with several different anticancer drugs produced better results than use of any single drug. Thinking about this idea of synergy brought me back to the idea of multidrug therapies for the treatment of HIV. If only I could get a protease inhibitor, which attacked HIV's protease enzyme, and use it in combination with an AZT-like drug, which attacked the virus's reverse transcriptase enzyme, I might see more powerful effects.

And so I redoubled my efforts to contact Hoffman La Roche, the drug company that was manufacturing the first of the protease inhibitors, Saquinavir. At that time, the spring of 1994, Saquinavir was reputedly showing great promise in small clinical trials. As soon as I'd heard about the drug, I'd started calling Hoffman La Roche every week, never managing to reach anyone who could tell me how to get it. Now I threw decorum to the wind and began to badger the company twice a day, until finally I got through to a Dr. Danzo, one of the top pharmacologists. Introducing myself as an AIDS researcher at Vanderbilt, I explained that Vanderbilt had an "unusual patient" who'd responded poorly to AZT and Delavirdine. Having used these drugs, he was now ineligible for many trials, but he hoped to try Saquinavir. Did Hoffman La Roche have a "compassionate-use" program for its protease inhibitor?

"No," the doctor said abruptly, as though he'd heard this request many times before.

"But he's an occupationally infected health care worker," I said. "Isn't there any chance we could get some Saquinavir for him to try?"

He told me that the company had barely enough of the drug for clinical trials, since it was difficult to manufacture. "We aren't making any exceptions," he said. "Once we start, we'll have to make exceptions for everyone."

"But this man is a physician himself," I pleaded, in case that fact would sway him. By that point I was desperate.

"Look, I'll have to ask our research director and call you back."

I waited a week for him to respond, and when he didn't, I called back. But I couldn't get through to Dr. Danzo. Over the next three weeks I called repeatedly, but never managed to reach him.

By then it was June 1994, and Stevens was off to the Tenth International Conference on AIDS in Yokohama, Japan. Before he left, he promised to let me know about any new treatments that looked hopeful. While he was gone, it became my daily ritual to phone Hoffman La Roche to no avail, and then to check the pathology fax machine for word from Yokohama, which never came. Growing increasingly demoralized, I kept dogging the on-line services and press releases, but all the reports I read lamented the paucity of new therapies. Indeed, that June was a bleak time in the history of the AIDS epidemic.

When Stevens returned from Yokohama, he held a lunch seminar for the infectious disease fellows to brief them on the conference. I asked to sit in, and Stevens agreed. The conference had yielded reports of some hopeful new treatments for opportunistic infections and one real ray of hope: data suggesting that if HIV-infected women took AZT during pregnancy, they could significantly reduce the chances of transmitting the virus to their fetuses.

And then Stevens dropped what to me felt like a bombshell:

news of a different approach to AIDS treatment, the preliminary results of a study done on a small number of patients by Dr. Clifford Lane at the National Institutes of Health using interleukin-2 (IL-2, as it was known in oncology circles).

IL-2 was a protein produced by T lymphocytes that stimulated the proliferation and maturation of T lymphocytes (particularly CD4 cells), B lymphocytes, and other attack dogs of the immune system. Originally, IL-2 had been used to mobilize the immune system against metastatic kidney cancer and melanomas. Now Lane was deploying it to help maintain or rebuild the immune system while simultaneously treating patients with antiviral drugs such as AZT and DDI to inhibit HIV. The study noted pretty impressive rises in the CD4 counts of patients who began the study with counts above 250. The downside was that the side effects were fairly severe, the most worrisome being a possible triggering of HIV replication.

Still, it was the newest angle on treatment that I had heard. I couldn't even wait until the meeting ended to dash to my office and get some background on IL-2. I called one of Vanderbilt's respected oncologists, a Dr. Weinberg, who had treated many patients with renal carcinoma, the disease for which IL-2 was FDA-approved. Learning that she wasn't available, with reluctance, I paged her. When she came on the line, she sounded busy and a bit miffed that a stranger would interrupt her so boldly. I apologized for doing so but implored her to give me five minutes of her time.

"We don't use IL-2 much anymore," she explained after listening to my questions. "The side effects are so bad."

She went on to say that her patients had suffered from "capillary leak syndrome," caused by fluid leaking out of blood vessels into tissues. A few had developed such bad pulmonary edema they went into congestive heart failure. "One, who was already quite sick, even died," she said, still sounding horrified by the memory.

I asked about the dosage she'd used and was told that it had been fairly high, somewhere around forty million units per day. Having heard that in Dr. Lane's study they were using doses one third that magnitude, I asked if the side effects would lessen with lower doses. They probably would, Dr. Weinberg said.

"Do you know of anyone using IL-2 for AIDS?" I asked.

"AIDS? No, I don't keep up with that."

After thanking Dr. Weinberg for her time, I immediately began calling the NIH. It took me a day to get through to Dr. Jones, a member of Dr. Lane's team, who was kind enough to take my call. He answered my first few questions with appropriate caution, but once I told him the story of my infection and my quest for treatment, he grew concerned and solicitous. No doubt he could hear in my voice how committed I was to treatment, and he probably wanted to do what he could to keep me from killing myself.

I asked him if people were taking IL-2 as outpatients.

"They do, eventually, but we always have our patients try the drug in the hospital first."

"Because of the side effects?"

"They can be bad. Usually patients are in for at least five days. And we monitor them carefully."

Like Dr. Weinberg's patients, the NIH's study group members gained between ten and fifteen pounds from edema. They also suffered rashes, diarrhea, severe dehydration, and lowered blood pressure; and they risked kidney and liver toxicity. "Most importantly," Jones warned me, "IL-2 can trigger a burst of viral replication. So you better be on at least AZT and DDI . . . and get double-branched DNA amplification before and after IL-2 to make sure you're not making things worse.''

''I'm on AZT and Delavirdine,'' I told him. I was moved by Jones's willingness to help me, to share unpublished data, which he discussed with me as an equal. I had scribbled frantically as he spoke, now writing down ''get on DDI.''

''I can't thank you enough,'' I said.

''You may change your mind once you start IL-2,'' Jones said, laughing. ''Good luck to you.''

And so I resolved to try IL-2. I had to get Stevens to monitor me—it would be foolish not to, of course, and I needed his objective assessment of my progress—but I decided to go ahead and get the drug, which I could do as a researcher, before I cleared it with him. Though he had been kind enough to tolerate my increasingly aggressive pursuit of new therapies, any responsible doctor would hesitate before attempting such an experimental course of treatment as IL-2. I didn't want to put Stevens in the position of having to write the prescription and, by implication, giving me his blessing.

As I picked up the two clear vials of the IL-2 from the oncology pharmacist, I felt elated. At last I was taking charge, becoming a full partner in my own treatment.

Cradling the precious vials in my lab coat pocket, I went directly to Stevens's office. Pulling them out, I held them before him. ''Look what I have.''

''Whoa, Mahlon.''

''I also brought the protocols, which I just got from the NIH. I'd like to get started on this right away.''

Stevens remained silent, thinking.

"Jim, you know I'm going to do it anyway," I said, which was, admittedly, a bit of a bluff on my part.

"It's crazy to take responsibility into your own hands."

"I know—and that's why I want your help. I'm going to write you a letter for my chart, a letter explaining my decision and absolving you of liability if anything goes wrong. I know I'm asking a lot. I'm putting you in an awkward position. But it's my life that I'm trying to save, and I'm going to grab any chance I've got."

Jim was blinking at me, clearly moved by what I'd said. And for just a moment, we ceased to be two doctors, or doctor and patient, but were rather two men facing an uncertain, perhaps perilous, future. "Ah, who can blame you?" Jim said at last with a sigh. "However, one thing we probably should do right now is get you on DDI."

"That was next on my agenda."

And so together we reviewed the protocols and mapped out a strategy of how much IL-2 I would take and for how many days. I told Stevens that I wanted to try the drug as an outpatient—if I was going to have diarrhea all day long, I'd rather have it in the privacy of my condo. More important, if IL-2 was going to become a regular part of my life, I wanted to find a dosage that was high enough to be effective yet would not be so debilitating that I couldn't work. Jim agreed to let me try the drug at home on the condition that I check in daily with the clinic.

And so I was ready to begin. Already IL-2 was producing in me a significant side effect: hope.

CHAPTER 22

THE PLAN WAS that I would get two inaugural injections of IL-2 at the clinic, so Madeline could get baseline weight and blood pressure data. Then I would self-administer the rest of my injections at home. The morning of my first injections, I arrived at the clinic early, startling Madeline, who was just walking in.

"Am I late for you?" she asked.

"No, it's me. I'm the early bird."

Motioning me into an examining room, Madeline shrugged off her coat and went immediately to get a syringe, which she loaded from one of my little vials. "I just pray this helps you," she said.

"Me too." I watched the needle sink under my skin, which I could feel contracting in pain.

"You may be sore a little for a few days."

"So be it."

"Have you ever given yourself sub-Q injections, Dr. Johnson?" she asked me with mock seriousness.

"Not since medical school."

"Well, don't try to stick yourself in the arm. I'd suggest the upper thigh."

The first forty-eight hours passed without incident. All I felt was a few aches and pains. The next day I felt worse, a little fluish, and figured the storm of symptoms was finally approaching. Knowing that I probably would be laid up for at least a couple of days, I decided to stop at Davis Kidd, a bookstore near my house, to pick up a few things to read. One was a book recommended by my mother called *My Own Country,* an immigrant specialist's account of the emergence of AIDS in eastern Tennessee.

By the time I got home I felt achy and fatigued. After making myself a light, high-protein dinner, I drew out my bag of syringes and vials of IL-2 with a certain apprehension, a little fearful of the side effects to come. I half wished that I'd asked someone to look in on me, but I hadn't wanted to impose on others. So after a moment's hesitation, I injected myself in my right thigh and then settled down on the couch with my new book to wait it out.

This doctor's story was a poignant one, an account of the plight of HIV-infected people and their families during the early years of the epidemic, facing both the disease and small-town prejudice in the sometimes inhospitable South. In caring for them, the doctor, Abraham Verghese, had undergone a moving metamorphosis from medical tradesman to true healer.

One of the characters in the book particularly engaged me—a remarkable woman named Vickie McCray, who had been unknowingly infected by her husband, yet managed to forgive him and even nurse him faithfully until his death. I fell asleep reading about her, and then awoke during the night feverish, shaking uncontrollably, with my teeth chattering. My muscles ached, and just the thought of moving hurt—even lying against a feather pillow pinched my neck. Now I knew what it was like to be "locked in," a syndrome seen in stroke victims who are left completely paralyzed except for the ability to move their eyes. All I could do was think, and so I mused on Vickie's story, eager to resume reading.

The next day, day four, was the worst yet. Still I managed to drag myself out of bed and get dressed. My joints were swollen and stiff, but I decided—more as a matter of discipline than fitness—to try to go to the gym, on the off chance that a workout might help and to prove to myself that I had the stamina to withstand the rigors of the side effects of treatment. Although fatigued, I managed to do a light workout, then showered and drove the few blocks to the AIDS clinic for a friendly once-over from Stevens and Madeline.

"You seem to be doing okay," he said. "How are you feeling?"

"A little achy," I said. "But not so bad."

"Get on the scale. I'm just curious to see how much weight you've gained."

Stepping on the scale, I exclaimed, "I've gained five pounds!"

"Five pounds in four days!" Stevens said. "Not bad. I guess we can assume the drug is working."

That night I dosed myself with extra Tylenol and Motrin to help control my fever. The following morning Madeline drew my blood, as recommended in the NIH's protocol, to see how the treatment was affecting my CD4 counts and viral load. Within twenty-four hours of taking my last dose of IL-2, I'd rallied enough to cut back on the Tylenol—and to pick up *My Own Country* and continue tracking Vickie McCray.

The daughter of an alcoholic father and a strict mother, she had grown up in the Greystone housing project, near Johnson City, Tennessee. When she was five, Vickie's father abandoned the family, and so from a very early age Vickie had to work to help support her mother and younger sister. Still, she excelled in high school and even dreamed of college. But when Vickie reached the tenth grade, her mother was diagnosed with cancer, and Vickie had to drop out to work and to care for her. She died when Vickie was seventeen.

Not long after her mother's death, Vickie married a handsome handyman named Clyde McCray and moved with him to a tiny place in Tester Hollow, on the outskirts of Johnson City. Though the marriage was never blissful, it was a cruel shock when, during her second pregnancy, Vickie discovered that Clyde was having an affair with her sister, who ended up also carrying his child. Somehow, Vickie found the strength to forgive them both, but then suddenly, mysteriously, Clyde began to lose weight and to exhibit strangely childlike behavior. Diagnosis proved elusive until Vickie insisted that Clyde be hospitalized and seen by specialists, including a neurologist who, as part of a thorough workup, ordered an HIV screen. Much to Vickie's horror, the test came back positive. Clyde had AIDS. Once his diagnosis was made, Clyde confessed to having had an affair with another man. And in the ensuing flurry of testing it was discovered that Clyde had infected both Vickie and her sister.

The day she received her results, for the first time in her very difficult life, Vickie nearly succumbed to despair. Her children were visiting a family friend, and so, alone in her trailer, she got out Clyde's gun, intending to kill herself. As she tried to load it, she spilled the bullets on the floor, and while collecting them heard the voices of her children calling to her. She searched in vain for her children, but the voices persisted, reminding Vickie that her suffering was not their fault. When she realized that she was imagining the voices—and when she thought about how much pain it would cause her children if she took her life—she started to cry.

And so did I. I put down the book and wept.

Yet, after all this, she refused to banish her husband from the house. She put aside her feelings of anger and betrayal and allowed him the dignity of dying surrounded by his family. In 1988, when Clyde developed dementia, AZT was only just becoming available in eastern Tennessee. There was no treatment that could slow his rapid, inexorable decline.

And so the nightmare of her childhood returned. For two years, Vickie struggled to keep a factory job at night, caring for a progressively demented and incontinent Clyde and their two children during the day. In 1990, Clyde Sr. died, leaving Vickie to raise Clyde Jr., their two-year-old son, and Danielle, their twelve-year-old daughter, on her own.

I closed the book at midnight, too haunted by Vickie's story to sleep. I marveled that anyone could undergo such grievous hardships without bitterness and—even more astonishing—retain such a heroic degree of compassion. Vickie's courage seemed almost superhuman, and it deeply inspired me. I couldn't resist flipping through the rest of the book, trying to find out what had happened to her. At the end, I was gratified to see, she was still alive.

I was still buoyed by Vickie's story when I went to check my posttreatment counts the next morning. Although Dr. Jones warned me that they might drop temporarily after IL-2, I didn't know how low they could go. The number rolled off the screen with startling indifference: 270! I shuddered. This was the lowest count I'd ever had, only 70 away from AIDS—a chilling reminder, as if I needed one, of what the stakes were in this experiment. Fortunately, the more telling blood test, the one that would more accurately reflect the effect of IL-2 on my CD4 counts, was a month away. Within two days my aches and fatigue disappeared, so I knew that I could withstand the side effects of IL-2. The big question was whether the drug would work.

After a little over a month, I got my blood drawn again, and, the following day, counted the minutes until lunchtime, when I could sneak into the neuropathology office to check the lab computer. With trembling hands, I typed in my patient number, hoping, even praying, for a little good news.

The values flashed on the screen like Christmas lights.

T-HELPER CD4%   45
T-HELPER CD4 #/CUMM   720*

"Seven-twenty!" I was stunned, breathless. Finally, I had seemingly reversed my downhill slide. Only now, with my first flush of success, could I fully allow myself to realize just how terrified I had been during those months of falling counts. I found tears welling up in my eyes, tears of relief and gratitude for the reprieve.

---

* One month after my second IL-2 treatment, my CD4 counts jumped up to 910 (45 percent) and have averaged over 1,000 ever since.

I still had to wait for my viral load measurement, now being determined through a sensitive technique called branched DNA amplification (BDNA). Until a year before, the BDNA test had been performed only in the most sophisticated of laboratories; and so the previous assessment of my virus, by Mike Saag at the University of Alabama, had been done by less sensitive viral co-culture method. The BDNA test could detect concentration of virus as low as 1,000 copies per milliliter of blood, a minuscule number in light of the fact that some people with HIV have viral loads in the millions of copies per milliliter. So it was well worth the six weeks' wait for the test results.

Finally, I got the call from Stevens.

"Well, I have some good news," he said.

I remember closing my eyes and praying.

"Both BDNA tests, before and after IL-2, failed to detect virus," he said.

I was flabbergasted. I'd expected to have at least some detectable virus, since I'd been infected for more than two years and had watched my counts drop from 821 to 320. "What do you think this means?" I asked Jim.

"Well, for one thing, it means the IL-2 didn't hurt you. Beyond that, I have no idea. Undetectable virus in someone on AZT and DDI—I don't know what to say."*

"Do you think the drugs could have beaten the virus back to below detectable levels?"

"I suppose, but we don't really know enough about drug

---

* Studies on combined use of AZT and DDI (such as ACTG175), presented in September 1995, suggested that the two drugs together were more effective than either drug taken alone.

combinations yet to be sure. All I can say is, I guess, congratulations. So far you're doing extraordinarily well.''

I thanked Jim and hung up the phone, elated. Even without any further IL-2 treatments—we'd had to wait for the BDNA results—my counts were still at 720 and 45 percent, a celestial level as far as I was concerned. And now the BDNA result, whatever it would ultimately prove to mean, could only be considered positive news. Over the next few days I kept trying to tell myself that this was only a momentary triumph, one that offered no concrete reassurance as to my prognosis. Previous ''magic bullets'' had looked promising, only to fail after the virus became resistant to them, and at this point there was no data showing a long-term benefit from IL-2. So I struggled to be realistic; that is, pessimistic. But now—I couldn't help it—an unwanted, irrational sense of hope was forcing its way to the surface.

CHAPTER 23

——— ∞ ———

THROUGH THE WEEKS of waiting for my test results I continued to wonder about Vickie McCray. Sometimes when I was feeling particularly low I'd go back to *My Own Country* and reread her story as if it were a parable from the Bible. One passage in particular always moved me: "It's almost like I'm still looking for Clyde. I'll be driving and I'll see a dark-haired man with a mustache and my head will spin." I could hardly bear the thought that this noble woman, with such a miraculous capacity for love, could be facing imminent illness and even death. I prayed that her counts were stable and that she was getting excellent care.

Then, as luck would have it, I happened to read that the author of *My Own Country,* Dr. Abraham Verghese, would be appearing in Nashville at a book festival. Eager to meet him, I attended and waited out the crowds to tell him how affecting I'd found his book, especially the story of Vickie McCray. I asked him if I could write to her, and though he was understandably protective, he sensed that he could trust me and wrote down her address.

I dashed off a short note:

October 20, 1994
Dear Ms. McCray:
    Every battle, every struggle against human suffering,
begets heroes who teach us of courage and offer us hope.
In the battle against AIDS, that hero is Vickie McCray.
All of us at Vanderbilt who know of your story thank you
for the inspiration and pray that you remain healthy.
Mahlon Johnson, M.D., Ph.D.
(infected from an autopsy)

I jotted a P.S. with my phone number, adding: "Please call if I can be of help."

Weeks passed without word from Vickie. I might have called if I'd had her phone number, but I didn't even know her real name. "Vickie McCray" was a pseudonym.

Then one night in early January, while I was unlocking my front door, I heard the phone inside ringing. I struggled to free my key as a low, smoky voice emerged from the answering machine. "Dr. Johnson? I bet you won't guess who this is."

The voice sounded tentative and wistful. It paused, as if by some telepathy the caller knew that I was there in the dark room listening—as if it was daring me to pick up the phone.

"This is Vickie . . . ya know . . . Vickie McCray," she went on, sounding amused by her new notoriety. "Your letter was very nice. I would have called you sooner but I didn't know who you were, and since Abraham was in India, I couldn't ask him.'' She stopped talking for a moment, and again I got the eerie sensation that she could tell that I was there listening. But I still couldn't force myself to pick up the phone, almost afraid to meet the woman who'd become an inspiration.

"I hope to meet you someday," Vickie was saying. "And if you're ever in Kingsport I hope you'll stop by." She started to rattle off her phone number, and then, suddenly afraid of losing the connection, I lunged for the phone—and missed. She was gone, and the recorder was clicking and maliciously whirling into rewind.

I stood there for a few minutes, paralyzed, convinced on some deep, instinctual level that if I called Vickie back it would transform my life. Finally, I found the courage to dial her number.

"Well, well, you must've been there listening to me make a fool out of myself," she said, her voice softly drawling.

"I was just coming in when the machine was on. I can't believe you called. So how are you?"

"I'm okay," she said. "Fred died in September, so I'm the last survivor in the book—you know."*

A little unsure of what to say next, I sought the familiar turf of medicine. "Are your counts okay?" I asked.

"At one point they dropped as low as one-eighty, but they're back up to two-eighty right now," she said with pride. "I believe it's all a matter of attitude."

My heart sank at the thought that her counts had already reached the range where she'd be clinically diagnosed as having AIDS. She hadn't had any major opportunistic infections, she told

---

* Fred (the Bear) was a character from *My Own Country*.

me, although she had been hospitalized for bronchitis during the previous autumn. I suspected from the timbre of her voice that she smoked, which would make her lungs more vulnerable to the pneumonias that plagued the immunosuppressed. She went on to say that she was taking the reverse transcriptase inhibitor, DDC, and that she'd tried AZT but couldn't tolerate it. At least she seemed to be responding to one antiviral drug, I thought with relief.

I asked about her children.

"Clyde Junior is ten now. He's Mr. Fix-It," Vickie said with a chuckle. "He's always taking something apart. The problem is it's not always broken. . . . Danielle's eighteen and only has a half year till she goes to college, thank God."

I tried to imagine her life as a single mother, taking care of two strong-willed children, supporting them while trying to go to college. "And are you in nursing school?" I asked—the book suggested that this had been her future plan.

"Part-time. But that's all I can manage with the kids. And you?" Vickie asked after a pause. "What about you?"

I told her I was healthy and working and that I'd been trying different regimens with experimental drugs, particularly IL-2, which I'd been taking every two months. I told her that my CD4 counts had jumped from 320 to 920.

There was a stunned pause. "That's amazing," Vickie said quietly. "I've never heard of anything like that. What did you call that stuff you took?"

I explained about IL-2, as well as its history in cancer treatment.

"I thought I was up on things, but I've never heard of that one," she said.

"Well, it's quite new," I said. "And it's a little controversial." I didn't tell her about my "undetectable" viral loads because I wasn't sure how it related to my IL-2 therapy. And I couldn't help worrying that, since Vickie's counts were so low, her immune system might be too far gone to respond to this very promising treatment. Yet I didn't want to sound discouraging. "We should talk about it," I said. "Maybe it's something you want to consider for yourself."

"I'll have to ask my doctor about it."

We continued talking for an hour with such an easy familiarity that it seemed as if we were picking up where we'd left off rather than speaking for the very first time. She kept asking me about myself but I was too curious about her to provide more than a brief outline. "Tell you what," I said. "I've kept a diary of my experiences since my accident. I'll let you read it if you like."

"Please send it to me," she begged.

"I don't know how to say this," I said, "but I'm terribly sorry about what's happened to you. And I would like to help if I can."

After we hung up, I lay down on the sofa and put on a piano concerto, feeling more serene than I had in a long time. My tranquillity lasted the whole next day. And I did send her my diary, with a note:

Dear Vickie:

I've read your story like I read the Bible, trying to comprehend what you've faced and lost over the last eight years. My story's too long and twisted for a call . . . or several so I'll send it to you. The writing's still quite lifeless after an eternity of weekends. But at least we'll be on equal footing this way.

I'll call again tonight.

But she beat me to the punch. No sooner did I get home from work than the phone rang.

"Hey, what are you up to?" said the now-familiar low voice.

"Vickie!"

"I just thought I'd say hello again. I've been rereading your nice letter."

She asked me how my day had gone, a question I barely answered while trying to steer the conversation back to her.

"Mahlon," she said, "I talked enough about myself last night. I want to talk about you."

"I mailed you my diary so you'll know everything—more than you'd ever want to," I teased. "But, to tell you the truth, today was a hard day. I just did an AIDS autopsy on a guy. His brain was completely rotted."

There was a meaningful pause and then she said, "One of the things that frightens me most is getting that dementia."

"It's a terrible thing," I agreed.

"Can I ask you something?" she said.

"Sure."

"After everything that's happened, how can you face autopsies? Don't they disturb you?"

I almost trotted out my knee-jerk response: that it was part of my job. But just then I got a rush of insight. "You know, Vickie," I said, knowing I'd stumbled on some truth, "I like doing them because I feel like I'm getting revenge. You take out that brain filled with virus, you put it in formaldehyde, and you kill the virus once and for all.''

A moment or two passed before Vickie said, ''Gee, I thought I'd just give you a call and make some chitchat.''

I laughed. ''I guess that sounds pretty grisly. But you can understand how fighting this disease has become a big thing in my life. In fact, I've been thinking about our conversation last night, about the drugs you're on. I think you should try AZT again, this time in combination with DDC.''

''You really think that'll make a difference?''

I briefly outlined the idea of multidrug therapy.

''Tell you what, I'll talk to my doctor,'' she said. ''But only if you promise to coach me.''

''Done.''

The next day I received a card in the mail, and inside it was a photograph. Vickie looked sweet and cuddly—as warm as she sounded on the phone—and on the back of the picture she had written ''Here I am with my mischievous grin.'' I was completely charmed. From my desk I excavated a wallet-size snapshot that Alexis had taken of me in the garden. Hoping that she would find it at least somewhat appealing, I sent it off to Vickie with a note.

ON MY ADVICE, Vickie did broach the issue of AZT with her AIDS physician, Dr. Armstrong, whom Vickie had started seeing after Dr. Verghese moved to Iowa. Once a family practitioner, Armstrong had out of necessity over the years become a de facto infectious disease doctor, one of the few practicing in eastern Tennessee. He had agreed to start Vickie on AZT.

"That's great," I said.

"So, how many weeks is it going to take for me to get used to this?"

"Well, it depends on the individual. But I'd say it's going to take at least two or three weeks. By then the worst was over for me, though the nausea bothered me for months. For the first day or two, make sure you're always near a bathroom."

"Tell that to my kids. They expect me to drive them everywhere," she said, laughing.

Within a day of starting the drug, Vickie reported attacks of diarrhea and nausea, but she claimed they were mild. I called her nightly with doses of support and sympathy and sent her a get-well card with a forlorn-looking bassett hound on the front. The day she received it, she sent me a funny card back. And thus started her custom of mailing me a card each week, making sure that it would arrive on Saturday. Inside she'd place cartoons or funny pictures or just amusing notes about life in the McCray household—her anecdotes about Clyde Jr.'s and Danielle's trying antics always made me chuckle. I wrote her back, telling her stories about life at Vanderbilt or about the high jinks of my mother's dogs. Over time our notes got more serious, with Vickie thanking me for caring for her, for watching over her health. "No," I'd protest. It was I who had to be grateful, for she was leading me out of my isolation.

And we talked on the phone every night—warm, long, colorful conversations that were becoming the focus of my days. I would picture us united across the miles, like two kids with tin cans pressed to their ears, connected by a line of string.

Sometimes it grew laughably obvious that we were tussling over who was going to take care of whom. "I want you to promise me something," she said to me in one of our early conversations.

"I promise."

"You don't even know what it is."

"Doesn't matter."

"When I come up there to visit you I want to cook you a meal."

"No, I want to take you out to dinner."

"No, you can't . . . besides, you already promised."

"Well, then, I break the promise. I want to take you out to dinner. You never get a chance to go out to dinner."

As it turned out, I won that one.

During the day, Vickie would sometimes leave messages on my machine to greet me when I got home. "This AZT better be doing me some good," she'd say. "A few more weeks on this and I'm going to be skin and bones." She meant it, too—apples were all she was eating. Since *My Own Country,* Vickie had slimmed down to "look good for my fans," as she jokingly put it. But one night I came home to find a particularly discouraged message. "Mahlon," Vickie said, "I need to talk to you about some tingling and numbness in my hands. Please call me when you get a chance."

Tingling and numbness in the hands or feet were symptoms of nerve damage or neuropathy, a notorious side effect of DDC and DDI. Alarmed, I called her back immediately and asked her how long it had been going on.

"It's been going on for a while."

"What do you mean? How come you haven't said anything?"

"Because I thought it went away. It seemed to. But in the last few days, it's been getting worse."

Vickie, I had quickly discovered, was the opposite of Dawn— the sort of person who would automatically minimize any discomfort. It was part of her stoic nature, part of her belief that a positive attitude was the key to survival. But these symptoms were too serious to play down, for the toxicity of some anti-HIV drugs could cause permanent nerve damage. To prevent it, Vickie would have to stop taking DDC immediately—which, of course, would leave her more vulnerable to HIV.

That was a frightening prospect because Vickie had been infected for at least eight or nine years and her CD4 counts were already low. AZT alone was not that effective at slowing down the virus. There were antibiotics that could help protect her against Pneumocystis pneumonia and other opportunistic infections that could crop up when a person's counts dropped into the 200 range. But I'd seen people succumb to lymphoma or cryptococcus with counts higher than Vickie's, and her years of smoking certainly wouldn't help. I began to fear that my dear new friend, my cherished confidante, might soon approach the point when she'd get sick and never recover. I couldn't begin to contemplate that loss.

I urged her to make an appointment with her doctor immediately. On the appointed day, after the appointed time, I started calling her house every fifteen minutes, praying that Dr. Armstrong would find another explanation for the numbness. It wasn't until six that evening that my office phone rang.

"Dr. Armstrong took me off DDC," Vickie blurted out, too scared to even say hello.

"What does he plan to do instead?" I asked.

"Just keep me on AZT, I guess. You know, I was fine for years without taking anything."

I was consumed with guilt for planting the notion that multidrug therapy could buy Vickie a lot more time—for awakening in her a hope for survival, only to see it dashed. Confounded hopes, I knew, were much worse than no hope at all, which could breed resignation.

"Look, Mahlon," Vickie continued, "I'm not afraid to die, but I'm afraid to think about what might happen to my children if I do. There's nobody in my life who can really take care of them."

"Don't say that," I countered, trying to think of options but feeling panicky myself.

"Okay," she said softly.

"There is something else that's coming soon," I recalled. "It's a drug called 3TC. It's like AZT and DDI, a reverse transcriptase inhibitor. But in combination with AZT it seems to be quite potent."

Several months before, long after I had started IL-2, Glaxo Pharmaceuticals had started a final "open label" clinical trial of 3TC. That meant that patients could receive the active drug rather than blindly hope to avoid the placebo. Before the AIDS epidemic, such compassionately straightforward drug trials were fairly rare. Now, thanks to the tireless agitation of AIDS activists, the "stockyard" mentality of drug trials was slowly being eroded, it seemed—and thank God.

I had studied the 3TC protocols a month before, hoping to get on the drug myself. I was ineligible, however, because the study was limited to people with counts below 300. But Vickie could qualify.

"Why don't you ask Dr. Armstrong tomorrow about 3TC?" I suggested. "I'm sure his clinic could participate in the study."

I figured that Dr. Armstrong would jump at the chance to participate in a new study, especially one that would give his patients direct access to a potentially effective treatment.

Vickie confirmed that Dr. Armstrong was interested but said that it could take several months to get approval for his participation through the drug company's internal review board.

"That's ridiculous!" I snorted. "It takes one month for these kinds of things to be approved."

"Wouldn't he know that? Maybe things are done differently with private clinics," Vickie said.

"I don't think so," I said in frustration.

Over the next several weeks, with my gentle prodding, Vickie kept calling Dr. Armstrong to find out how the 3TC application was going. Armstrong was always too busy to come to the phone, but his office assured Vickie that the approval process was well under way.

A month went by, and then I received a letter from Glaxo stating that, due to a huge demand for the 3TC, after May 1, 1995, enrollment in the trial would be limited to patients with CD4 counts of less than 100. It was imperative to get Vickie on the drug before then so that she wouldn't be disqualified. Now, with Vickie's permission, I called Dr. Armstrong myself.

"Hello, this is Mahlon Johnson," I said, refraining from referring to myself as Dr. Johnson. "I'm a friend of Vickie McCray's."

"I know who you are," Armstrong assured me.

I asked about the 3TC application, and he said that it was "in the works."

"Look, one of the reasons I'm calling is that I've just received a letter from the 3TC study director." I explained the situation. "So if Vickie doesn't enroll in time, she'll be out in the cold."

"Dr. Johnson, as I said, it's out of my hands," Armstrong told me. "We have to wait for approval."

I couldn't get a reading on Dr. Armstrong, who not only

seemed officious, but, I suspected, resented my intrusion, the intrusion of a pathologist, into his practice. Of course, I didn't even want to consider that Dr. Armstrong's ego might be getting in the way of his judgment and his professionalism. I had to give him the benefit of the doubt. And, at this particular point, I felt that it would be far too aggressive of me to urge Vickie to switch doctors, particularly because Dr. Armstrong was one of the few physicians in the area with good credentials and expertise in AIDS.

Vickie agreed that she was in a tight spot. "But I don't want to make Armstrong angry," she said. "That's why I don't push. I was brought up to believe in what doctors say."

"I guess we just have to keep agitating."

"He probably thinks you're some kind of fanatic," Vickie teased me.

"Did he say that?" I asked suspiciously.

"No, of course not."

"I guess I am a bit fanatical," I said. "But it's been paying off . . . so far, anyway."

"I know it has," Vickie said. "And that's why I believe you when you say this drug will help me."

And so we waited for Armstrong's clinic to be sanctioned by the drug company. But by the third week of April, one week before the enrollment deadline, there was still no word.

Now I was feeling desperate. I feared that, with no significant antiviral drug protection, Vickie's counts might be dropping. During one of our nightly calls, I said, "It looks like nothing's going to happen in time. I think if we scramble we might be able to get you enrolled through the AIDS clinic here at Vanderbilt."

"Well, it sure doesn't seem to be happening in Kingsport," Vickie said sadly.

"It's your call, Vickie. I've rocked the boat enough. You're going to have to decide."

"I've decided," she said. "Let's try and get it through Vanderbilt. I'll call Dr. Armstrong tomorrow and tell him."

First thing the next morning, after a restless night, I called Jim Stevens to find out if he'd accept Vickie as a patient. After giving him the necessary medical history, I hatched my plan to fly Vickie up to Nashville and enroll her in the 3TC program at Vanderbilt.

"Well, I don't know."

"Jim, this woman is very important to me. You've got to help me."

"I understand. But she'd have to be seen every three months. Can she come up that often? Why doesn't she want to enroll over there? Surely someone in eastern Tennessee is participating in the study."

"No, not yet."

As an AIDS doctor who had spent years in the trenches, Stevens knew all too well what awaited Vickie if her counts spiraled downward. So he agreed to take Vickie on, provided that her enrollment was sanctioned by Dr. Armstrong and that her latest blood counts be sent to Vanderbilt. Stevens would have to show the drug company evidence of at least two CD4 counts below 300 in the last three months for Vickie to be eligible to get the 3TC.

"Don't forget," Jim said. "They're closing enrollment after May 1, so we need to get her labs right away."

I was elated—and Vickie was thrilled—that Jim had agreed to help. We had only a week to get Vickie's lab sheets from Kingsport and send them off to the enrollment office in New Jersey. I just hoped that Armstrong would be cooperative.

Vickie called him immediately.

"So, what did Armstrong say?" I asked.

"He didn't say much . . . but he said okay. I guess that's the important thing."

"What was his tone? Did he sound resigned, angry, relieved, anything?"

"He sounded very busy," Vickie said. "But he said okay."

By Thursday afternoon, April 27, I thought I had all the arrangements set for Vickie's enrollment in the 3TC study. But a call to the AIDS clinic proved me wrong.

"No, Mahlon," Madeline said. "We haven't received anything from Kingsport."

"Are you sure?"

"I'm positive, don't you think I've been keeping an eye out?"

"I'm sorry, it's just that they were supposed to send it overnight."

"I guess maybe they forgot."

As soon as I got off the phone with Madeline, I called Dr. Armstrong's office. He was busy, I was told. "This is Dr. Mahlon Johnson," I said. "I'm calling because we were supposed to get some data for Vickie McCray here at Vanderbilt and it hasn't arrived."

"I don't believe it has gone out as yet, Dr. Johnson."

"But it was supposed to have arrived today," I said.

"I understand. But we've been short-staffed."

"My problem is we need this by tomorrow if Vickie is going to be enrolled by May first, which is Monday. That's the cutoff date for the drug trial."

"Okay, then we'll get it out to you overnight."

But by Friday afternoon at three the data had still not arrived.

I called Armstrong's office again and got a different receptionist, who said she had no record that the information had been sent. She, too, promised to send the material Federal Express for Saturday delivery. But on Saturday no package arrived.

I had to call Vickie and tell her the bad news. "What's going on?" she said. "I don't understand why this is happening."

It was infuriating that, despite the clear urgency of Vickie's situation and all our prodding, Armstrong's office had dropped the ball. Though I was probably being paranoid, it was hard not to suspect that the repeated screwups reflected some sort of resistance.

On Monday morning I called Kingsport once again, only to be told that there had been a mix-up and Vickie's data had been sent by regular mail. I then called the enrollment office in New Jersey, pleading for a day's grace period, but that proved to be futile. I was told that if they made an exception for one person, then they'd have to make exceptions for everyone else. Vickie's lab sheets didn't actually arrive until Tuesday morning, May 2. We missed enrolling her in the 3TC trial by a single day.

I knew how devastated Vickie would be, and again, I reproached myself for getting her hopes up. But there were other drug trials in the works at Vanderbilt, notably an upcoming study of one of the new protease inhibitors. If I could get Vickie enrolled, I knew, it would cushion the blow of missing the 3TC trial. So I ran over to the AIDS clinic to check the protocols and see if I could get her signed up.

I found Madeline in the break room unwrapping a small sandwich for a hasty lunch between patients. She told me that, to be eligible for the trial, Vickie would have to have a CD4 count of less than 500 and have less than two weeks of prior treatment with

AZT (I, of course, would be disqualified from the trial on both counts).

Now Madeline asked me how long Vickie had been on AZT, and I hedged, claiming that I wasn't quite sure. There was only compassion in Madeline's gaze, but I wondered if she suspected that I wasn't being entirely candid. Many health care workers in her position were understanding enough to look the other way if it meant that someone could receive a life-prolonging treatment. Still, not wanting to put Madeline on the spot, I scheduled an appointment for Vickie, promising to pin down how long she had been on AZT.

That night I called Vickie to break the crushing news about the missed deadline, then quickly sidestepped to explain the protease inhibitor trial.

"But we'll have to be careful what you say when you fill out the forms," I told her, "since you can't have been on AZT for more than two weeks."

"But I have been."

"Just tell them you can't quite remember, but that it's only been about that long."

Admittedly, my advice was not in the best interests of research and medicine, but keeping Vickie alive was more important to me than observing the arbitrary rules of a drug study.

Vickie sighed. "Mahlon, you know how much I appreciate everything you're doing for me, but I have a problem with lying. . . ."

"Even if it'll save your life?" I exclaimed.

"I just don't feel right lying. I've never lied in my life. That's how I was raised. Lying to a doctor would be even harder than lying to the next person."

"We can talk about this later. But for the time being, Vickie, just let me fill the stuff out. Protease inhibitors are the most promising new drugs to be developed, much more promising even than 3TC. If you could just get on them, it might buy you time. Vickie, this is our only hope except for IL-2. And your counts may be too low to respond to that. Think of . . . I don't know, think of Clyde Junior, for goodness' sake."

"Are you going to be in there with me?" she asked, searching for reassurance. "I'm not good at fibbing."

"Yes, I promise, I'll be there with you."

CHAPTER 24

NOW VICKIE AND I began to plan, excitedly, for what would be our first face-to-face meeting. Through our months of nightly phone calls, I had felt almost afraid to meet her, wary of testing the strength of what was becoming such a deeply sustaining bond. In the early stages of our relationship, I would have been crushed if somehow our chemistry was different, less potent, in person; and I couldn't risk losing my warmest and closest emotional attachment. But now I felt more confident in Vickie's affections; and besides, she was coming for treatment, not just to see me, which took the pressure off.

I had suggested that Vickie fly to Nashville, but she kept quietly insisting on driving. Then one day when I called, her daughter, Danielle, answered the phone and clued me in to the reason.

"Ma doesn't want to tell you, but she's never been in a plane before. I think she's a little afraid to fly."

"What about you? Have you ever been on a plane?"

"No, but I'm not afraid. I'd love to fly."

So I suggested that Danielle accompany her mother. In my travels around the country to conferences, I'd accumulated a lot of airline mileage vouchers and could easily spare one for Danielle.

At first there was silence on the other end of the line. "You don't have to do that; she can come by herself."

"No. This would be easy—unless you're more afraid of flying than you're letting on."

"No way," Danielle said. "But I should probably ask Mom."

Vickie called me later on that night. "I hear you've got our itinerary all planned." She sounded bemused.

"I did it because Danielle told me you were afraid of flying."

"She wasn't supposed to tell you that!"

"She also thought you might need a chaperone," I teased.

"That'll be the day."

I assured Vickie that I'd earned more free trips than I could use, and so she agreed to fly if Danielle came along. I made the reservations, and when I called the next day to confirm the flight time with Vickie, Danielle once again answered the phone—this time all out of breath.

"Danielle? Are you all right?"

"Why?" She sounded a little paranoid.

"You sound like something's wrong over there."

"Well, I just came in from doing some stuff outside."

"You didn't wreck your Mom's car, did you?" I said, joking.

"How did you know?" Danielle said in utter terror.

"Uh oh." Vickie had made her beloved Camaro off limits to Danielle until she showed more responsibility and could pay for her own insurance.

"Mahlon, please help me. She's going to kill me. That's the only car she's ever had. Her first."

"Are you all right—at least?"

"I am till Ma gets home."

"What happened?"

"Oh, I don't know. We were just taking it for a little spin in the church parking lot and a big rock jumped out."

"We—you mean you and Clyde Junior?"

"No. Friends."

At that point I could hear a commotion at the door. Someone had dropped Vickie off early—in front of her newly remodeled Camaro.

"Danielle!" I could hear her shout.

"Here, you talk to her," Danielle said. There was a thunk as she dropped the phone and made her escape.

Vickie came on the line.

"Hey. It's me."

"Damn, you wouldn't believe what Danielle did."

"I heard Danielle had some trouble with jumping rocks."

"She what?"

Despite Vickie's distress, I couldn't help laughing at the image.

"So you think this is funny," she said in mock annoyance. "You should see the car. She's busted out a headlight and torn up the whole bumper. That kid . . ." I'd never heard Vickie sound so exasperated.

"Well, look at it this way," I said, trying to cheer her up, "it's better that she had a little mishap in the church parking lot now and learn from it than have her first accident on the highway. Besides, now you've got a good reason to say no when she starts begging to borrow your car."

"Boy, do I!" Vickie's voice was softening a bit.

"Ma, I got to talk to you," I heard Danielle calling to her. "It's not as bad as you think."

"I don't want to hear it!" Vickie said sternly. But she let a forgiving chuckle escape into the phone.

Vickie and I had often discussed her dealings with her children. She knew that her illness frightened them and that they worried about losing her, as they had their father. So she found it hard to discipline them, for fear of being too tough. She was especially concerned about Clyde Jr., who was doing badly in school. Vickie claimed that she did everything she could to induce him to study.

"Have you tried bribery?" I asked her.

"What do you mean, bribery?"

"You know, like giving him twenty dollars for every *A*, ten dollars for every *B*."

"He'll probably get straight *A*s and break me," Vickie said.

I had wanted more of a connection with Vickie's family, and Clyde Jr. in particular, knowing how troubling it could be for a boy to grow up without a father. So I suggested to Vickie that I be the one to bribe Clyde.

"Oh, Mahlon, that's not necessary."

"Would you mind terribly if I made a little deal with him?" I asked.

Vickie protested, perhaps feeling awkward about my making a financial contribution to her household, but I insisted that the experiment would give me pleasure. Finally she gave in, saying, "Well, hell, Mahlon, if that's what you really want to do. It's your money."

"It's for a good cause," I told her.

So the next time Clyde Jr. answered the phone, I made him an offer. "For every *A* you get, I'll give you twenty dollars; for every *B*, ten; and for every *C*, five."

"What about for a *D*?" he queried.

"Nothing. *D*s are no good."

"Hmmm," said Clyde, thinking it over, tempted but no doubt a little embarrassed that his mother had discussed his bad grades with me.

"What do you have to lose?" I said.

"Nothing, I guess."

"So do we have a deal?"

"Sure, I guess."

I asked him to put Vickie on the phone.

"Ma," he yelled teasingly, "guess who wants to talk to you. Now she's going to get all giggly," he told me, man-to-man. I was amused and a little touched. I felt that perhaps we'd made some kind of breakthrough, and I was glad.

THE DAY OF Vickie's trip to Nashville was fast approaching. So I was surprised to get a call from Zac, saying that the AIDS clinic wanted to interview Vickie over the phone for the protease inhibitor trial. I didn't quite understand this sudden change of tack, in light of the fact that I'd already set up an appointment for her at Vanderbilt. More than that, the change confounded my plans to be present at the interview, to coach Vickie on what to say.

"Are you sure you just don't want to wait until she arrives? It's only two days," I said.

"Yes, Dr. Johnson, we're sure." When Zac called me Dr. Johnson, he was usually waggishly trying to put me in my place. "Just tell her to expect our call."

The moment I got off with Zac, I dialed Vickie's number, praying that she'd be home. Instead, I got her answering machine. Explaining that there had been a change of plans and that the clinic was going to interview her over the phone, I exhorted Vickie to say that she'd been on AZT for only two weeks. She never got my message—the kids heard it but forgot to play it back for her—but she did get one from Zac and called him back. Later that evening, I heard from her.

"Mahlon, I hope you're not mad at me," she said, sounding inconsolably distressed. "I guess I messed up."

"Oh no," I said.

"I didn't know they were calling to do the interview, so I just wasn't prepared. I slipped up and told them the truth . . . that I'd been on AZT longer than two weeks."

I stifled a sigh, not wanting to say anything that would make her feel worse.

"I got so nervous and confused," Vickie was saying tearfully, "I couldn't remember whether it was two or three weeks. I just couldn't fib."

"And they told you that being on AZT disqualified you from the protease inhibitor trial?"

"Yes, this one and every other trial, even that drug you were on—Delavirdine. I also told them I'd been on DDC."

"Oh no!"

"I'm sorry, I didn't know what I wasn't supposed to say."

"It's okay, it's okay," I reassured her. "You didn't do anything wrong. You just told the truth. We'll get you on something somehow."

There was a significant pause, and then Vickie said, "I guess we don't need to come to Nashville now."

"What are you talking about? Of course, you're still coming. I want to see you anyway . . . after all this time."

"Are you sure?" Vickie said.

"There's just one thing. My place is pretty small. So I went ahead and booked you and Danielle into a hotel."

"Mahlon, that's ridiculous. I can sleep on the couch. Hell, on the floor, for that matter."

"No, I want you both to be comfortable."

"But you don't understand," Vickie said. "We're not used to all that fuss."

"Please, let me do this for the two of you. It'll make me happy."

ON THE DAY of Vickie's arrival, I reached the airport early and settled into one of the lounges overlooking the tarmac so I could watch the American Eagle flights unload their passengers onto the shuttle buses that brought them in to the gate. But the planes were too far away for me to spot Vickie. When I heard that their flight was in, I waited at the gate for the shuttle bus. Out came Danielle, stumbling off the last step as she swung a knapsack over one shoulder. Having already seen my photograph, she recognized me first and waved as she came into the terminal. "Ma's coming," she said. Then, behind her, I spied a woman with curly brown hair and wearing sunglasses, which she took off, gazing at me with the palest gray-blue eyes. Without a word, we reached to one another for a long-awaited hug. And our moment as strangers quickly passed.

"I see you made it through the flight all right," I said.

"Well, I'll be all right in a minute," Vickie said, fanning herself. "I'm still feeling a little queasy."

"Did the plane ride make you nervous?" I asked.

"Not really," Vickie said.

"Oh, come on!" Danielle said. "You were worse than I was."

Vickie laughed uneasily. "Well, let's put it this way. I feel sorry for that poor woman sitting next to me. I'm sure she thought I was crazy. I had my fingernails dug so far into the armrests it's a wonder I still have them."

There were so many things I wanted to say to Vickie, so many things I wanted to ask, that I hardly knew where to start. As we walked to my car, we kept stealing glances at each other. Finally I reached down and took her hand. She raised my hand up to her eyes. "You have nice hands, Mahlon," she said. "You really do autopsies with these? They look like they belong to a musician or an artist."

I told her that when I was a child, one great disappointment was that my hands were considered too small for me to become a successful cellist or pianist.

In the car Danielle filled the silence with excited chatter until we pulled up to the Vanderbilt Holiday Inn. There I waited in the lobby while they checked in and changed. Vickie emerged wearing a stunning red pantsuit, which Danielle made a point of telling me was her best, just to tease her mother. I took them to dinner at the Sunset Grill, one of Nashville's trendier restaurants, and Danielle exclaimed over its courtyard, which was covered by a glass-and-metal geometric roof. I was pleased at her enthusiasm, and I asked Danielle if she had been to the "big city" before.

"Yes," she said, a little hesitantly, glancing at her mother. "We came here once . . . when my dad was alive."

"Oh yes," I recalled.

Vickie nodded. "One of Clyde's last requests was to see Opryland." Then she sighed. "It was one of the most difficult things I've ever done."

Clyde had lived in Tennessee his entire life but had never been to the theme park, museum, and auditorium that housed the Grand Ole Opry, the cathedral of country music. And so, before he deteriorated too much, Vickie took Clyde Jr. to her aunt's house and piled Clyde and Danielle and Clyde's wheelchair into the Camaro. She drove six hours from eastern Tennessee in an oppressive August heat, having to stop several times to tend to her husband's incontinence. The journey itself proved to be very taxing for Clyde, and as they got closer to Nashville, he grew feverish and dizzy.

Still, he was determined to continue. Vickie got Clyde situated in his wheelchair, but when she began to push him around the grounds at Opryland, he fell into a deep sleep. And although Danielle loved her father, she kept making excuses to go off on her own, unable to cope with the sight of her addled and incontinent parent out in public. The trip had been a nightmare.

"I'm so sorry," I murmured, taking Vickie's hand. All I

could think was that if anyone in the world deserved a measure of happiness, it was Vickie; and internally I vowed to redress the sorrows of her life in any way I could.

The next morning, I took Vickie and Danielle to brunch at the Cakewalk Cafe, a stylish but comfortable restaurant decorated with modern watercolors done by local artists. Our waitress appeared, modishly clad entirely in black, and when I caught sight of her face, I must have visibly jumped. She looked exactly like Dawn.

Immediately, I looked away, unsettled by the discovery that, after so much time and despite the tremendous dissatisfactions of our relationship, Dawn still had the power to haunt me. Vickie, picking up on my distress, looked at me quizzically. I smiled at her.

"Why are you so quiet?" I asked after a moment.

"Oh, no reason," Vickie said.

"Tell me, what is it?"

"It's really nothing."

"If I guess, will you tell me?"

"Okay."

"You saw me react to that waitress, was that it?"

"Well . . ."

"I'll tell you why. I don't know that woman, but she looks so much like Dawn that it startled me for a second."

Vickie nodded but still looked glum.

"I haven't spoken to Dawn in almost a year."

"You don't have to explain all that," Vickie said. "It's just that I had this nightmare right before we came to Nashville. I'd pretty much put it out of my mind till now. But in my dream, I drove up here to see you and parked at the back of your condo. Then I noticed that you'd thrown all the cards I'd sent you into the Dumpster. I looked up at your window and I saw a woman's face—

a very pretty woman's. I don't know what Dawn looks like, but somehow I knew it was Dawn.''

"Vickie, you're pretty, too. You have beautiful eyes. And I have every one of your cards. I cherish them.''

The waitress returned, cutting short our conversation, and this time I made certain not to glance at her. When she left, I began to reassure Vickie again. "It's okay, Mahlon, I don't want to talk about it,'' she said. "It was just a dream. Let's enjoy ourselves.''

It struck me then that Vickie probably didn't want to discuss such touchy matters in front of Danielle. So I shifted the subject to more familiar ground, the question of treatments.

"You know, I've been thinking that you might want to try IL-2,'' I told Vickie, "since the other drugs out there right now will probably be tied up in the rigamarole of trial criteria.''

"Do you think I can?'' she asked.

"I could call Dr. Jones at the NIH to see what he thinks of the idea,'' I said. "I'll tell him about your counts and then find out how long the waiting list is for their program. It would be easier for you to try IL-2 here at Vanderbilt, but Dr. Stevens and some others have already said they won't try IL-2 on patients until it becomes FDA-approved for HIV. There are some serious liability issues.''

"Why did he agree to do it for you?''

"He was concerned, but he knew that I could get the IL-2 and treat myself. By agreeing to let me try it he could at least monitor the situation. Besides, I was in a better position to understand the risks and take it carefully.''

"I guess I can't get it from you, huh?''

"Vickie, trust me, you don't want to. With your history of

bronchitis and counts where they are, taking IL-2 may not be so simple. I can take responsibility for myself, but it would be crazy—and unethical—for me to get you the drug and start administering it without an AIDS specialist involved.''

''So, what do we do?'' she said.

''Do you think we can get Armstrong to give it to you?''

Vickie shrugged. ''I haven't really spoken to him since all the mix-up with the 3TC.''

''I guess it wouldn't hurt to ask. I mean, I could call him again on your behalf.''

''Okay.''

An awkward silence fell, and then she gazed at me. ''Why are you trying so hard to help me?'' she asked me point-blank.

I was taken aback—astonished that, after four months of nightly calls and weekly cards, Vickie didn't realize that she had become the focus of my life. Our relationship was, admittedly, unusual; but as I flashed back to the discomfort ignited by the waitress who looked like Dawn, I recognized that, even long distance, my connection to Vickie was far more sustaining. In that moment, ruefully, I saw my attraction for Dawn as almost a cliché—I had been beguiled by her beauty, of course, but I was also spurred on by Dawn's rejection and inability to love. Vickie, by contrast, had accepted me from the outset. No acrobatics had been required to gain her affection. But how could I articulate what Vickie had come to mean to me?

''Well, I'm doing okay right now,'' I began. ''My counts are up, and I feel like I'm holding my own against the virus. I've done everything I possibly can for myself, so I can afford to concentrate on you, to help you fight, if you want me to.''

''I do want you to, and I'm grateful to you, Mahlon.''

"I'm not doing it only for you," I told her. "I'm doing it for myself. You've—well, you've become very important to me."

"But why have I become so important?"

"A lot of reasons." I was almost stammering. "For one thing, I admire your courage, your will to keep fighting after all you've been through. You're an inspiration to me."

"Well, I really didn't do anything special," Vickie said.

"Well, you've done something special for me. . . . Every night when we started talking you would always tell me something funny—about Clyde Junior, your dogs, the skunk out back. You made me laugh."

Vickie chuckled softly.

Then I continued a little self-consciously, fearing that what I was about to say might sound hokey: "It's hard to keep up the will to fight just for yourself. I have my parents and my sister, of course, but there's no one whose life I affect on a daily basis. Since I've gotten this disease, I've realized for the first time that it's really other people—our connections with them—that we live for. Does that make any sense?"

"Yes," Vickie said, "it does."

"More than Dawn, more even than Alexis, the woman I thought I would marry, you've made me feel connected—that I really matter to you."

"You do, Mahlon," Vickie said, taking my hand.

"That's why you've become so important." Moved to tears, I had to stop for a moment, aware that Danielle was watching.

THE NEXT DAY, Vickie and Danielle had to leave. I'd shyly asked if, on the way to the airport, Vickie would like to drop by my old house, "the cottage" she'd heard so much about. It had been a year since I'd sold the house, but it had remained a powerful symbol for me, of a future that perhaps I would never have. Knowing my feelings for the cottage, Vickie was curious to see it.

As we drove toward Green Hills, I described how carefully the gardens had been laid out and how much pleasure tending them had given me. We soon reached my old familiar street and I could see that my former driveway was empty. The occupants—renters, as it turned out—were not at home, so I stopped the car next to the row of hemlocks I'd planted. Most of them were dead now, starved of water and care.

Getting out of the car, I went around and opened up the doors for Vickie and Danielle. "Come on," I said. "I want you both to see the stuff I planted, at least the stuff that's still alive."

"You two go on. I'll stay here," Danielle said, sensing that her mother and I needed a few moments alone.

I led Vickie between two brown, needleless hemlocks into the backyard. Checking the house again to make sure nobody was home, we then went and peeked in the windows. From what we could see, the place was scantily furnished and now appeared more like a dormitory than a residence.

Vickie put her arm around my shoulder. "So, this was the last place you were happy."

"Yeah, that's why I wanted to show it to you. . . . I just can't believe that the people who bought this place turned around and rented it to people who don't give a damn," I said. "If I had known this would happen, I never would've sold the house. Just look at the gardens."

I waved a hand toward a flower bed that was a stand of

withered stalks choked with weeds, then toward another that lay completely barren. "Believe it or not, in the spring of '92 and '93 this yard was wall-to-wall tulips. And normally at this time of year all the rhododendrons would be blooming like crazy." I scoured the property for a single pink flower. "It's been a few months since I've come by here, and even then it looked like no one was bothering to water the plants. Now, everything has just died a slow death."

Vickie turned to me. "Maybe you should have called and reminded them?"

"What was I going to say? 'I'm the guy who used to own this house. You're ruining the garden!'"

"Maybe," Vickie said.

I laughed. "I don't think so. I'd sound like a crackpot."

"No, you wouldn't. You'd sound concerned."

"And then they'd say, 'If you're so concerned, then why did you sell the place to begin with?'"

"So?"

"And what would I tell them?"

Vickie was silent as I kicked away some vines and some clusters of leaves, hoping to uncover even one daisy.

Then she squeezed my hand. "I'm very sorry, Mahlon. This must've been a beautiful place. I'm sure you'll have another garden someday."

"You better hope not," I said. "Or I'll have your butt up here helping me plant trees and bulbs."

"I'll come," Vickie said with a laugh. "You can count on it."

"I'm going to hold you to that," I replied, though we both knew better than to hope that such a day would ever come.

CHAPTER 25

THE NEXT MORNING, I called the NIH to see about getting Vickie on IL-2.

"I'm really sorry, Dr. Johnson," the research nurse told me after listening carefully to my description of Vickie's situation. "But there's almost a six-month waiting period for this study."

"And there's no other way to get the treatment?" I asked.

"I'm sure you understand how strict protocol has to be here," she said, referring to the fact that the NIH was under constant scrutiny from all sorts of watchdog organizations. "However, from what you've told me, I don't see why your friend can't have a local doctor prescribe the IL-2 and monitor her treatment."

"It's hard to find someone who is willing," I explained.

"Well, if you do, we'd be happy to help."

Filled with dread, I then called Dr. Armstrong in Kingsport. As Vickie's primary doctor, and a highly trained one at that, Armstrong seemed our best hope for trying IL-2 in Tennessee. It took two days of phoning before I finally managed to reach him.

After reintroducing myself, I expressed my concern about Vickie and gently pointed out that, due to certain unspecified delays and to the fact that Vickie had already been taking other drugs, she had been unable to enroll in the 3TC study or any of the other ACTG trials at Vanderbilt. That left her with very few therapeutic options. I told Armstrong of my own experience with IL-2—how much my CD4 counts had risen. I explained the side effects Vickie might encounter on IL-2, including the risk of a burst of viral growth, and told him that Dr. Jones at the NIH might be willing to offer some advice. Then, with fingers crossed, I posed the question: "I was hoping you might let Vickie try IL-2."

There was a long silence. Then Armstrong said, "Dr. Johnson, I too want the best for Vickie. I hope to put her on a protease inhibitor when they finally become available."

"But that could be a year from now. She's been infected for at least eight or nine years and has already had her counts dip down toward two hundred."

"I know that, and I'm sorry. But I can't use a drug that's not FDA-approved for HIV. I'd be liable, and besides, who'd pay for it? TENNCARE certainly won't."

"It will be expensive, but don't worry. I'll pay for it, if that's the problem."

"And what if Vickie gets worse? What if she develops pulmonary complications?"

I assured Armstrong that I had discussed Vickie's history,

including her smoking and rare bouts of bronchitis, with Dr. Jones's office at the NIH and with an oncologist who'd overseen IL-2 trials on cancer. At the dosages the NIH used, I had been told, IL-2 shouldn't pose much of a problem, even for a heavy smoker. I pointed out that if Vickie did show signs of bronchitis he could always just stop the treatment.

"Dr. Johnson," Armstrong said with a sigh, whether of exasperation or resignation, I wasn't sure, "I've followed Vickie for years. She has terrible pulmonary function. It wouldn't take much to tip her over. I wouldn't try her on anything like this until she stops smoking."

"But—"

"Dr. Johnson, what would you have to say if Vickie tried IL-2 and wound up in the ICU on a ventilator?"

"Both the oncologist and Dr. Jones's office don't think that will happen," I repeated. "Besides, all I'm asking is whether you'd be willing to try. You can start Vickie at an even lower dose than what they recommend if you want."

By suggesting a dosage, I had overstepped, and now I painfully realized how presumptuous I must sound. I could hear from Armstrong's harsh tone as he replied that he was out of patience.

"Dr. Johnson," he said with brutal frankness, "Vickie is a country woman who has been infected for a long time. She has accepted the fact that she will die of AIDS. To give her false hope is wrong, very wrong. Why don't you leave her alone and let her die in peace?"

For a moment I couldn't answer, for at the mention of Vickie's death I was seized by a paroxysm of grief. I had just seen her, so warm and real, and now I had a vision of her slowly wasting, then being locked on a ventilator for pneumonia, three hundred miles away, unable to hear my pleas on the phone to stay alive until I got there. I moved the receiver away from my mouth, hoping that Armstrong wouldn't hear my sudden silent weeping. At last I recovered my voice enough to thank Armstrong for his time and say good-bye.

Was Dr. Armstrong right? Was I actually being reckless with Vickie's life? IL-2 had helped me, but it was still an experimental treatment. Nobody knew what the long-term effects might be, or whether Vickie and I would destroy our bodies trying to kill a virus that, so far, had eluded all efforts at eradication. Much as I resented Armstrong's counsel that I should let Vickie ''die in peace,'' I could understand the state of exhausted hopes that some AIDS doctors seemed to reach after seeing promising treatments fail again and again. But unlike Vickie and me, Armstrong wasn't on death row. To have any hope of survival—if it was possible, even to dream that our death sentences might be commuted—Vickie and I had to mount the best defense we could, no matter how risky.

So I realized that I could no longer be the passive bearer of treatment tidings. From now on I would have to take the reins of Vickie's treatment as I had my own. To do so, I would have to find a doctor who wasn't yet beaten down by the struggle, someone with the vigor to help Vickie fight.

But having excluded the NIH, Vanderbilt, and Dr. Armstrong, I was running out of options. My last hope was Beth Ann Jamison, now in private practice in internal medicine and AIDS care at St. Thomas Hospital, an affiliate of Vanderbilt. It was politically touchy for me to turn to her instead of our colleagues at the AIDS clinic, but I had no choice. Vickie had been disqualified from all of Vanderbilt's current drug trials, and it was far from certain when other treatments would become available. IL-2, which Vanderbilt wouldn't use until it was FDA-approved for HIV, was her only hope.

After rehearsing my plea, I called Beth Ann's office. It had been nearly a year since we'd talked, but she had kept abreast of my progress and now congratulated me on doing so well.

"Thank you," I said, "but I'm calling you about someone else."

I launched into Vickie's story, the nightmare she'd lived, the children she'd orphan if she died, the concerns I had about her neuropathy and use of DDC, and our struggle to get her some kind of treatment before her immune system deteriorated beyond repair.

Beth Ann asked why I didn't get Jim Stevens to treat Vickie, and I explained his reluctance. "I see," she said. "Well, why don't you fax me over the protocols and any new articles you have? I'm not promising anything until I study the treatment. But if I do give Vickie IL-2, I'll want to do it in the hospital so we can watch her carefully. Would she be willing to go along with that?"

"Sure, anything," I said, knowing that I could convince Vickie. I quickly faxed over the information. The next morning Beth Ann called me back, sounding cheerful. She planned to check with the NIH and consult other colleagues, but she would give Vickie a chance on IL-2.

Vickie was elated at the news, but then grew a little nervous when she began to think over the possible dangers and side effects.

"Do I really have to go in the hospital?"

"I'm afraid so. But it won't be so bad. I'll come and stay with you."

"It may take me a while to find someone to look after the kids."

"Beth Ann said that you could come anytime."

"Well," Vickie said with new hope in her voice. "Well, then let's go for it!"

CHAPTER 26

———————— ∞ ————————

MY STAUNCH FRIENDS, the Archangels, had applauded my relationship with Vickie, recognizing that in caring for her and being
nurtured in return, I was edging from introversion toward sociabil-
ity and self-assurance, even regaining a sense of pleasure in life.

As Carol would say, "Nothing takes you out of yourself like
taking care of someone else. Someone who deserves it," she would
add, glancing away, not wanting to resurrect the memory of our
argument about Dawn.

She and Shannon and Bart had encouraged me in my frustrating dealings with Dr. Armstrong and would have rejoiced with me
now that I had succeeded in getting Vickie treated. But sadly,
during that spring and early summer, both Carol and Shannon
suffered terrible tragedies of their own.

Carol had called me early one morning in May, crying, "Mahlon, oh Mahlon, Craig got killed in a car crash!'' She had already lost one son, her oldest, so it seemed cruelly unfair that history was repeating itself. Worse yet, Craig was her soul child, who not only looked most like her but was closest to her in temperament. It was an unimaginable loss. Carol was sobbing, gasping, choking out ''I can't believe it'' over and over. ''I just can't believe it would happen to me again.''

''What can I do? Can I help? Do you want me to come over?'' I asked.

''No,'' she said. ''Thanks. We're about to leave for Georgia, where Craig died, to straighten things out. But could you tell Shannon and also Bart, when he gets home? I don't know when I'll get to talk to them.''

''I will, don't worry. We'll all be sending you our love,'' I said, and then she was gone, leaving me with a droning dial tone.

I tried calling Shannon, but I couldn't reach her or find out how to contact Bart. I kept trying, but I was very shaken by Carol's news. I had been plotting to rescue Vickie and myself from death, as if it were something I could control; and this accident, this appallingly random occurrence—lightning striking the same family twice—seemed to reveal to me my helplessness and my hubris.

Now I began to obsess about my need to control our treatment, wondering miserably if my blind faith that Vickie and I could stay alive was a delusion. I had gotten my counts up, and my viral load was seemingly negligible, but could these encouraging signs be merely the eye of the hurricane? HIV was nearly always lethal, as far as anyone knew. Were Stevens and the others just indulging me in my belief that I might save my life, and Vickie's, unwilling to rob a dying man of hope? Were my colleagues seeing me as a maverick who would try anything that showed the slightest promise? Were they afraid to tell me about new treatments for fear I'd try something unproven that might cause my demise? Or had they begun to think of me as a pest, an arrogant threat—a pathologist insisting on learning as much about early HIV treatment as they knew? And for what? Carol's loss of her son was proof of the uncertainty of life, a reality that I had been doing my best to deny.

"You're just depressed by Carol's news," I told myself. But I was still wrestling with dark thoughts when I spoke to Vickie that night. She was saddened by Carol's tragedy and commiserated with my inability to come up with a way to comfort her. "I don't know how Carol will ever be able to get over the deaths of two sons," I said. "But look at you, at all you've been through. You're not even bitter."

"Well, I guess I used to be," Vickie said. "I used to think that I had gotten more than my fair share of bad things in life. But then I stopped."

"But how did you stop?" I wondered, wanting to know for Carol's sake and for my own.

"I figured that somehow I had to focus on the future, on making things better for my kids, at least for as long as I could. And when my time was up, it was up."

"Oh, Vickie . . ."

"Really. We don't know how bad death is, because we don't know what comes after death. But we do know that suffering is bad. Clyde suffered. And if Carol's boy had to die, I'm glad he could die quickly and not be in pain day after day. That's the worst thing, watching somebody you love be in so much pain over such a long time and not being able to relieve their agony. Quick death is a mercy. And so if I could die without suffering—and if I've done all I can for the kids and for you—then maybe it won't be so bad."

As much as her words—simple but eminently wise—Vickie's quiet conviction comforted me. How much easier and more natural it would be, after witnessing Clyde's suffering, for Vickie to succumb to fear. Again I marveled at her ability to stay focused on the positive even when tangled almost inextricably in a web of trouble. By the time we said good-night, my dark mood had lifted.

A minute after I hung up the phone, it rang again, and I assumed it was Vickie calling back with another reassuring thought. But it was Shannon, who had just returned from visiting her mother in eastern Tennessee.

"Did you get my message at work?" I asked.

"No, not yet. I'm calling you for another reason. I'm really worried about my mom."

Shannon's mother had been losing weight, and a visit to the family doctor revealed mild abdominal distension from fluid. So she had an MRI, which showed an ovarian mass and liver abnormalities, the telltale signs of ovarian cancer.

"Oh, Shannon," I said. "You're going to bring her to Nashville for treatment, aren't you? She should come right away."

"I want to," she told me in a shaky voice. "But I don't know too many of the oncologists personally. Will you help me find Mom a really good doctor?"

"Of course," I assured her, and offered to help her research the treatment options.

"What were you calling me about?" Shannon now asked. I hated to burden her with more bad news, but I had made a promise to Carol. So I explained about Carol's son. Shannon broke down and wept.

Bart, meanwhile, had gotten the news from Carol's husband, and planned to drive back to Nashville from Texas, where he was working, to be with Carol when she returned from Georgia. But when he heard that Shannon's mother would be in Nashville—and why—he got someone to cover his route and came back a few days earlier. He and Jo, Shannon's mother, had a history. Whenever he was on the road and passed within reach of her home in eastern Tennessee, he'd stop by for a meal and to ferret out amusing anecdotes from Shannon's childhood that he would strategically deploy when they would embarrass Shannon the most.

Bart was eager to visit Shannon's mother, who was now in the hospital, but his pickup truck wouldn't start, so he called me to ask for a ride. I was happy to oblige, if only to get the chance to witness the hilarious banter that I'd heard Bart and Jo shared.

When we got to Jo's room, Bart poked his head in the door, unleashing his gravelly laugh.

"Mom, your boyfriend is here," Shannon said.

"Some boyfriend I am," Bart retorted as we entered. "I never come to see you anymore."

"You don't hear me complaining," Jo joked weakly from where she lay. Shannon had repeatedly told me how tough her mother was, a stoic fighter who, whatever happened, refused to complain.

"Mom, this is Mahlon," Shannon said. "I've told you about Mahlon."

"Oh yes." She reached out a warm, bony hand to shake mine. "It's nice to meet you." She nodded toward the bedside chair, so I sat down.

Though drawn by her illness, Jo was still a handsome woman with huge soulful brown eyes and a dreamy smile. In her face I could see the ravages of a cancer that burned more calories than her tiny body could provide. Since I had never met her, I didn't know what to expect, but clearly her changed appearance distressed Bart. Uncharacteristically, he lost his composure and began to clown, flopping down next to Jo on the bed. A contorted frown gripped his face as he tried to suppress a sob. "You look beautiful as ever," he told Jo, a tear rolling down his cheek. Jo smiled, as though to reassure him, and he responded by stroking her thinned gray hair.

"You better be careful. I got into trouble once that way," Shannon said to ease the sadness.

"What happened?" I asked.

There was a certain AIDS patient, one of many she'd befriended, whom Shannon shopped for and visited in her spare time. One evening when she dropped off his groceries, Shannon found the man in bed, body aching, needing a massage. So, climbing under the covers, she began to rub his neck, and just then his grandmother unexpectedly arrived. "I've never seen someone so embarrassed and excited in all my life." Shannon laughed. "I'm sure she thought the guy had finally turned straight at the end of his life."

Bart and Jo burst out laughing at the story, and Shannon and I joined in. "I can't believe you never told me that one, Shannon," Bart said indignantly. "I can't wait to repeat it. I just love that story!"

Now Jo turned to me, and giving her hand a squeeze, I asked what her oncologist's treatment plan was. Shannon outlined the possibilities—cis-platinum and maybe Taxol with Marinol, the marijuana derivative that was an antinausea drug.

"Oh, boy, we'll all come by for a little of that," Bart said.

"Well, only if you get here in time," Jo replied. "I'm expecting some other visitors."

"Oh really?" Bart asked. "Like who?"

Shannon smirked. "That painter who's been visiting her—he's coming, isn't he, Mom?"

"Well, I don't know. He says so."

"Oh, that guy," Bart said, feigning disgust. "That guy is just too young for you."

"Well, he's not half as young as that wild thing you brought by the last time you came through," Jo shot back.

All eyes turned to Bart. "And who might that be?" Shannon inquired.

"I don't know what she's talking about," Bart protested, looking innocent.

"Is that the one who hugged you and accidentally bruised your ribs?" I asked naively.

"What?" Shannon howled, delighted to have the goods on Bart.

He looked at me, horrified. "Who told you about that?"

"Maybe it was me," Jo teased.

We all laughed again, and after we quieted down, Jo turned to me again. "Shannon says you're doing really well. She says she thinks you're pulling through."

"I'm doing everything I can."

"If it works, your treatment, will you be the first one in the world to beat it?"

To encourage her, I replied that all I could do was fight and not worry about the future. She nodded. Then I picked up a stuffed frog that someone had sent Jo. "These things can be therapeutic, too, you know."

"I realize that," she said. "But I kissed it and nothing happened."

"I'd keep trying," I told her. "You never know."

Jo laughed, but it was clear that she was tiring. With a glance, Bart and I told each other it was time to leave. "I'm betting on you," I said to Jo in parting.

"For me, I'm afraid, it's going to take a miracle," she whispered back. "So I'm betting on you."

I left the hospital heartbroken at what Shannon's wonderfully spirited mother was facing, for ovarian cancer at her stage was often fatal. Still brooding, when I got home I was surprised to find a message from Carol waiting on my machine. Shannon had heard from her, I knew, with condolences about Jo, but Carol had asked that no one be told she had returned. She still needed a few days to herself.

I called her immediately and was encouraged by the awe in her voice. "I've got to tell you something, Mahlon," she said.

"What is it?" I prayed that perhaps there had been some mistake and that her son was still alive.

"The most amazing thing happened. You just won't believe it."

When the news of her son came, Carol had mass-mailed a single message to all the people with AIDS whom she'd been counseling on the Internet. She'd wanted them to know that she'd be unavailable for a while since she'd be in Georgia collecting her son's body. The response from her clients was swift and overwhelming.

By the time Carol returned, her mailbox was stuffed with care packages of food and beautifully written condolence cards. Her answering machine was filled with messages from local florists who had phone-ordered arrangements on hold, waiting to be delivered. Her E-mail address was deluged with notes from well-wishers. And then, out of the blue, two men with AIDS from Texas, whom she had counseled on-line but had never met, appeared on her doorstep. Neither of them was healthy, but they had driven all the way to Nashville to see her in person and to do whatever they could to help out. They had insisted on cleaning her house, doing her grocery shopping, and cooking her meals. "Right now I have so much food in my refrigerator and freezer that we could all live for the next year!" she exclaimed. "And, believe me, my house has never been so clean!"

"That is amazing," I said, touched by the poignant image of two emaciated men listing through Carol's home like an infirm whirlwind.

"And you know what, Mahlon?" Carol was saying. "If this hadn't happened to me, if Craig hadn't died, I never would've believed that people had this kind of capacity for generosity—that it was possible to receive such an outpouring of love from strangers."

"It's like a miracle," I had to agree.

CHAPTER 27

———— ∞ ————

IT SEEMED THAT bad luck was dogging Vickie's trip to Nashville for her first IL-2 treatment. The day before her departure, her trusted baby-sitter was injured in a car accident, and so Vickie had to call on her twenty-four-year-old niece to pinch-hit and look after the kids. But since her niece got off from work at the same time school let out, Vickie would have to worry whether she'd reach home before disputes broke out between the bossy Danielle and the stubbornly independent Clyde Jr.

"Well, try to forget that for a while," I said as we sat in Beth Ann's waiting room, ducking the curious stares of a woman weighed down by gold bracelets. She seemed torn between the pictures in her *People* magazine and us, a real-live tableau. "You're here, and all you have to think about is how well I know you're going to do."

I'd made it a point to talk frankly with Clyde Jr. and Danielle about Vickie's risk of pulmonary problems, while stressing the potential lifesaving benefits of IL-2. And yet I could tell by their polite yet disengaged responses that nothing I said, no matter how hopeful, would alleviate their fears. Privately they'd confided to their mother that they were afraid for her to go so far away to try an experimental treatment. To them, after all, she seemed perfectly healthy. Why, they asked, would she take a drug and run the risk of hurting herself?

The doorway to the exam room swung open and there stood Beth Ann, smiling radiantly. She had cut her hair shorter since I'd last seen her, and there were more streaks of gray in it. But before even saying hello to me, she headed for Vickie with her hand extended.

"It's an honor to meet you," Beth Ann said. "I read *My Own Country* when it came out, so I almost feel like I know you." Vickie laughed shyly, embarrassed by the compliment. Now, I could see, we had the gold-braceleted woman's undivided attention.

Patting my shoulder, Beth Ann greeted me warmly, then grabbed Vickie by the hand. "Come with me," she said. "Mahlon, let Vickie and me talk for a moment."

An eternity of fifteen minutes passed, during which I prayed that Vickie wouldn't say anything that might discourage Beth Ann from going through with the treatment. At last Beth Ann returned alone to request some documentation we'd brought along. By then the bracelet-laden woman had been summoned into the office, so we could talk freely about my experience with IL-2. "That's just great," Beth Ann said when I told her that for nine months straight I'd managed to keep my CD4 count average well above 1,000.

Beth Ann invited me back to the examining room, where

Vickie sat nervously, combing her fingers through her hair. "I thought I'd tell the two of you together," Beth Ann said. "I think we can begin the treatment." Vickie and I just grinned at each other with relief.

"But I want to proceed very cautiously," Beth Ann continued. "We'll start with an intermediate dose and administer it for four days rather than the usual five. I'll monitor you very carefully, Vickie, to make sure that you're tolerating the drug. If you are, we can increase the dosage toward the end of the treatment. So, are you ready to check in to the hospital?"

"Sure!" Vickie said.

Much to Vickie's chagrin, St. Thomas's had a rule that patients admitted to the hospital from a physician's office had to be transported by wheelchair. Vickie resisted this, but finally allowed me to push her to her room.

"Hell, I'm healthier than most of the people walking around here," she said in disgust as she settled herself in the metal contraption and I began to wheel her along.

"Shush," I admonished. "The nuns run this place, and they'll throw our butts out if they hear you cussing."

Vickie reached back and took my hand and squeezed it.

A small wooden cross graced the wall in Vickie's room, which, it struck me, looked very much like Jo's. Jo was dying now, wasting away, devoured by another illness that our best drugs couldn't stop. The grim thought crossed my mind that if we couldn't stop cancer, how could we ever hope to fight AIDS? Impatient with myself, I suppressed the question, reminding myself that Vickie and I were here in the hospital on a mission of hope.

I turned to find Vickie staring raptly at the IV pole. "What are you thinking?" I asked.

She gave me a smirk. "I was wondering where the back door was."

"Are you scared?"

She shrugged. "I don't know what to expect. So, yeah."

"Well, at least you're in the hospital, in case there are any complications."

"Just so long as they don't give me the wrong drug."

"They won't, don't worry. Anyway, I'm going to be here, looking out for you."

Just then the nurse arrived with a bag of saline and a clear bag of IL-2. She gently suggested that Vickie put on her nightgown and get into bed before she started the IV. Vickie headed to the bathroom to change, and when she emerged, I said, "You know, you're not bound to go through with this. You can back out right now if you want to."

Bemused, Vickie looked at me. "Mahlon, I've come all this way. Why would I back out now?"

"I just want you to know that you can. You won't be disappointing me or Beth Ann or anyone else if you change your mind."

"Thank you for saying that, Mahlon," she replied. Then she told the nurse, "He's more nervous than I am." She rolled up her sleeve. "I'm ready. Let's get a move on."

At first Vickie's forearm presented a challenge to the nurse, who had trouble finding a vein. "Maybe I should take this as a sign, what do you think?" Vickie joked after the third misplaced stick. I had winced with every one, but Vickie had remained sanguine, suspecting that the nurse was embarrassed. "Look," Vickie said finally, "I've had IVs put in before. I was a problem last time. But don't worry, I know you'll get it."

The nurse managed to find a vein on the next attempt, in-

serted the catheter, and taped it smoothly. "Well, here goes nothing," Vickie said as the nurse bled the IL-2 solution into the IV
line.

"So, what should I expect to feel?" she asked me.

"You'll see. All I can say is that sometime after twenty-four to
forty-eight hours, I felt really achy. And by seventy-two hours I
didn't want to get out of bed. We'll have to watch your blood
pressure, because the drug tends to lower it. And we'll have to
keep an eye on your lungs to make sure you're not getting any fluid
accumulation. That's the most dangerous possibility. But don't
worry. I'm ready to man the cutoff valve at the first sign of a bad
reaction."

Vickie laughed. I sat in the chair next to her, holding her hand
as the drug dripped into her vein. I'd offered to turn the television
on for her, but she shook her head. "Lord, I'm tired of that idiot
box. It's always on at my house."

"Can't you get the kids to turn it off?"

"If they don't watch television, they'll bounce off the walls. I
hate the TV noise but I prefer it to the sound of all their bickering
and banging." She paused for a moment and then said, "You
know, this quiet is awfully nice. Too bad I had to go into a hospital
to get it."

Four hours after the infusion began, a male nurse knocked on
the door, then pushed it open slowly, with a wary glance at the
infectious precautions sticker posted on the outside. Pulling on his
latex gloves, he announced his intent to check Vickie's vital signs as
well as the infusion site. After ascertaining that the infusion was
going smoothly, he solemnly took Vickie's temperature and pulse
and checked her blood pressure. "Hmmm," he said, "your blood
pressure's . . ." He held back, supercilious, assuming we

wouldn't fully understand. "What is it?" I demanded, and he told me. To our relief, it hadn't changed. We could hardly wait until he left the room to start laughing at his imperious routine.

Suddenly, the phone rang, a jarring, clanging, disconcerting sound. Hoping it was Beth Ann, I lunged to take the call.

"Let me speak to Ma!" Danielle screamed.

"What's wrong?" I asked, keeping my voice calm. But Danielle kept demanding to talk to her mother.

Rolling her eyes, Vickie reached for the phone. In her deep, patient voice, she quizzed Danielle, trying to extract the facts from Danielle's hysterical rambling.

"Go get Clyde. I want to hear his side. . . . No, Danielle, *go get Clyde,*" Vickie said with a firmness that seemed to work. Then she covered the receiver and looked up at me. "You won't believe it—they're trying to kill each other. Danielle pissed off Clyde. She tried to drag him into the house by using a stranglehold. Now he's threatening to run away."

"But where's your niece?"

"She called the police—can you believe that? Now she's outside waiting for the cops to come and break up the fight."

"Why did she call the police?"

"God only knows . . . she can't handle the kids, I guess. Oh, Mahlon, I can't believe this is happening now!" Vickie was growing tearful with frustration. "Of course, I know why they're acting up. They're just afraid something's going to happen to me."

"Let me try to talk to Clyde," I said, taking the phone. "It's important for you to relax." In the background I could hear a commotion, a man's stern voice, and Danielle ordering Clyde to the phone.

"Hey, Clyde," I said when he finally got on, "what's going on over there? Are you okay?"

"Danielle tried to choke me," he raged. "Where's my mom?"

"She's right here."

"Is she okay?"

"She's doing just fine. Now, what's all this about a fight?"

Clyde started to catalog his complaints about his sister, and I listened closely, injecting only an occasional "Hmmm." When he paused, I said carefully, "Clyde, there's something your mother really needs right now. She needs to have you be the man of the house."

"Oh, yeah?"

"Yes. You've got to take care of things until she gets back. Otherwise she's going to worry and not get the most out of her treatment."

"Has she started it yet?"

"Yep, and she's doing great, much better than I did when I took it."

"She's really okay?"

I reassured him again and then put Vickie on the phone so he could hear for himself that she was fine. After she soothed him, Vickie told him to get her niece, whom she directed to apologize to the police and then send them away.

After hanging up, Vickie leaned back in bed with a weary sigh. "Are you all right?" she said to me.

"Am I all right?"

"This is what having kids is all about. Do you still wish you had some?"

"Sometimes."

"Come stay with me a few weeks and I'll definitely cure you of it. Though, you know," she said, "this is the first time I've ever been away from them. I can't blame them for being upset."

"It's not like you went on vacation. You went into the hospital for a treatment that may keep you healthy longer—keep you healthy for them."

"I know, and I've got to do this whether they understand or not. I just don't have a choice."

I stayed with Vickie for another half hour and then gave her a good-night kiss. On my way out of the hospital, I stopped at a pay phone and called Clyde Jr., to reassure him once again that his mother was doing well and to assure myself that everything was still calm in Kingsport.

Thursday was day two of Vickie's treatment. At seven o'clock in the morning, sure that Vickie would be awake, I called her room. She had slept peacefully, apart from a four A.M. checkup by the nurses. The fever and aches caused by IL-2 hadn't set in yet. "I'm okay so far," she reassured me.

"Just you wait," I said.

Having arranged to take the afternoon off, I worked all morning and hurried over to St. Thomas Hospital at lunchtime. By then Vickie had called home and was relieved to hear that the kids had settled down. "I hate to think what they'll be serving us for lunch," she said. "From what I've seen so far, I don't much care for this hospital food."

"It's all cooked by nuns," I told her.

"I don't believe you."

"Well, luckily we won't have to eat it. I've come prepared." I closed the door to Vickie's room. In violation of hospital rules,

I'd stopped at a famous Nashville deli and bought two overstuffed beef sandwiches and a couple of Coca-Colas.

I opened my briefcase and showed Vickie my bounty. "Oh, my God, how did you know that's what I wanted? You angel!" she exclaimed.

At first Vickie's appetite seemed to be fine, but right after she finished eating her sandwich, her eyes turned glassy and she turned pale. "I don't feel so good all of a sudden," she said.

"You don't look so good either," I told her.

"I wonder if I ate the sandwich too quickly. Or maybe it's the drug. Do you think it could be the drug?"

Then she started to cough. I asked if she was all right and she nodded, although she couldn't answer. I made her sit up straighter and started rubbing her back. When the coughing continued, I pushed the buzzer for the nurse, then dug out Beth Ann's number. But by the time the nurse arrived, Vickie's coughing fit had passed. "So, what's going on here?" the nurse said, taking Vickie's blood pressure and listening to her lungs with a stethoscope.

"I feel like I'm going to vomit," Vickie said.

The nurse examined her further. "You seem fine to me. Your lungs certainly sound pretty clear." Then her brow wrinkled with suspicion and she peered at both of us with mock severity. "I could swear I smell deli food."

Vickie and I just laughed and tried to look innocent.

By Friday morning, day three of her treatment, Vickie had become achy and tired but had no other noticeable side effects. "For heaven's sake, Mahlon," she told me, "you said that this drug is so terrible, but so far this is pretty much of a breeze."

It concerned me that she was feeling so well. Beth Ann had prescribed a cautious dosage that, relative to Vickie's weight, was probably lower than the dosage I was taking, and I worried that Vickie might not be getting enough of the drug to stimulate her weakened immune system. I knew, too, that about half of the patients with counts as low as Vickie's didn't respond to IL-2 at all. So when I got back to my office, I called Beth Ann, who assured me that Vickie was getting a high enough dosage to make a difference. "Remember, Mahlon, we planned this primarily as a trial run," she said. "Let's meet in her room this afternoon and evaluate how she's doing."

When we arrived, Vickie was sitting up in bed, seemingly unfazed by the treatment. "Doesn't Vickie look great for someone who's been on IL-2?" Beth Ann remarked. "How are you feeling? Anything unusual since this morning?"

Vickie shrugged and looked at me. "I think Mahlon made too big a deal out of the side effects."

Beth Ann laughed and said that the drug produced more side effects in some people than in others. After examining Vickie and looking at her chart, Beth Ann said, "You're doing so well, I think you can tolerate a higher dose, especially since tomorrow is your final day. Are you ready for that?"

"I'm up for anything," Vickie said.

Because the IL-2 dosage was being elevated, I planned to stay with Vickie for her entire last day, Saturday, to make sure that there were no complications. The nurse, now Vickie's bosom pal, came in with a new IV bag full of IL-2 and swapped it with one that was nearly deflated. "Stick around, don't go too far," Vickie joked with her nervously. "In case I catch on fire."

After an hour on the higher dosage, Vickie started to cough, just a little, a dry short cough. I searched her face for any signs of troubled breathing, but she said she was all right. I stroked her hair for a while and then gave her a hand and foot massage. "You spoil me too much, Mahlon," she told me.

"You can't spoil anybody too much," I said.

"I guess I deserve to be spoiled after letting you talk me into this ordeal." Vickie laughed.

Another hour passed, and the nurse returned to check Vickie's vital signs. So far, so good—she didn't seem to be suffering any pulmonary congestion. Encouraged by her clean bill of health, Vickie said, "Mahlon, you know, I've been dying to go for a walk. I've been lying here for four days."

"You sure you feel up to it?"

"Hell, you went to the gym on your fourth day."

"That's true."

She put on her bathrobe, and with me pushing her IV pole, we strolled down the hallway of the hospital, negotiating the traffic, and ended up in a family waiting room that had a good view of the creek across the street. The sun was going down behind the hills. "Isn't that beautiful?" Vickie exclaimed. "I hate to admit it, but I'm kind of enjoying getting a break from my kids. I almost feel like I'm on vacation."

I was amazed at her nonchalance. I had first started taking IL-2 bimonthly, at only a slightly higher dose, and I'd come to dread the side effects. In fact, that was why I'd experimented with a monthly lower-dose regimen; the aches weren't as bad. But it just wasn't in Vickie's nature to acknowledge feeling miserable. She could find a silver lining in every cloud.

"I like talking to the nurses," she was saying. "I've gotten to know quite a few of them—comparing notes and so on. By the way," she added, "in case you haven't noticed it, a lot of nurses smoke."

"Believe me, I've noticed."

"I'm dying for one so bad I could taste it."

"That might not be such a good idea, especially now," I said, referring to the fact that her smoke-damaged lungs were particularly susceptible to complications with IL-2.

Vickie sighed. "I know. I wish I didn't like smoking as much as I do." Then she turned to me with a stubborn look on her face. "Then again, with everything I've had to deal with—kids and school and money problems and this damned virus—it's one of the few pleasures that I have."

I put my arm around her reassuringly. "I know what you're saying. Everybody has their vices," I said.

"Oh, yeah, and what are yours?"

I started to laugh. "You won't believe it, frozen yogurt."

"That's hardly a vice," Vickie said.

"To me it is. I love it. I eat too much of it every day."

Now Vickie turned to me, looking serious. "You know, Mahlon, I really appreciate what you've done for me, getting me in here for treatment. I hope you realize how grateful I am."

"I'm just being selfish. I want you to stick around."

"Still, you busted your ass. I should do something in return."

"Please," I said, "I just want you to stay well."

The last of the sun was slipping down behind the hill, and the whole family waiting room took on a burnt glow—except for the watery blue emanations of the unwatched yet blaring television.

"No, now you listen to me," Vickie said, pulling me close. "I'll make you a deal. I'll try to give up cigarettes, how's that? From here on in I quit. And that's not easy because I'm dying for one right now and I sure don't want to gain any of that weight back.''

''Tell you what,'' I said. ''If you're really serious about doing that, I'll sweeten the deal.''

''How will you do that?''

''If you give up smoking, I'll give up frozen yogurt.''

''You're on,'' she said, laughing.

CHAPTER 28

—— ∞ ——

THROUGHOUT MY CRUSADE to get Vickie established on some kind of treatment, I had, of course, continued my own IL-2 therapy, which meant constant monitoring of my viral load. To my amazement, not one of the tests I got between the autumn of 1994 and the spring of 1995 ever detected the presence of the virus in my blood—even the BDNA assay, which could pick up the virus concentrations as low as 1,000 copies per milliliter of blood. By the spring of 1995, an even more precise test had become available, called quantitative RNA PCR, which could uncover smatterings of virus as sparse as ten copies per milliliter of blood. So I sent along my samples for a quantitative RNA PCR analysis—and once again the virus was undetectable.

What could all these negative test results possibly mean? No one really knew; and I could hardly dare to hope that perhaps the combination of IL-2, DDI, and AZT that I was taking had actually vanquished the virus. It had to be lurking somewhere in my lymph system, I knew. So I called Jack Templeton, a friend and AIDS researcher at Duke University, who had offered to run another sensitive test, called CD8 depleted cell cultures, on my blood.

I could hear the excitement in his voice when he phoned me with the results. "Mahlon," he said, "this is the first time in recent memory that our lab has had trouble isolating virus from somebody infected with HIV. Admittedly, most of our patients have AIDS, but still . . ."

"Jack, what do you think is going on?"

"Well, you certainly have a low viral load," he said, choosing his words carefully. "That's great news."

By 1995, there had been a few reports of HIV-infected newborns who had apparently cleared all traces of the virus from their blood. The conjecture was that, unlike adults who were exposed to HIV and then slowly but belatedly developed antibodies to the virus, the babies had inherited their mothers' antibodies along with HIV, which gave them a head start at fighting back. But as far as I—and anyone I consulted—knew, nobody who contracted HIV later in life had been able to drive it out. Could that be what was happening with me?

"It would be interesting to have a Western Blot done now and compare it to one you had closer to the time you seroconverted," Jack said.

At that time, the Western Blot test was rarely repeated once an HIV infection was diagnosed. The feeling was that retesting was pointless, that once the antibodies developed, it would be next to impossible to get rid of them. Antibodies to such diseases as hepatitis B and syphilis can be detected in the blood for many years—even decades—after the illnesses themselves are cured, and so it was assumed that the antibodies to HIV would persist as well.

Yet, following Jack's suggestion, I went to have my Western Blot run yet again. As I fully expected, it came back positive, but on my last Western Blot, done in January 1995, seven antibody bands had shown up. Now two of those bands, the p35 and p65 bands, had completely disappeared, and a third, the p32 band, had grown so faint as to be deemed "indeterminate."

Startled, I called Jack right away with the results. I knew that he was too good a scientist to encourage me falsely with speculations, so I got excited when he seemed to consider all the findings significant. "Mahlon," he said, "I think you need to bring your case to the attention of David Ho."

Dr. David Ho was the director of the prestigious Aaron Diamond AIDS Research Lab in New York City. He had achieved international recognition for his pioneering work on the kinetics of HIV replication, and his group also studied unusual cases, such as long-term nonprogressors. I wasn't in that group, since my CD4 counts had progressively declined from 821 to 320 in the year and a half after my seroconversion. Nonetheless, Jack thought that my case would interest Dr. Ho enough that he gave me Ho's direct phone number. And indeed, Dr. Ho not only took my call but immediately offered to analyze my blood if I'd send it along with the details of my therapy.

If my results were that unusual, it struck me that I should check with Dr. Jones at the NIH, who had been kind enough to guide me into IL-2 therapy. When I described my course of treatment and my recent lab findings, Dr. Jones, too, asked for blood samples. Then he said, "Dr. Johnson, would you be willing to come up here for more tests at your earliest possible convenience?"

I was honored. Dr. Jones had shown me great consideration. I looked forward to meeting him and providing any samples they could use. I gratefully accepted his invitation—and now, for the very first time, I allowed myself to imagine that maybe, just maybe, I'd made some kind of breakthrough.

As THRILLED AS I was with my new, tentative hopes, I wasn't yet ready to share them with Vickie. In fact, beyond what I'd told her in our first phone conversation, I had never discussed my viral load with her. One reason was that, to date, no one had been able to venture a guess as to what my series of "undetectable" results meant. Clearly, according to my Western Blot, I was still infected, and so—low as my viral load seemed to be—presumably I was still capable of communicating the disease. The thought of inflicting the physical misery and psychic pain of HIV on another person absolutely horrified me—so much so that I never let anyone scavenge a taste of food off my plate. Once, I remember, when Carol was visiting my office, she asked for a swig off my open bottle of diet Dr Pepper. Since my mouth had touched it, I refused. She thought I was crazy, and perhaps I was. But that's how deep my fear ran.

The second reason that I didn't tell Vickie my news was simply that our relationship was too important to me to rock the boat. Our bond was strong, but it was still relatively new and untested; and our illness and shared quest for treatment had been the crucible that forged it. If my HIV status changed—and I couldn't dare to think it had, except as a fantasy—she might no longer see me as a comrade in arms, might no longer trust me to help her. Worse yet, perhaps she'd assume that I would abandon her for the blissful world of the uninfected, as I had feared Dawn would.

Vickie would have good news of her own to celebrate, I hoped. When I finally got her pre- and post-IL-2 blood test results, I was almost afraid to open the envelope. As it turned out, my fears about her deterioration after stopping DDC seemed warranted— her pre-IL-2 CD4 count proved to be an unnerving 203 (20 percent), perilously close to AIDS. But I was surprised and delighted to see that her viral load before therapy was only 280 copies per milliliter, an extremely low level that remained unchanged after the IL-2 treatment. Mercifully, the drug wasn't making her worse. We'd know if it was making her better when we checked her CD4 counts in a few weeks.

Though Dr. Armstrong had refused to collaborate on the IL-2 treatment, he had agreed to do Vickie's follow-up lab work. At last the telltale results came in, and Vickie called me, sounding a little down.

"My count's three fifty-five. Is that okay?"

"What's your percent?"

"Let's see . . . twenty percent."

"That's not bad at all."

"But you got a much bigger jump, didn't you?"

"Remember, we had to be cautious the first time," I reassured her. "Now at least you know you can take IL-2 safely and respond."

"Hmmm," Vickie said, not wholly convinced. "So the next IL-2 treatment should tell the real story, right? Maybe next time there'll be a much bigger improvement."

I was touched by her determination and hope. "We'll have to see," I said to encourage her. "But there should be."

CHAPTER 29

September 1995. Washington, D.C.

A skycap, watching the limousines stuck in traffic, gestured with his head when I asked him where to get the NIH shuttle. Unsure of what this signal meant, I asked another skycap I saw leaning over the guardrail, who acted as if the NIH shuttle were either unmentionable or irrelevant. Perhaps to him critically ill patients didn't rate in a world of foreign dignitaries.

Finally I found the appointed spot, and soon a dirty white van pulled up, piloted by a muscular black driver wearing jeans. With dignified gentility, he opened the side doors and ushered us in, four pilgrims on the road to Oz. Besides me, there was a bald, broad-shouldered man wearing a Marine's jacket and accompanied by a beautiful woman who looked thirty-five years his junior. I couldn't help stealing a few glances at her tight jeans and clinging green sweater earlier, on the sidewalk, but stopped when I spotted her huge diamond ring. Now I heard her call the ex-Marine "Dad" and risked giving her a smile. She smiled back warmly, seemingly unoffended by my attention. The fourth passenger was a slightly rotund woman with a closed, sunken right eye socket who nonetheless seemed quite cheerful.

"My name's Sheila," she announced sunnily. "I'm from Alabama."

"We're the Jacksons. We're from New Orleans," said the beautiful young woman.

"Have you been to the NIH before?" the one-eyed woman asked.

"Yes, my father was treated for leukemia there three years ago. He's been in remission." The daughter put her arm around the ex-Marine, seeming proud of his toughness.

"So, you're going back just for follow-up?" the older lady inquired.

"No. They think Dad may have a recurrence now."

"Well, I'm going back for more chemo and IL-2." The one-eyed woman sounded quite chipper, as though she hadn't quite taken in the daughter's ominous news. Or maybe she was just indefatigably upbeat. From the looks of her recessed socket, I surmised that she had lost the eye to cancer, and I shuddered to imagine the whopping doses of IL-2 she must be getting. "Did you have an ocular melanoma?" I asked her, speaking for the first time.

She screwed up her one good eye at me. "How did you know?"

I explained that it was just a guess, since IL-2 was sometimes used for melanoma.

"So, how do you know so much about IL-2?"

Now seven eyes were trained on me, not so much with suspicion but with curiosity, for I was the only one in this ad hoc traveling support group who had revealed nothing of his story. "I'm a doctor," I said, and left it at that. The answer seemed to satisfy them.

By now we were well on our way to Maryland, and the driver, only half listening to our conversation, butted in to tell us he was taking the scenic route. We wound along the Potomac River, where rowing sculls glided along the surface like water spiders. As the spires of a cathedral came into view, the ex-Marine's daughter confided that she'd been diagnosed with breast cancer two years before. Her prognosis was good, since she'd had localized disease and negative lymph nodes. Then the one-eyed woman described her past surgery and pending therapy with an enthusiasm that seemed untainted by the trauma and pain she had undoubtedly suffered.

"My husband always wants to come with me but I won't let him," she added with a laugh. "You know how it is. When you're that sick, you don't want nobody mothering you."

"I know what you mean," the daughter said. "My father wouldn't leave my room when I had surgery."

I wondered where her mother was—if, besides coping with their own illnesses, this father and daughter had already had to weather her death. The ex-Marine sat quietly, watching the Potomac the whole time, as if possessed of a quiet confidence that he could deal with whatever awaited him.

As we rounded a bend, I could see a distant glimpse of the Washington Monument, a reminder that we had just left the capital of the most powerful country on earth. And I couldn't help wondering why we had spent all our energy on technologies of destruction rather than on those that preserved life. Surely a country that could reach the moon and develop atomic bombs could find a cure for cancer, or for any other disease, if it had the will to do so.

Our route was now lined with the baronial estates of the Maryland gentry, and the lady from Alabama interrupted my musing. "My goodness, how much do you think these places cost?"

"Oh, Lordy, a bundle, near a million, I guess," our driver said, faking a plantation accent. We all laughed.

Finally we pulled up to the entrance of a twelve-story building of smoked glass and brick that could have passed for a suburban office plaza or a computer center rather than a hospital. But, for all of us, it was the veritable Emerald City, the premier medical center in the country, which, despite dismal salaries, employed many of our nation's preeminent scientists—the wizards we hoped could give us a heart or a brain or courage or a way to get home to Kansas.

To the left of the outpatient registration desk stood a huge aquarium filled with black angelfish the size of Frisbees. This scene of captivity—in this shrine where people came to be liberated from their diseases—at first seemed perverse to me. But as I watched them, the fish were so mesmerizing that I was sure that they had soothed many an agitated, fearful patient who had trekked across the country for treatment of a dark, incomprehensible disease.

I was fairly uneasy myself. So, as the registrar, a soft-spoken Asian man, reviewed the details of my life—now reduced to addresses, insurance numbers, and a living will—I tried to slip in the fact that I was a physician who was just visiting to give blood for some experiments, not someone who had to be processed like a regular patient. The registrar seemed to recognize my state of disquiet; no doubt he'd seen it countless times before. Nodding knowingly, he completed my paperwork and with quiet tact wished me well.

My first step was the phlebotomy station, where I was to have blood drawn for various lab tests. There, in the open waiting area, I encountered an emaciated young man with a crew cut and three days' growth of beard. Nestled next to his bony leg was a carefully folded leather flight jacket. He sat alone thumbing slowly through a magazine as if that exercise required more energy than he could muster. He looked at me and smiled sheepishly, as though embarrassed to be in the predicament he was in. I was sure that predicament was AIDS.

After my blood work, I was directed to Clinic 8, on the eighth floor, where cutting-edge research was being done on AIDS. Its waiting room was graced with floor-to-ceiling windows offering a panorama of the pine trees and parking lots of the NIH campus. As I gazed out the windows at the antlike scientists coming in to work, I overheard a nurse talking to two healthy-looking fellows seated near a cooler full of soft drinks. "The thalidomide has been sedating for the people who have tried it, but that's the only side effect," she was saying.

I turned around, hoping to learn more, suspecting that she was talking about the latest way to block some of the side effects of IL-2. The NIH had, after all, pioneered the treatment.

"You guys on IL-2?" I asked.

"I was for a while," one told me. "I'm just starting up again." His manner seemed circumspect, as if my question was intrusive. I suppose it was, but there so much I wanted to learn. Still, if he was going to be cautious, so would I, saying, "I've heard that some people do amazingly well on IL-2."

"Yeah," he said. "I was on it for six months, and my count went to three thousand."

"Three thousand?" I looked at him in disbelief. "What did you start with?"

"About five hundred."

"Do you know how long you've been infected?"

"Probably since sometime around 1988."

I'd read about a patient who had shown an exaggerated response to IL-2, and now realized that I was talking to him. No wonder he had such an air of excitement. He was like a boy eagerly waiting to open his presents on Christmas.

A slim physician with graying hair and wire-rimmed glasses hurried through the room. From pictures, I was sure this was the famous Clifford Lane, who'd developed the studies on IL-2 treatment for HIV patients. He embraced the two men I'd been talking to as if they were old college buddies visiting from out of town. I watched in awe as he hurried off down the hall until a nurse collared him and, with a furtive whisper, glanced at me. Lane spun around and came back.

"Dr. Johnson?" he asked. I stood up. "Cliff Lane," he said, shaking my hand vigorously. "We're so glad you could come up."

"Why, thank you. It's an honor to meet you," I answered, meaning it. "I can't thank you enough for your work. It may not be the whole solution but it's sure given me some hope."

"Good luck to you," he said. "Sorry, but I'm running late for a meeting." And with that, Lane raced off again, leaving me standing, a little dazzled, in his wake.

I turned toward the other two men, hoping to resume our conversation and find out more about the elusive Clifford Lane. But they had moved away from me, perhaps discomfited by hearing me addressed as "Dr." They probably thought that I was there to do research, not to seek help for the same problem they had. And so they closed ranks against me, a supposed emissary from the world of the uninfected.

Fortunately, a nurse soon arrived to usher me into the sanctum of Dr. Jones. I found him surrounded by mounds of papers, data sheets, and a computer in a small room the size of a closet. He was a square-jawed man with a robust build who seemed somewhat younger than Dr. Lane; I put him to be around forty. He didn't look up from his work until the nurse cleared her throat, startling him, and said, "This is Dr. Johnson."

"Oh, come in, come in."

As he rose to greet me, I began to thank him for his research. He accepted my compliments modestly while protesting that no one yet knew if IL-2 would do any long-term good. "That's the question—can it really make a difference over time?" he told me. "But at least we're seeing that, at our doses, it doesn't seem to do any harm."

"But there's more to this than long-term survival," I found myself saying. "Psychologically, it means a lot to walk around with a CD4 count of a thousand."

He smiled.

Still a bit in awe, I asked about his career, and we began talking about our medical training, how we'd each ended up where we were. We talked as physicians, and as before I was grateful that he spoke to me as an equal, as a colleague. But when it came down to discussing my treatment, I clearly was a patient, which seemed to sadden him.

"You probably have some questions," he ventured.

I grinned at him. "You bet! Several."

He nodded. "So do I. I just wish we had more answers."

"So what do you think about my recent test results? Have you seen other people with negative blood cultures, BDNA and PCR tests that failed to detect virus, and weakening bands on the Western Blot? Is this just something that happens?"

"It's a bit unusual," he said cautiously. "But until now we haven't really been checking Western Blots over time."

Looking at me closely, he went on. "Dr. Johnson, there may come a day—sooner than we think—when HIV may become a chronic disease, something like diabetes, thanks to multidrug cocktails and immunotherapy."

"You think so?" I asked. I suspected that Dr. Jones was even more confident than he sounded, for doctors at the NIH had to be especially circumspect in their pronouncements, since they were held in such high regard. Then, too, most medical breakthroughs never quite lived up to their original promise. Cautious hopes had begun to crop up in the AIDS journals, hopes for a new era in which some lucky number of the infected could, for the first time, entertain the possibility of survival. Hearing these hopes articulated by somebody at the NIH, albeit with a note of caution, was elating.

"Any other questions?" Dr. Jones asked.

"I could use some advice about my friend, the country woman I talked with you about three months ago—you know, the Vickie McCray in *My Own Country*."

"Oh, yes. How's she doing?"

"It's hard to say. Her counts are up from two-oh-three, twenty percent, to three fifty-five and twenty percent while on AZT, after a trial of intravenous IL-2 for four days."

As he listened to the familiar data, Dr. Jones frowned, which worried me. "We've always treated for five days. You get a better effect with five days continuous infusion rather than four."

"I know. I guess we should have held out for five days but there were extenuating circumstances and the doctor was appropriately cautious the first time. Vickie has been a smoker up until now so we were worried about her bronchitis."

"Is she still?"

"She's given it up for the time being."

"That will help," Jones said. "So how did she actually do on that first infusion?"

I told him everything went fine, that there were no complications.

"Well, at least she seemed to respond," Jones said. "Which is good news, because, as you know, some people don't. In time, we may try to vary the dosages here, too."

Shaking hands, I said good-bye to Dr. Jones, who promised to call me when he got the results of all my blood work. He also suggested that I send blood to his lab in three months and then visit again in six.

I made my way to the shuttle bus stop. There, waiting on the bench, was the emaciated fellow with the flight jacket whom I'd seen at the phlebotomy lab earlier in the morning. He was tilting his head back to let the fall sunlight warm his face. To my relief, he didn't look so ill now and seemed in good spirits, undoubtedly in anticipation of going home.

Dropping my briefcase, I leaned against the bus stop sign, and he glanced up at me.

"Heading out?" I said.

"Yeah, at last. You going back to California?" he asked me.

"No. Nashville. I'm from Nashville."

"Oh. Sorry. You look like a guy I just met from California."

Savoring the hope I'd gleaned from my meeting with Dr. Jones, I wanted to offer whatever encouragement I could to this man who looked so much like a fellow HIV sufferer.

I couldn't, of course, ask him outright what he was being treated for, so I casually mentioned that I had just come from a hopeful session with Dr. Jones, the immunotherapy researcher. My surmise that the man had HIV was confirmed when he recognized Dr. Jones's name. Now he began to confide in me, telling me that he was part of a study being done on patients with uninfected twin siblings. "My brother was up here for almost a week. They gave me a bunch of his CD4 cells and put me on a new protease inhibitor to get my counts up. Then they tried me on IL-2."

I was fascinated to hear about the protocols. "You take the IL-2 okay?"

"Better than okay," he said. He'd arrived with CD4 counts of 50. Now his counts were up to 1,000.

"Whoa. That's incredible," I said.

"I know the jump in my counts is from my brother's cells," he said. "It probably won't last, but still . . ."

"It may last. IL-2 really helped my counts. We've got to be hopeful now."

The man smiled ruefully, acknowledging our common condition, our bond. "I'm trying. My wife is infected, too, though. She's not as far along as I am. Her counts are three hundred. Still, I'm worried about her, and I'm hoping I can get her on the same treatments."

I felt a warm rush of identification with the man. Not only was he the only other heterosexual male with HIV I had ever met, but he was trying to save his wife just as I was trying to save Vickie.

Wondering if he felt the same sense of isolation that I did, I asked him where he lived.

"In Wichita," he told me. He'd moved back there after taking disability from the navy, where he'd served as a fighter pilot. I asked him how AIDS was viewed in Kansas.

"We've had to keep it a secret," he explained with great sadness. "None of our neighbors know. I haven't even told my boys the whole thing. They just think I'm sick with some kind of cancer. I'm afraid of what their friends would do if they found out."

"How about medical care?"

"They're behind there, way behind. No one even knew about IL-2. I found out myself, calling that NIH Clinical Trials deal."

I marveled at his nerve. Even for me, a doctor, it had been a tremendous struggle to find out about all the latest treatments and to procure them for myself and Vickie. And yet this man, a Wichita-based pilot without my advantages of medical training and affiliation with a major research hospital, had somehow managed to claw his way to the cutting edge of treatment at the NIH. He must have been an incredible scrapper with an extraordinary will to live.

I began to tell him a little about my own situation—about my quest for treatments and my relationship with Vickie. Then, too soon, the shuttle bus arrived. Tacitly, we agreed not to continue such an intimate conversation in front of other people; and I could sense that, like me, he regretted the abrupt ending to our camaraderie.

His airline terminal came before mine, and as he prepared to disembark from the van—searching for his ticket, pushing down the bottle of pills that popped up in his duffel bag—we locked eyes in a moment of silent communication.

''See you at the NIH sometime,'' I said, hoping that I would, wondering at the last minute if I should invade his privacy by asking for a name and an address.

''Okay, see you then.'' He said good-bye with the same lingering reluctance as he stepped out of the van and slowly headed inside the gate.

CHAPTER 30

———— ∞ ————

VICKIE WAS SCHEDULED to receive IL-2 every two months. Just before she was due to come to Nashville for her second treatment, I received some excellent news from Kern McNeill, the distributors of 3TC. They were reexpanding the open label trial of the drug, which would be offered to patients with CD4 counts of 300 who couldn't tolerate or who weren't responding to FDA-approved anti-HIV treatments. I wasn't eligible, of course—my CD4 counts were too high—but the trial was tailor-made for Vickie, since her counts had averaged well below 300, since she couldn't take DDI or DDC, and since she had never responded well to AZT. Being on IL-2 wouldn't disqualify her because the treatment wasn't FDA-approved for HIV.

Vickie's data was already in the company's computer, so she

wouldn't even have to reapply for the trial, which was a relief because her last post-IL-2 count had been 355, slightly above the requirement of an average count of 300 in the past three months. Her counts had probably dropped in the interim, but we couldn't be sure.

"Let's just hope that the 3TC people don't ask for any preliminary blood work," Vickie said.

"I'll see what I can find out about trial rules," I promised.

So, when I scheduled Vickie's appointment with Madeline, I subtly fished for information on any lab work that would be required. The AIDS clinic had records of all Vickie's tests, except for the recent count after her IL-2 therapy. Since there was no telling which treatments would disqualify Vickie from future drug trials—and since I didn't think IL-2 would exclude her from the 3TC study—I hadn't mentioned it to Madeline at this point. So when she didn't rise to the bait and fill me in on the trial procedures, I didn't push it for fear that she would get suspicious.

I had arranged for Vickie to come to Nashville on a Friday, when she would be seen by Madeline and start 3TC. Over the weekend, her blood levels of 3TC could build to the therapeutic range, which would further protect her against the possible virus-boosting effects of IL-2, which she would begin taking the following Monday. When I picked her up from the airport, she looked better than I'd ever seen her, sporting an attractive new haircut and a glowing smile. We walked arm-in-arm out of the terminal to where my car was parked and headed directly for the AIDS clinic. As we sat down to wait beneath the memorial quilt, it struck me that I had first come to this clinic alone, then with Dawn, and now I was here with Vickie. It was as if I was a little boy who kept bringing injured strays, including myself, to the vet's for care.

"God, I'm nervous," Vickie whispered. "I just pray she doesn't draw any blood."

"Try not to worry," I said. "You're already enrolled in the trial. If they do take blood, they might not drop you just because your counts have risen a little." I was trying to reassure myself as much as Vickie.

Finally, Madeline, cheerfully garbed in a flowered nurse's jacket, emerged from the inner offices. "Hello, Vickie," she said, extending her hand eagerly. "It's great to finally meet you. I've heard a lot about you."

"And Mahlon's told me that you're terrific," Vickie replied. "That you practically run this place."

Madeline laughed. "Come along with me," she said.

Vickie rose to follow her, giving me a furtive, uneasy glance. I hid my own apprehension behind an encouraging smile.

Ten nerve-racking minutes passed before Vickie and Madeline returned, giggling—which I took to be a good sign.

"Everything okay?" I asked with feigned nonchalance.

"Everything's just fine, Mahlon," Vickie said, knowing that I would interpret this to mean there had been no blood test.

"Then what are you two laughing about?" I asked.

The two women exchanged a look. "Nothing . . . just the ways of men."

"Please, go easy on us," I begged.

"You'll be happy to know, Mahlon, that I've given Vickie a two-month supply of 3TC," Madeline said. "She should do fine. Side effects seem to be pretty rare on this drug."

I knew that this was true from the literature. And now that Vickie had the pills safely in hand, I could relax.

As Vickie headed toward the clinic's exit, Madeline pulled at my sleeve.

"I'm dying to know how it went at the NIH," she said. "Your cultures are still negative, aren't they?"

"I'm still waiting to hear," I whispered. "If it's okay I'll call you about this later—I don't want Vickie to feel she's being left behind. Getting her counts up is all that matters right now."

"I understand," Madeline replied.

I caught up with Vickie just outside the door. "Madeline was so nice!" she exclaimed. "Now I feel silly for worrying."

"So, what happened? Did she say anything at all about drawing blood?"

"I think they'll need it later."

"Well, we'll worry about it then. Hey, let's see the stuff."

Vickie pulled the small round bottle out of her purse and broke the seal to reveal the diamond-shaped white pills that, combined with AZT and IL-2, might buy her more time.

"After all we've been through," she said. "They're even more precious than real diamonds."

Staring at the pills—the actual pills, not placebos—that we'd fought for so many months to get, I was exultant. After all the pleading calls to Dr. Armstrong, the anxious wait for Vickie's results, the frantic appeal to the drug company when we'd missed the deadline by a day, the fear that with a simple blood test Vickie could be disqualified from the 3TC trial at the last minute, I felt as triumphant as if we'd pulled off the jewel heist of the century.

·   ·   ·

SINCE VICKIE HAD come through her first round of IL-2 so well, Beth Ann had promised that subsequently she could be treated as an outpatient, rather than be trapped in the hospital. Not wanting to impose on me, Vickie tried to insist on staying in a hotel, but I wouldn't hear of it. Not only did I want to monitor her condition when she was on IL-2, but since I saw her so infrequently, I wanted as much of her company as I could get.

Having Vickie stay with me did pose some rather delicate questions, for while we were mentally very intimate, physically we had been merely affectionate. Vickie had spent the night at my apartment once, the night after she'd completed her first IL-2 treatment. Then there had been no question that in her fragile state of health she would be better off sleeping in my guest room. But now that we had a whole weekend together before she went back on IL-2, the question of where she would sleep loomed uncomfortably large.

I knew that it was up to me to take the initiative, but I was worried how Vickie would respond if I made an overture. As loving as she was, as forgiving as she had been of Clyde, I still couldn't believe that she could feel comfortable with sex. Sex, after all, had infected her with the disease that had already robbed her of so much. For Dawn, in her wounded state of betrayal, physical contact had been deeply traumatic, as if sex were tantamount to rape. The single time we engaged in it, at her behest, it had shattered our relationship. So I had an almost visceral fear that once sex entered the equation it might undermine what had become the most important emotional connection I had. I couldn't bear to lose it.

There were medical issues to consider, too. I had become Vickie's adviser on treatments, and it was already hard to be objective. To do so in the midst of a sexual relationship might be well nigh impossible; at the very least, sex would alter the balance of trust we had so carefully established. More disquieting still was the risk we would both run of infection with each other's strains of HIV, no matter how careful we were. During my intimate encounter with Dawn two years before, I had employed more than adequate safeguards. But at the time the outlook for HIV-infected people was different; effective treatment was just a dream. Now, however, with multidrug therapy, we had real hope of survival; it seemed we could keep the virus at bay. So sex at this point just wasn't worth the risk to me.

Admittedly, many people would feel differently, take the necessary precautions, and go on with their sexual lives. But not me, not after all Vickie and I had been through to get the antivirals and the IL-2; and not now, when my viral load was coming up "undetectable" on test after test. If Vickie and I were building a life partnership, sex could wait until our medical conditions were such that both of us would be able to lead relatively normal lives again.

And so I made up the bed in the guest room, piling plenty of pillows and blankets at the end of the bed to prepare for when Vickie began IL-2. Vickie didn't seem surprised or hurt; I even thought that she seemed a little relieved to set aside the very complicated issue of sex for the time being. But to make sure that she didn't feel rejected, and because my test results were taking such precedence in my thoughts, I decided that the time had come to tell her about them.

At one point during the weekend, I was lying on the floor and she came over to snuggle, laying her head on my shoulder.

"I haven't told you this," I began awkwardly, "but over the last few months I've had all kinds of tests done to determine my viral load."

Vickie said nothing. I could feel her waiting.

"None of the tests have been able to detect any virus in my blood. I'm sure it's still in my lymph nodes, but . . ."

"That's absolutely incredible," Vickie exclaimed. Then there was an uncomfortable pause. "But why were you afraid to tell me?"

"Because I didn't want you to interpret my news to mean that I'd be any less committed to you."

"I wouldn't necessarily think that."

"I guess maybe I would think that, be afraid of it, I mean, if the roles were reversed. You know, I did think that with Dawn."

"I trust you more than that," she said.

A powerful affection for her welled up in me, bringing me close to tears. I turned sideways, leaning on an elbow, and faced her. "You know," I said, "I would do anything for you or your family."

"I know that."

"I even think that I would die if I absolutely knew that my dying would somehow save your life."

"Don't say that, Mahlon. You don't have to."

"As horrible as all this whole HIV experience has been for me, I would just as soon go through it again as not, if I had to do it to meet you."

"Oh, Mahlon," she said.

"But running the risk of infection again, after coming all this way and thinking that just maybe I could have a chance to live, I'm afraid I just don't have it in me.''

She put her hand against my cheek. ''Mahlon, I understand that, of course I understand. I feel the same way.''

''You do?'' I asked her, barely able to speak.

''Yes, I think I do,'' she said with sad conviction.

CHAPTER 31

———— ∞ ————

"HAVE YOU HEARD anything?"

"No, and it's driving me crazy. Have you?"

"Not yet." For a few weeks Vickie and I seemed to be parroting these questions over and over, for both of us were waiting anxiously for news. I was anticipating the results of my recent blood workups by David Ho, Jack Templeton, and the NIH; and Vickie was eager for her post-IL-2 CD4 counts. Her second round of treatment had been blessedly uneventful, and now, I knew, she was determined to see her counts skyrocket. She would cite her slogan, "A lot of it is attitude," while I gently tried to lower her expectations so the disappointment wouldn't be too crushing. But she would not be deterred from her hopes.

As it turned out, Vickie's news came through first. One afternoon around four o'clock my phone rang, and, picking it up, I heard the familiar voice. "Hi, it's me." There was a long pause. I waited.

"Well, I got the news," Vickie said in a very flat tone.

I nearly panicked. Immediately, I began to scramble for the reassuring facts. "You know it can take a few treatments to get your counts up, so if they're not that high you shouldn't get discouraged. . . . Remember that your viral load was low the last time, and that means a lot . . ."

Vickie said nothing.

"Uh, Vickie, are you there? What are the counts? Come on, tell me," I said, my heart fluttering.

Then came a burst of hysterical laughter. "Five-oh-four!" she cackled.

"That's spectacular!" I said. "I'm so thrilled for you."

"Five-oh-four," she said again, sounding awed.

"I don't know how you could tease me like that," I chided accusingly.

"Mahlon, I just couldn't resist."

"Well, I guess I'll forgive you this time. Just as long as the news is good."

"Mahlon, I can't believe it," she said. "I really can't. I mean, I never thought I'd ever have counts like this again."

Then her voice dropped. "And you know, I never could have done this without you."

MY NEWS STARTED trickling in the following day, starting with a phone call from Jack Templeton at Duke. He told me that my CD8-depleted cultures were negative and asked me if I'd heard from David Ho. I said I hadn't but planned to call him next. My fingers were crossed as I dialed: getting through to someone renowned and busy as David Ho twice in a row would be a miracle in itself. But to my surprise, he took the call.

"Dr. Johnson. Our CD8-depleted cultures and PCR are negative."

"Amazing," I murmured. "That's what they found at Duke, too."

"Good for you," he said. Then he intoned the same judicious words as Dr. Jones and everyone else had: "It's still too early to tell, of course, but your results are very promising."

A week later, Dr. Jones called with some results from the NIH. Their tests revealed the same thing as everyone else's—nothing. Neither branched DNA amplification nor DNA PCR, another HIV test, had detected any virus in my blood. And the Western Blots they'd run to compare my early and more recent blood samples suggested that there might be a slight reduction in antibodies to HIV, but nothing definitive yet.

I told Dr. Jones that his results confirmed the findings of both Jack Templeton and David Ho. "What should I do next?" I asked.

"Well, we've got a protocol for tonsil and lymph node biopsies to evaluate tissue changes and to try to isolate virus that way. It would mean spending several days up here in the hospital if you want to try it."

"I think I'll do that. By the way, I already talked a colleague into doing a spinal tap on me, and we couldn't detect any cells or virus in that."

Then I posed the big question, the one that I knew no researcher could answer responsibly but that I couldn't help but wonder.

"Is there a chance, do you think, that I have cleared the virus from my body?"

Dr. Jones paused. "There have been a couple of reports of people seroreverting, but those cases were poorly documented and I believe the patients are showing signs of infection again. Your case is a bit unusual. But . . ."

"He didn't say no!" The thought came pulsing into my mind. "He didn't say it was impossible." I could feel blood rushing into my head, as if my brain was struggling to mediate between my rational scientific understanding and my insurgent, renegade yearning to be blessed with a miracle.

I was too restive to work when I got off the phone. I knew I couldn't reach Vickie until later, so I decided to call my mother. In the three years since my accident, I had kept up a constant litany of hopeful platitudes, assuring her that I'd be well for a long time, that some new treatments held tremendous promise, and so on. It hadn't always been easy to put such a positive face on my situation, and I knew my mother was too wise to believe me wholeheartedly. But I could never really level with her, for I still regretted having aroused her anxiety about the autopsy accident so soon, causing her years of worry before I'd even gotten sick. In my effort to keep dropping little encouraging scraps of news at her feet, I had told her about my invitation to the NIH.

"Guess what," I told her now. "The NIH has finally gotten back to me."

"So you're definitely negative," she said without waiting to hear my news.

"No," I had to tell her. "Their Western Blots are still positive, but the BDNAs and other tests they've done so far look negative."

"I think you've turned this around—that you're not infected anymore," she said firmly.

"No, Mom, I am sure I'm still infected and I still register antibodies. But no one seems to be able to isolate virus in my blood."

"What's the difference?" she said. "They can't detect the virus."

"Well, it's probably still hiding in my lymph nodes."

"Not necessarily," she said.

My mother had read the story about the HIV-infected babies seroreverting and hoped that the NIH would confirm the same process in me.

"Mom. It's not clear what my data means and it won't be for a while."

"I think it means that you're no longer infected, that you've driven it out."

I could only shake my head at her persistence, which I had to recognize as the optimistic fruit of seeds I had sown myself. "No adults have ever cleared the virus, Mom. We can't jump to that conclusion," I told her.

"Maybe you can't," she said boldly, "but mothers have a certain intuition."

"Maybe I should make you talk to Dr. Jones at the NIH," I threatened.

"I'd be happy to!"

"I'm sure you would," I said. "And you know what, you'd probably be the first mother they'd ever listen to."

CHAPTER 32

❧

DECEMBER 22, 1995.

As always, despite my mother's entreaties, I'd be spending Christmas on call. But before that, I planned to have an early Christmas with Vickie and her family. It would be my first visit to her home and also to eastern Tennessee, which had taken on mythical stature for me since I'd read *My Own Country*. From the airplane window I could see miles and miles of rolling hills dotted with naked trees and patches of pasture that looked like blankets spread out on the winter-stripped earth.

On this trip, I'd be meeting my phone pal Clyde Jr. for the first time. He'd come to tolerate me long-distance, it seemed, but I suspected that I'd encounter more resistance when he actually saw me in person with Vickie. At his age, ten years, I remembered being very protective of my mother, rebuffing every suitor she had with disarming coldness. I knew from Vickie how seriously he was taking his role as man of the house—unstopping sinks, cutting the grass, and tirelessly fixing every mechanical device he got his hands on. I understood that, in his own way, Clyde was trying to reassure Vickie that she wasn't facing the world alone. Thirty years earlier, I had tried to do the same.

Clyde was with Vickie when she picked me up at the airport. I could feel his wondering brown eyes on me as I embraced his mother, and he shook my hand with a trace of reluctance, tugging nervously at the buttoned collar of his starched white shirt. Then, reaching for my suitcase, he declared, "I'll carry that." Stifling a smile, I let him take charge.

"So, was the flight smooth or rocky?" Vickie asked. She still hadn't gotten used to her commuter flights to and from Nashville.

"Well, we hit this cloud right out of Nashville and then— *boom*—down we went, dropped about a thousand feet. I nearly had an accident."

Clyde Jr. looked down and giggled.

"Oh, you're just pulling my leg," Vickie said. "Well, wait till you see how well I've tuned up the Camaro." She liked to play on my fear that she drove too fast.

"Uh oh. Maybe you should let me drive," I teased back.

"Not a chance. I'm going to give you the grand tour."

We approached a spotlessly clean blue car with beads of water still clinging to the bumper. A new Christmas tree air freshener hung from the rearview mirror. Clyde Jr., with a grunt, swung my suitcase into the backseat, politely averting his eyes from the brightly wrapped presents bulging from its side pockets.

"You can hardly tell that this car was in an accident," I said. "It looks like Danielle got her money's worth at the body shop."

"Yeah, right," Vickie replied sarcastically.

I had to nag her a little to buckle up, and then we roared out onto a winding two-lane road that snaked through wooded hills and past small farms with fading red-and-white Winston ads on the collapsing old barns. As Vickie whipped around the curves, I pressed my back against the seat. "Hey, take it easy now, Ms. Andretti," I said.

"What, am I driving too fast?" she asked innocently. "This isn't fast, is it, Clyde?"

"No, Ma," Clyde said, taking the cue. "I wish you'd speed it up. I'm getting hungry."

"I told Danielle and Clyde you hardly eat anything," Vickie said to me. "I'm just warning you that we'll all be insulted if you don't stuff yourself today."

I'd begged Vickie not to go to any trouble for me, to let me take them all out for turkey and fixings at a restaurant. But she wouldn't hear of it. She was determined to cook me a Christmas dinner that would make up for all the ones I'd missed while in training or on call. I knew that if I protested any more about her cooking, she'd get offended, so I changed the subject. "Hey, I tried calling you guys a couple of times last night," I said. "There was no answer."

"Danielle was out, and Mom and me were painting the bathroom," Clyde Jr. said.

I looked over at Vickie, who was staring intently at the road, just about to roar past a slow-moving tractor crawling along in front of us. "Now, I really hope you didn't do that just to impress me."

Vickie chuckled. "We were just tidying the place up for the holidays."

I smiled to myself and wondered if Vickie could understand how grateful I was to be spending this day with her, how honored I was to finally meet her son.

Vickie lived in a little clapboard house near a bend in the road. The front door opened onto a dark, small living room crowded with an old TV, two fraying royal-blue love seats squeezed against the back and side walls, and a massive Christmas tree, limbs bowed down under the weight of red lights and big ornaments. The tree completely blocked the only living room window, but bright winter light edged around the top.

As I entered I spied Danielle, lankier than I remembered her, sitting on the floor of the adjacent dining room. Above her head hung a picture of Jesus. When she saw me, she got up, hands in the pockets of her baggy jeans, to give me a shy kiss on the cheek. Trying to put her at ease, I told her how good she looked. Her response was a self-conscious shrug.

Clyde Jr. had charged ahead into the kitchen, where a large bronze bird lay tented under aluminum foil, flanked by cans of green beans, three pumpkin pies, and a large plastic bowl filled with naked white potatoes waiting to be mashed. I secretly hoped Vickie's potatoes would turn out better than my beloved mother's creations, which, invariably, were runny, despite her determined efforts to get them right.

Vickie squeezed her way into the kitchen, shedding her worn coat while barking at Clyde to leave the pies alone.

Foiled in his scheme to get a head start on dessert, Clyde looked at me and snickered.

"Well? What do you think of our home?" Vickie said, sweeping her arm across the air like a model displaying a new car.

"It's great, really cozy."

"It's not much, but it's a hell of a lot better than the trailer. And the yard is nice. I'll show you."

Grabbing my hand, Vickie led me over the worn parquet-patterned kitchen linoleum and pulled me out the back door. There, she threw her arms around me and we embraced again. "So, how're you doing with the 3TC?" she whispered, not wanting the children to overhear. The drug had been FDA-approved in November, so I'd been taking it, too. Vickie was proud that she'd tried it out first and could now give me advice.

"So far I'm feeling okay."

Vickie waved a hand out over her backyard toward a large open space. "These fields are where guys come hide out after they bust out of the local jail," she told me. "Clyde Junior claims that he's heard a few of them rustling in the bushes."

"Really?" I said, a little alarmed.

"I never saw anybody. Hell, for all I know, Clyde could've heard a big raccoon." Vickie laughed.

We headed back into the house, edging past the chipped table that partly blocked the back door. "Usually we don't have the centerpiece on the table," she said. "But this is a special occasion."

I followed her down a narrow hallway with four open doors barely separated by a few steps. We reached Danielle's room in two.

"Danielle's room is a real pigpen, even now that she's in college." Somewhere under a heap of jeans and T-shirts lay a single bed surrounded by a montage of magazine pictures of bare-chested hunks. An old child's dresser and rocking chair filled the remaining space. The next stop was Clyde's room, another cubbyhole, jammed with a bunk bed and a small desk, its wall adorned with an old Dallas Cowboys poster.

"And here's my room," she said, motioning me into another small space dominated by a queen-size bed with a headboard containing a snapshot of the two of us taken during the summer.

"We're hungry, Ma . . ." Clyde Jr. was protesting. "When do we get to eat?"

"Right now," Vickie said. "Go wash your hands while I mash the potatoes."

Despite my protests, I was placed at the head of the table, between Vickie and Clyde Jr. and facing Danielle. Clyde Jr. demanded that I demonstrate how to carve the turkey, apparently thinking that someone who cut up people for a living would know how to handle a measly bird. But turkey carving was a skill I had never mastered; in fact, given my fatherless adolescence and holidays on call, I wasn't sure that I'd ever seen it properly done. But under Clyde Jr.'s scrutiny, I took up the knife and plunged in, carving the turkey as I had sections of brains, into thick, even slices. To my relief, Clyde Jr. didn't object to my technique and held out his plate for the first serving.

"Don't start eating yet," Vickie chided. "You know we have to make a wish first."

"Yeah, make a wish, make a wish," Danielle chimed in.

"Mahlon, you and I will do it," Vickie said.

It had been decades since I'd handled the wishbone of a turkey. Carefully grasping my half of the bone, I positioned my thumb advantageously at the vertex.

"No cheating," Vickie said. "Now, close your eyes and get ready."

Peering through my lashes, I could see that Vickie's eyes were shut tightly as she concentrated on her wish. And I wished with all my heart that I would find whatever it took to help her survive, be it an antiviral drug, a magic spell, even fervent prayer.

"Ready?" she asked.

"Yes," I said, silently intoning "Please let Vickie live."

With a gentle tug, the bone snapped.

"Damn," Vickie said, staring at her smaller half, "I lost."

I chuckled with relief, as if the wishbone really could fulfill my dream.

Without further ado, Clyde Jr. dug in, shoveling huge mounds of turkey and potatoes and gravy into his mouth. Ravenous, I followed suit, and so did Danielle. The food was delicious, and I told Vickie so.

"Yeah, Ma, everything's great," Clyde Jr. said, not to be outshone at paying attention to his mother.

"So, how are your grades this term?" I asked Clyde Jr.

He grinned and said, "I got to talk to you about that."

"Oh?" I said.

He glanced sharply at his mother and then at me. "Not here," he said. "We need to wait until later. It's a secret."

"Now what do you have up your sleeve?" Vickie asked.

"Nothing," he said. "Don't worry about it."

"Okay, but it better be nothing."

Much to Vickie's delight, I ate two helpings of everything— the most I'd eaten in a single meal since my track years in college.

And once the dinner plates were cleared, Vickie brought out her famous pumpkin pie and cut a huge slice for me, passing it over with pride.

"Bet you haven't had good pumpkin pie in a while," she said with a smile.

I passed the plate of pie over to Clyde Jr., knowing how eager he had been for dessert.

"No, Mahlon, I cut that for you," Vickie said. "Clyde gets his next."

"Okay, okay," I said.

After we finished Vickie recruited the reluctant Danielle to help her wash the dishes. While the two women were gone, I turned to Clyde Jr. "So what did you want to talk to me about?"

"I got two *As*, a *B,* and two *Cs*," he crowed proudly.

"That's fantastic. That means you've earned yourself sixty dollars."

"I know," Clyde Jr. said. "And I'm going to use the money to buy Mom a Christmas present."

"That means you need it right now."

Clyde Jr. suddenly looked uncomfortable. "Well . . ." he began.

"What is it?" I glanced at the kitchen. "You better hurry."

"I want to buy her a garbage disposal."

"A garbage disposal?"

"Yeah, she needs one really bad. If I can just get it I can put it in myself."

Then I realized why he seemed so edgy. Sixty dollars probably wouldn't be enough to buy the garbage disposal. I was touched by what Clyde Jr. wanted to do for his mother. "If it costs more than sixty dollars, I'll help you out," I said. "Don't worry."

Clyde Jr. glanced toward the kitchen, where Vickie was still safely engaged in conversation with Danielle. "I could do it before Christmas. I could get it and put it in tomorrow or whenever."

"Tell you what. You pick out the one you want and then call me. And then I'll call the store and give them my credit card. How's that?"

"And you'll put the sixty dollars you owe me toward it, right?"

"Well, we'll worry about that later," I said, getting out my wallet. "For the time being, you can just hang on to it."

Vickie had promised the kids an after-dinner ride, so we all piled into the car.

"You know, I'm a good driver," Clyde Jr. told me.

"You are? At your age?"

"He not only drives cars, he fixes them," Vickie said. She explained that on weekends he'd been helping his cousins change oil and spark plugs and even rebuild cars. In the process they'd discovered that he had an uncanny sensitivity to engines and could determine the diagnostic significance of every ping and grind. Once when my car developed speedometer trouble, he had pinpointed the problem over the phone, but I thought that he'd just made a lucky guess. Vickie had often described how Clyde Jr. loved to tinker with everything, and now I realized that his mechanical ability was truly a gift.

"That's great," I told Clyde Jr.

"Yeah," he said modestly. "But I want you to see how well I drive."

Vickie pulled into the church parking lot, the site of Danielle's disaster, and let Clyde Jr. get behind the wheel.

With great seriousness and concentration, he fastened his seat belt, and then, hand on the ignition, asked, "You ready?"

"I guess, but take it easy," I said.

He gunned the motor, scorching the parking lot with rubber. I cringed, Danielle screamed, and Vickie broke out laughing. "I told him to do that," she said. "To get back at you for your 'jumping rocks' comment when I was laid up at your house."

I held up my hands. "Never again," I said submissively.

Once Clyde Jr. had calmed down and demonstrated his ability to negotiate the church's parking lot, Vickie let him drive us home. And although he was remarkably competent, I sat there white-knuckled, expecting to meet death around every bend. But I kept my fear to myself, knowing how much it meant to Clyde Jr. to impress me.

When we reached Vickie's driveway, a red Mustang pulled in behind us. The driver turned out to be a friend of Vickie's, and with a wink she announced her desire to take the kids out for ice cream. To my surprise, Clyde Jr. and Danielle obediently switched cars without even a complaint about Clyde Jr.'s insistence on riding shotgun. Obviously, this plan had been hatched before-hand.

Vickie confirmed my suspicion as we went into the house. "I thought we should get a few minutes to ourselves," she said. "The kids can get pretty rowdy."

"I enjoyed them," I said, "especially Clyde."

"He's a handful, all right." She sighed. "I wish you didn't have to leave so soon."

"Me, too, especially since you've got all those great leftovers. But I think we have about half an hour, don't we?"

We settled down on the couch in front of the Christmas tree, our hands and heads touching, looking at the winking lights. I couldn't help but think how different this Christmas was from the disastrous one I'd spent with Dawn two years before, when I was so hurt by her distance and her depression. Ironically, after all this time, Dawn had recently called me to let me know that Jan had died. She herself had been in and out of the hospital with bouts of depression, but her physical health was still fine. I wished her well, and as I hung up I marveled that I could talk to Dawn without much of a sense of regret—that my passion for her equivocal brand of affection had finally ebbed. I was healthier now, in mind and body, than I'd been in those lonely and desperately illness-obsessed days before I met Vickie.

"What are you thinking about?" she asked, snuggling closer to me. "Are you wondering what I got you for Christmas?"

"Your wonderful dinner was a gift in itself."

"Well, remember our agreement—no peeking until Christmas Day."

"Good luck keeping Clyde away from the presents," I said. "I saw him sizing up the shoebox-sized one, and I think he suspects that I got him a pair of Nikes."

"Oh, Mahlon, did you? He'll be so thrilled."

"I'm not admitting anything until Christmas."

I envisioned the three of them in front of the tree on Christmas morning, in a tableau very much like the one of my childhood—mother, son, and daughter. I wondered what it would be like to be there with them and what role I would come to play in their lives, the closest thing to a family of my own that I would ever have. And it struck me that, for the first time since my accident, I was actually conceiving of the future, almost believing that I—or we—could have one.

AFTER THE BUSTLING warmth of Vickie's house, my own apartment seemed empty and too quiet. At least I had a Christmas tree, a live spruce that my mother had sent, despite my protests. After setting down my bags, I arranged Vickie's gifts beneath the tree and hung up the red knit stocking she had given me. I was about to call her to say I'd made it home safely when I noticed the light blinking on the answering machine. Hoping it wasn't a summons to the hospital—or worse, Mother calling to make good on her threat to visit for the holiday, even though I was on call—I played the tape. I was surprised to hear an unfamiliar female voice.

"Dr. Johnson? This is Cheryl at Hoffman La Roche Pharmaceuticals. Dr. Danzo asked me to call and tell you that the FDA just approved saquinavir," she said. "The drug should be in the pharmacies by tomorrow."

For the past two years I'd been seeking protease inhibitors as if they were the Holy Grail, because they attacked HIV at a different point in its life cycle than any of the available antiviral drugs. If they were used alone, the virus could mutate and defeat them, as it did AZT, DDI, DDC, and all the rest. But the combination of a protease inhibitor and conventional antivirals dealt HIV a powerful one-two punch. Forced to fend off two different foes at once, the research suggested, the virus might be too disabled to fight back effectively.

Whenever there had been a protease inhibitor trial, I had tried to enroll myself and Vickie, but for various reasons we had both been ineligible. I had called the drug company assiduously, trying to get the drugs directly on the "compassionate use" basis. And apparently I'd been enough of a pest that Dr. Danzo took pity on me and called to let me know they were being released.

I had to tell Vickie.

She answered the phone on the first ring, as though she'd been waiting for my call. "Hey," I said. "I'm home."

"Flight okay?" she asked tentatively.

"Like a roller coaster. We nearly crashed twice."

"Oh, you, you're just trying to scare me." Vickie laughed. "Remember, I'm getting used to flying now."

"So, anyway, you and I will have a Merry Christmas this year," I said teasingly. "Santa left us an unexpected gift."

"Oh, yeah, what's that?"

I told her that the protease inhibitors had just been FDA-approved and would reach the pharmacies by the next day. "Now, all we need is a prescription and we're there," I said.

"Oh, my God, what great news!" she exclaimed. "I can't believe it, it finally happened." Then she paused. "Mahlon, now we really do have a chance, don't we?" she asked.

"I think so," I said. "Yes, I think we do." And with that we both burst into tears and wept there, to each other, on the phone. We had waited so long for this moment to arrive.

E P I L O G U E

————— ∞ —————

As we approach our second Christmas together, Vickie and I enjoy a state of grace, blessed with health that was once unimaginable. Her latest count was 568 (24 percent), the highest it has been in many years. Though far from normal, it's certainly a heartening rally by someone infected with HIV for close to a decade, whose counts, pre-IL-2, had hovered on the brink of AIDS. Vickie's viral load on her last RNA PCR was almost undetectable, down from her pre-IL-2 level. She's holding her own with a kind of quiet strength she shares with me.

As for me, my last count was 1,269 (70 percent). Over the past year I've maintained an average monthly count of 1,134 (55 percent), a far cry from the 320 I'd dropped to in October 1994. In early 1996, BDNA and RNA PCR analyses of my viral load were still negative, meaning that I had less than 10 copies of the virus per milliliter of my blood. I did schedule the recommended tonsil biopsy at the NIH, but it was determined that I had too little tonsil to biopsy. I repeated my Western Blot in May and October of this year. Only four bands show up now, and two of them seem to be growing fainter.

Vickie and I have gotten to this point through ongoing experimentation under the guidance of wise doctors. We have both continued our IL-2 therapy, Vickie on a modified form of the NIH's bimonthly regimen, and I on a monthly cycle of low-dose treatments, developed through trial and error, that holds side effects to a minimum. On this regimen, in concert with antivirals, I saw my viral load become "undetectable" and my counts soar, long before I ever started taking protease inhibitors.* New studies being published by the NIH and other groups† now confirm that IL-2, taken in combination with AIDS drugs, may be a powerful weapon in the war on HIV.

In March 1996, when a new, more potent protease inhibitor, ritonavir, became available, Vickie and I both switched to it. Vickie moved on to still another protease inhibitor, indivar, while I stayed on ritonavir with the idea of conducting yet another experiment on myself: to begin taking saquinavir again in tandem with ritonavir (along with AZT and 3TC). I was inspired by news that this combination, when applied to HIV cultures in the lab, might delay resistance and completely stop viral growth—not just slow it down, but actually stop it.

---

* Anyone pursuing IL-2 therapy must do so under the careful supervision of an AIDS doctor experienced with the drug and able to devise a safe and effective, individualized therapeutic program.

† Kovacs et al., *N. Engl. J. Med.,* 1996, 335:1350–6; and Jacobson et al., *Proc. Natl. Acad. Sci.,* 1996, 93: 10405–10.

Could this combination be the desperately hoped-for magic bullet, perhaps a so-called "cure" for AIDS?

The answer is, probably not—not yet. For one thing, no one yet knows whether this or any drug combination can eradicate the virus in living human beings, as opposed to in the lab; and for another, the doses it could take might harm the patient as much as HIV. Then, too, in some HIV-infected people the most promising drug "cocktails" have proven ineffectual; there are even reports of patients who have initially radically improved on protease inhibitors, only to relapse. The regimen itself is rigorous and requires tremendous discipline. By August 1996 I was taking at least twenty-eight pills a day—breakfast and dinner doses of six ritonavir, three saquinavir, two AZT capsules, and one 3TC; plus a late-night snack of an additional AZT, a gram of vitamin C, a super B-complex, and a beta carotene capsule. Because HIV mutates into drug-resistant strains extraordinarily quickly, protease inhibitors and antivirals must be taken scrupulously on time so that the levels in the blood never drop enough to let the virus regrow. And so, for Vickie and me, our "bombing runs" have become focal points of our days, the topic of our nightly conversation, another expression of affection: "Did you take your medicine on time?"

And there are side effects—certainly tolerable, especially in view of the stakes: a burning tongue, and in my days on IL-2, fatigue, body aches, and chills. These side effects are positive signs in a sense—constant verification that the drugs are potent—but they are also reminders of the toxicity of our treatments. No one knows how damaging these drugs may be in the long run, what toll they may ultimately exact from us—anemias, liver damage, slow death by poison in the quest for life.

And yet they offer the best hope that we have ever seen in the history of the worst pandemic of our time. Most researchers now believe that we have reached a new era when HIV may be managed like a chronic disease, like diabetes. A few have even gone so far as to suggest that perhaps we can drive it from our bodies altogether, if we can completely arrest its growth for about three years.* The body, including the lymph system, is, after all, an assemblage of remarkable self-renewing organs that continually replace dying cells with new ones. And with this turnover, it is theoretically possible that the last vestiges of the virus, immobilized by drugs, might be slowly rousted from their secret hiding places. But how will we recognize this blessed day, should it ever come? When will it be safe to stop bombarding ourselves with drugs? And what if our efforts fail? What if suboptimal treatments select for or create new ultravirulent mutant strains of virus resistant to all treatments? The specter of such a supervirus, ravaging vengefully unchecked, is hideous to contemplate.

As it is, more than 1 million Americans are infected with HIV—one out of every 92 men, one out of every 800 women. Since 1981, when the Centers for Disease Control first identified the mysterious disease, 500,000 have developed AIDS and more than 319,000 have died. AIDS is now the number one killer of Americans between the ages of twenty-five and forty-four.

Worldwide, the wrath of the virus has been ever more destructive, claiming some 22 million infected victims, 7.7 million of whom have full-blown AIDS. Of those infected, 18.8 million live in sub-Saharan Africa, India, or Southeast Asia, regions where poverty, sexual customs, illiteracy, and limited access to health care

---

* Pennisi et al., *Science,* 1996, 272: 1884.

confound the noblest efforts to prevent or treat the disease.* In such countries as Zambia, ravaged by HIV and tuberculosis, the estimated life expectancy will be halved by 2010, from 66 to 33 years. And every minute, five more people in the world become newly infected with HIV.†

So it is essential that research continue. Better drugs are needed, drugs that block HIV's entry into cells, drugs that block the integrase enzyme and prevent chronic infection. Ongoing studies must refine how and when we use the armamentarium and find ways to make it affordable for the millions who need it. My current regimen, including IL-2, costs almost $2,000 a month, charges largely paid for by medical coverage; treatment with two reverse transcriptase and one protease inhibitor, a more standard combination, can run to $1,400 a month or more. No doubt these prices will drop as the drug companies recover their extraordinary development costs, but what about those in need now? And what about those who were born in lands gripped by poverty, where the annual per capita income doesn't even cover the cost of a month's supply of AZT? Even in the United States, what will become of those HIV-infected for whom these new treatments—and the hope of life—will be an unattainable luxury?

I think of us, the lucky few with access to the new therapies, as Orpheus, granted a chance to rescue Eurydice from the realm of death. Will we falter, as Orpheus did, and reconsign Eurydice to the underworld?

Thus, as a physician, I view the new era with only cautious

---

* Joint United Nations Program on HIV/AIDS, July 1996.
† World Health Organization estimates through June 1996.

hope, hope that the carnage will stop. But as a patient, as a human stalked by HIV, I feel the grateful joy that I might live. Just four years ago AIDS hovered like an endless storm, with effective treatments too far off on an overcast horizon to offer hope. HIV meant despair, life without a future, certain premature death. But now, almost incomprehensibly, we're being given a glimpse of longevity.

What will we make of this life restored, if we can dare to believe in it? Before my accident I was an isolated man, withering in a world of work and study. I managed to endure through persistence and the ministrations of my medical colleagues, Stevens, Jones, Beth Ann Jamison, Madeline, and the rest, to whom I owe so much. But it took the nurturance of the archangels Carol, Bart, and Shannon, whose tremendous humanity taught me the power of compassion; of my mother, who taught unswerving faith to an unsure son; and especially of Vickie, my blessed Vickie, who taught courage in the face of death, forgiveness in the face of betrayal, and devotion in the face of hesitance—to give me the capacity to do more than survive, to live.

I pray that Vickie and I—that we all—can see a renewal of life in this new era, an age of miracles, when perhaps the war on AIDS can be won.

ABOUT THE AUTHORS

MAHLON JOHNSON, M.D., Ph.D., is an associate professor of pathology and cell biology at Vanderbilt University Medical School and visiting adjunct associate professor of neuropathology at the University of Tennessee Medical Center at Knoxville.

JOSEPH OLSHAN is the author of five novels, including *Clara's Heart* and the current highly acclaimed *Night Swimmer*.